KINGSFORD
GREAT BARBECUES

KINGSFORD®

GREAT BARBECUES

GREAT BARBECUES

CONTENTS

ISBN: 0-88176-822-7

This edition published by:
Publications International Ltd.
7373 N. Cicero Ave.
Lincolnwood, IL 60646

8 7 6 5 4 3 2

ACKNOWLEDGMENTS

The Kingsford Products Company would like to thank the following companies and organizations for the use of their recipes and photographs:

Alaska Seafood Marketing Institute, Salmon Division
American Lamb Council, Inc.
Beef Industry Council
California Apricot Advisory Board
California Beef Council
California Strawberry Advisory Board
California Tree Fruit Agreement
The Catfish Institute
National Broiler Council
National Fisheries Institute
National Hot Dog & Sausage Council
National Live Stock & Meat Board
National Turkey Federation
The Potato Board
Weber-Stephen Products Co.

Printed and bound in U.S.A.

HOT OFF THE GRILL

TO BARBECUE LOVERS EVERYWHERE

Kingsford's Great Barbecues is all about sensational barbecues, from easy crowd-pleasing favorites to elegant grilled suppers. If you're new to the world of authentic charcoal cooking, we've included all the basics for starting off like a pro. And for the experienced outdoor chef, we offer plenty of intriguing menus to keep your grill fired up all summer—and winter—long!

These mouth-watering recipes are all cooked over charcoal briquets—the heat of choice for 70% of grill owners. The reason charcoal is preferred for outdoor cooking is simple. It's the real wood char in briquets that helps deliver the rich, smoky flavor we associate with the true taste of barbecue.

We've even settled the controversy about which fire—charcoal or gas—grills a better burger. Results of controlled taste tests from across the country show the hands-down winner is the charcoal-grilled burger—ranked **number one** by the majority of tasters for best barbecued flavor.

Barbecuing may be synonymous with summer, but many outdoor cooks are discovering what passionate grill enthusiasts have known all along. Winter barbecue is a sensation. Discover how easy it is to barbecue a golden holiday turkey (see the recipe on page 64) and get ready to start a new family tradition. Turkey never tasted so good.

From our family to yours, here's to a great year of great barbecues!

Sandy Sullivan and the Kingsford BBQ Pros

A DASH OF HISTORY

Henry Ford gets credit for more than the Model T. His ingenuity is responsible for launching America's passion for outdoor cooking. You might say he's the original baron of barbecue—all because he couldn't tolerate waste.

In the early 1900s, Ford operated a northern Michigan sawmill that made wooden framing for his Model Ts. He looked on in frustration at the growing piles of wood scraps and wondered how they could be put to productive use. He came up with the idea to chip the wood into small pieces, convert it to charcoal, grind it into powder, then compress it into the now-familiar pillow-shaped briquets. These convenient briquets were originally sold through Ford automobile agencies.

Ford put his brother-in-law, E.G. Kingsford, in charge of the charcoal operation. Together, they helped make barbecuing an American tradition. Ford charcoal, later named **Kingsford®** charcoal briquets, is the original and still the number one brand sold in the nation today.

WHAT TYPE OF CHARCOAL?

Successful barbecuing starts with a good fire. Premium quality briquets, like **Kingsford®** charcoal, help deliver a perfect fire three ways. They light quicker so the coals are ready sooner. They burn more evenly to produce balanced heat, and they perform consistently—bag after bag. The renewed interest in authentic charcoal cooking has spawned extra convenience and new flavor in the types of charcoal available.

Instant Lighting Charcoal Briquets. An especially good choice for midweek barbecues when time is at a premium. Products like **Match light®** charcoal briquets already contain just the right amount of lighter fluid to produce a quick-starting fire. Simply stack the briquets into a pyramid and light several briquets with a match. The coals will be ready in about 20 minutes. Be sure to close the bag tightly after each use.

Charcoal Briquets with Mesquite Wood Chips. The perfect selection for cooks who enjoy the wonderful flavor of mesquite but feel less comfortable

grilling over pure mesquite charcoal, which burns hotter and less evenly. For example, **Kingsford®️ with Mesquite** charcoal briquets are compressed charcoal briquets with mesquite chips blended into them. These briquets produce real mesquite smoke to enhance the flavor of outdoor fare.

It's important to remember that charcoal is porous and will absorb moisture. Always store briquets in a dry area, and keep the bag in a tightly closed or covered container. Charcoal that has been exposed to humidity or moisture can be more difficult to light.

SAFETY FIRST

Make sure the grill is on a solid surface and is set away from shrubbery, grass and overhangs. NEVER use gasoline or kerosene as a lighter fluid starter. Either one can cause an explosion. To get a sluggish fire going, *do not add lighter fluid directly to hot coals.* Instead, take 2 to 3 additional briquets, place them in a small metal container and add lighter fluid. When the briquets have absorbed the lighter fluid (1 to 2 minutes), add them to the pyramid of briquets, then light with a match. These briquets will restart the fire.

Remember that coals are hot—up to 1000°F—and that the heat transfers to the barbecue grill, grid, tools and food. Always wear fireproof mitts when cooking and handling grill and tools.

BUILDING PERFECT FIRES

How Much Charcoal? A 5-pound bag of **Kingsford®️** charcoal contains 75 to 90 briquets; a 10-pound bag between 150 and 180; and a 20-pound bag 300 to 360 briquets. The number of briquets required for barbecuing depends on the size and type of grill and the amount of food to be prepared. Weather conditions also have an effect; strong winds, very cold temperatures or highly humid conditions increase the number of briquets needed for a good fire. As a rule of thumb, it takes about 30 briquets to grill 1 pound of meat. For example, you'll need 45 briquets to grill six 4-ounce hamburgers.

For grilling meat directly over the coals, you want enough charcoal—in a single layer—to extend 1 to 2 inches beyond the area of the food on the grill. Pour briquets into the grill unit to determine the quantity needed, then stack them into a pyramid.

When cooking in a covered grill using an indirect method, food is placed over a drip pan and the coals are banked either to one side or on both sides of the pan. This method is recommended for large cuts of meat (like roasts) and for fatty meats to eliminate flame flare-ups. Here's how to determine the number of briquets needed:

BRIQUETS NEEDED FOR INDIRECT COOKING, COVERED GRILL

	Diameter of Grill (inches)			
	26¾	22½	18½	14
Briquets needed each side of drip pan for cooking 45 to 50 minutes	30	25	16	15
Briquets to be added on each side of drip pan every 45 minutes	9	8	5	4

Using Lighter Fluid. Stack briquets into a pyramid. Soak briquets with at least ½ cup lighter fluid, like **Kingsford™️ Odorless charcoal lighter.** Wait 1 minute to allow fluid to soak into briquets. Then light with a match. Coals will be ready in 20 to 30 minutes, when they are about 80% ashed over. At night, they will have a noticeable cheery glow.

Using a Chimney Starter. This method is essentially failure-proof and no lighter fluid is required. First, remove the grid from the grill and set the chimney starter in the base of the grill. Then crumple a couple of sheets of newspaper and place them in the bottom portion of the chimney starter. Fill the top portion with charcoal briquets. Light the newspaper. Do not disturb the starter; coals will be ready in 20 to 30 minutes. Be sure to wear fireproof mitts when emptying coals from the chimney starter into the base of the grill.

Using an Electric Starter. Nestle the electric starter in the coals. Then plug the starter into a heavy-duty extension cord. Plug the cord into the nearest available outlet. After 8 to 10 minutes, when ash begins to form on the briquets, unplug the starter remove it, and carefully set it aside. Arrange the briquets in a single layer, close together.

How Hot is the Grill? If you don't have a grill thermometer, here is a quick, easy way to estimate the temperature on the grill surface. Hold your hand, palm-side-down, just above the grid. Count "one thousand one, one thousand two," etc., until the heat is uncomfortable. If you can keep your hand in place before pulling away:

- 2 seconds—it's a hot fire, about 375°F or more.
- 3 seconds—it's a medium-hot fire, about 350° to 375°F.
- 4 seconds—it's a medium fire, about 300° to 350°F.
- 5 seconds—it's a low fire, about 200° to 300°F.

FLAVORED SMOKE

Flavored smoke, enriched with heady aromas from hardwoods and fresh or dried herbs, is the latest sensation in barbecue flavorings. Outdoor cooks find it's both easy and fun to experiment with different meats and flavor combinations. Here are some suggestions for getting started:

As a general rule, a little goes a long way. Added flavorings should complement, not overpower, food's natural taste. Always soak flavorings, such as wood chunks, wood chips or herbs, in water at least 30 minutes before adding to the coals. You want the flavorings to smolder and smoke, not burn.

Hickory and mesquite chips or wood chunks are the most readily available flavorings. Other good choices are oak (good with heartier meats), cherry or apple wood (flavorful companions to poultry) and alder wood from the Northwest (marvelous with fish). Look for **Kingsford® Heart-O-Hickory smoke chips** in your store's barbecue section.

Grapevine cuttings and even shells from nuts like almonds, pecans or walnuts add interesting flavor. You can also try water-soaked garlic cloves and orange or lemon peels.

Small bunches of fresh or dried herbs, soaked in water, can add fragrant flavor as well. Rosemary, bay leaves, oregano and tarragon, for example, can be teamed with wood chips or simply used by themselves.

DRY RUBS AND MARINADES

Dry rubs are combinations of seasonings and spices rubbed onto meat before grilling. Basic rubs often include coarsely ground black or white pepper, paprika and garlic powder. Some include mustard and brown sugar—even cayenne pepper. Crushed herbs are other good choices—sage, basil, thyme and oregano, for example.

Marinades, like dry rubs, add flavor, but they also help tenderize less tender cuts of meat. Basic marinades include an acidic ingredient responsible for tenderizing—generally from wine, vinegar, soy sauce or lemon juice—combined with herbs, seasonings and oil. Fish and vegetables don't usually need tenderizing and should be marinated for only short periods of time (no more than a few hours). Beef, pork, lamb and chicken all benefit from being marinated for a few hours to overnight. Use leftover marinades as a baste while cooking. You can also serve leftover marinades as a sauce. However, follow food safety practices by boiling the marinade for a few minutes before serving.

A WORD ABOUT SAUCES

Sauces, rich and thick with tomato, or savory with garlic, onion and spices, add delicious flavor to almost any grilled fare. Premium sauces, like **K.C. Masterpiece®** barbecue sauce, capture real homemade taste and are a barbecue staple worth using often. Serve warmed sauce on the side for added zest. Here's how to protect the rich, deep color and spicy flavor of barbecue sauce, especially tomato- and molasses-based ones that can burn if applied too early:

- For grilled steaks and chops: Baste with sauce after meat has been turned for the last time, about the last 3 minutes of grilling.
- For grilled chicken: Baste with sauce the last 10 minutes; turn once.
- For hot dogs and sausage: Baste with sauce the last 5 to 6 minutes.
- For barbecued meats (cooked by indirect method): Baste with sauce the last hour of cooking.
- For smoked meats: Baste with sauce the last 30 to 45 minutes.

BARBECUE TIPS

- To keep food from sticking to the grid and make it easy to turn, rub the grid with vegetable oil before cooking.
- Always use tongs or a spatula when handling meat. Piercing meat with a fork allows delicious juices to escape and makes meat less moist.
- When making kabobs, if you use wooden or bamboo skewers, be sure to soak them in cold water 20 minutes before using.
- The secret to evenly cooked vegetable and meat kabobs is to parboil solid or starchy vegetables before they are threaded onto skewers for grilling.
- Foods wrapped in foil and cooked on the grill should be turned often to prevent burning and assure even cooking.
- When barbecuing food for more than 45 minutes, add 10 to 12 briquets around the outer edge of the fire as cooking starts. When these briquets are ready, add them to the center of the fire as needed to maintain constant temperature.

REGIONAL BARBECUES

America loves to barbecue. Featured here are favorites from all over the United States, including chili-pepper-stuffed chicken, smoked grilled salmon and succulent sauce-laden ribs. Suggested menus offer you great ideas for serving complete meals.

BUTTERFLIED LEG OF LAMB

Makes 8 to 10 servings

1 boneless leg of lamb (6 pounds), butterflied
½ cup olive or vegetable oil
½ cup chopped fresh mint *or* 2 tablespoons dried mint, crushed
2 cloves garlic, minced
4 teaspoons Dijon-style mustard
1 tablespoon black peppercorns, cracked
1 tablespoon chopped fresh rosemary *or* 1 teaspoon dried rosemary, crushed
1½ teaspoons finely shredded lemon peel

Remove excess fat and thin fat covering from surface of lamb. With meat mallet, pound meat to even thickness, about 1½ inches. Place lamb in large plastic bag. Place bag in shallow roasting pan. In small bowl, combine remaining ingredients; pour over lamb in bag. Close bag; refrigerate 2 to 5 days, turning occasionally.

Arrange medium-hot **Kingsford® briquets** around drip pan. Drain meat; reserve marinade. Put 2 skewers diagonally through meat to keep flat while grilling. Insert meat thermometer in thickest part of meat. Place lamb over drip pan. Cover grill and cook until thermometer registers 140°F for rare (35 to 40 minutes), 160°F for medium (about 45 minutes). Brush with marinade often. Turn meat once halfway through cooking time. Remove meat; let stand, covered, 15 minutes. Carve meat into thin slices to serve.

Northeast Barbecued Lamb Dinner:
Butterflied Leg of Lamb with Grill-Roasted Onions and Vegetable-Rice Salad
(recipes on page 8)

6

GRILL-ROASTED ONIONS

Makes 8 servings

4 medium yellow onions, unpeeled
1 tablespoon olive or vegetable oil
　Salt and pepper
8 teaspoons butter or margarine

Cut unpeeled onion into halves lengthwise. Brush onions with oil. Place onion halves on 18×18-inch piece of heavy-duty foil. Season to taste with salt and pepper. Place 1 teaspoon butter on each onion half. Wrap loosely in foil; seal edges tightly.

Grill packet, on covered grill, over medium-hot **Kingsford®** briquets 20 minutes or until onions are tender, turning packet once. Unwrap packet and serve onions in skins.

VEGETABLE-RICE SALAD

Makes 8 servings

3 cups cooked long grain rice
1¾ cups prepared Hidden Valley Ranch® Original Ranch® Salad Dressing
2 medium tomatoes, chopped
　Milk
　Lettuce
　Cooked green beans (optional)

In bowl, combine rice and salad dressing. Toss gently to coat. Cover; refrigerate. Just before serving, stir in tomatoes. Stir in 2 to 3 tablespoons milk if rice mixture seems dry. Turn into lettuce-lined salad bowl. Garnish with green beans and additional chopped tomato, if desired.

SKEWERED SHRIMP WITH LEMON

Makes 8 appetizer servings

16 fresh or frozen large shrimp, shelled and deveined
½ cup olive or vegetable oil
2 lemons
½ cup fine dry bread crumbs
½ teaspoon pepper

Thaw shrimp, if frozen. Thread 2 shrimp on each of 8 skewers. Brush with 2 tablespoons of the oil. With vegetable peeler, remove peel from lemons; shred finely. In bowl, combine lemon peel, bread crumbs and ¼ teaspoon of the pepper. Press crumb mixture firmly onto shrimp to coat evenly. Refrigerate until ready to grill.

For dipping sauce, squeeze juice from lemons (you should have about 6 tablespoons juice). Combine juice with remaining 6 tablespoons oil and remaining ¼ teaspoon pepper; set aside.

Grill breaded shrimp, on covered grill, over medium-hot **Kingsford®** briquets 4 minutes. Turn skewers; grill 4 minutes longer or until shrimp are pink and crumbs are slightly browned. Serve shrimp with lemony dipping sauce.

STRAWBERRY LEMONDRIFT PIE

Makes 6 to 8 servings

2 pints fresh strawberries
½ cup milk
1 envelope unflavored gelatin
⅔ cup granulated sugar
1½ tablespoons grated lemon peel
¼ cup fresh lemon juice
2 cups whipping cream
1 baked and cooled 9-inch pie shell
　Confectioners' sugar

Remove stems from strawberries. Place strawberries in bowl; cover and refrigerate. In 1-quart saucepan, combine milk and gelatin; set aside 5 minutes. Stir in sugar. Stir over low heat until gelatin and sugar are completely dissolved. Stir in lemon peel and juice. Cool to room temperature. Refrigerate until mixture is syrupy, about 15 minutes. Whip cream in large mixer bowl until stiff. Fold in gelatin mixture. Spoon into pie shell, mounding top. Cut strawberries into halves; cover pie with strawberries. Chill until firm, about 2 hours. Dust top lightly with confectioners' sugar before serving.

*Recipe courtesy of **California Strawberry Advisory Board***

GRILLED POTATOES

Makes 8 servings

6 medium potatoes
⅓ cup olive or vegetable oil
¾ teaspoon salt
½ teaspoon garlic powder
¼ teaspoon pepper

Peel potatoes, if desired, and cut each into 4 wedges. In large bowl, combine oil, salt, garlic powder and pepper. Add potatoes; toss to coat. Wrap potatoes in heavy-duty foil; seal edges tightly. Grill packet, on covered grill, not directly over medium-hot **Kingsford®** briquets about 35 minutes or until potatoes are tender.

NACHOS

Makes 8 servings

1 bag (8 ounces) tortilla chips
1 can (16 ounces) refried beans
  Pickled jalapeño pepper strips (about 24)
2 cups shredded Monterey Jack or Cheddar cheese (about 8 ounces)

Place half the tortilla chips in large iron skillet. Spoon half the beans over chips and arrange jalapeño strips on top. Sprinkle with half the cheese. Make a second layer with remaining ingredients. Grill, on covered grill, over medium-hot **Kingsford®** briquets 6 to 8 minutes or until cheese melts.

BLUE RIBBON PINTO BEANS

Makes 6 to 8 servings

2 pounds dried pinto beans
1 pound sliced smoked bacon, cut into 1-inch pieces
2 medium tomatoes, diced
1½ tablespoons ground cumin
1½ tablespoons chili powder
2 garlic cloves, minced
1 jalapeño or serrano chili pepper, minced
  Salt

Place beans in large heavy saucepan. Cover with water and bring to boil. Drain. Return beans to saucepan. Add enough water to cover by 2 to 3 inches. Add remaining ingredients except salt. Bring mixture to boil. Reduce heat to low and simmer about 3½ hours or until beans are very soft, adding more water as necessary to keep beans submerged. Season to taste with salt and cook 15 minutes longer, uncovered, if liquid is thin.

AVOCADO-TOMATO SALAD

Makes 8 servings

2 ripe large avocados, seeded and peeled
  Lemon juice
2 or 3 medium tomatoes
  Lettuce leaves
  Prepared Hidden Valley Ranch® Original Ranch® Salad Dressing

Slice avocados and sprinkle with lemon juice to prevent browning. Cut tomatoes into wedges. Arrange avocado slices and tomato wedges on individual lettuce-lined salad plates. Drizzle with salad dressing.

FAJITAS

Makes 8 servings

2 pounds beef skirt steak or flank steak
¾ cup beer
½ cup lime juice
2 tablespoons Worcestershire sauce
8 flour tortillas (6-inch)
Pico de Gallo Sauce (recipe follows)

Trim excess fat from steak. In shallow glass dish, combine beer, lime juice and Worcestershire sauce. Add steak; turn to coat with marinade. Cover and refrigerate overnight, spooning marinade over meat occasionally.

Drain steak; reserve marinade. Pat steak dry with paper toweling. Grill steak, on covered grill, over medium-hot **Kingsford®** briquets 8 to 10 minutes, basting meat occasionally with marinade. Turn and grill to desired doneness, allowing 8 to 10 minutes longer for medium. Carve meat across grain into thin slices.

Meanwhile, wrap tortillas in large piece of heavy-duty foil; place tortillas at edge of grill 5 minutes or until heated through. Wrap steak slices in warmed tortillas; top with chilled Pico de Gallo Sauce.

PICO DE GALLO SAUCE

Makes about 1¾ cups

3 medium tomatoes, peeled and chopped
½ cup chopped green onions
1 large fresh Anaheim chili pepper, seeded and chopped
1 fresh jalapeño pepper, seeded and chopped
2 teaspoons chopped fresh cilantro or parsley
1 teaspoon salt

In small bowl, combine tomatoes, onions, peppers, cilantro and salt. Cover and refrigerate 5 hours or overnight.

Tex-Mex Barbecue Dinner:
Fajitas with Pico de Gallo Sauce;
Avocado-Tomato Salad and Nachos
(recipes on page 9)

Southeast Pork Barbecue

- **Barbecued Pork Leg with Sam's Mop Sauce**
- **Southern-Style Squash and Okra**
- **Saucy New Potatoes**
- **Corn Muffins**
- **Peaches in Port**

To prepare this menu, you'll need to use about 134 Kingsford® Charcoal Briquets (about 8 pounds).

CORN MUFFINS

Makes about 14 muffins

1 cup all-purpose flour
1 cup yellow cornmeal
¼ cup sugar
4 teaspoons baking powder
¾ teaspoon salt
2 eggs
1 cup milk
¼ cup vegetable oil or melted shortening

In bowl, stir together flour, cornmeal, sugar, baking powder and salt. Add eggs, milk and oil. Beat just until combined; do not overbeat.

Grease muffin cups or line with paper baking cups; fill two-thirds full. Bake in 400°F oven 15 to 20 minutes or until done. Let stand 3 minutes in pan. Loosen muffins; remove from pan.

SAUCY NEW POTATOES

Makes 4 to 6 servings

1½ pounds new potatoes
½ cup K.C. Masterpiece® Hickory Barbecue Sauce
¼ cup water
Salt and pepper

Cut largest potatoes in half; arrange on 18×18-inch piece of heavy-duty foil. In small bowl, combine barbecue sauce and water; pour over potatoes. Season to taste with salt and pepper. Fold foil over potatoes; seal edges tightly. Grill packet, on covered grill, over medium-hot **Kingsford®** briquets about 30 minutes or until potatoes are tender. Turn packet over after 15 minutes.

BARBECUED PORK LEG

Makes about 20 servings

1 boneless pork leg roast, rolled and tied (8 to 10 pounds)
Sam's Mop Sauce (recipe follows)
K.C. Masterpiece® Hickory Barbecue Sauce

Arrange medium-hot **Kingsford®** briquets around drip pan. Place prepared pork leg over drip pan; cover grill and cook pork 4 to 4½ hours (adding additional briquets as necessary) or until meat thermometer inserted in thickest portion registers 170°F. Baste pork with Sam's Mop Sauce every 30 minutes, patting a thin coating of sauce on meat with cotton swab mop or pastry brush. Let stand, covered with foil, 10 minutes before serving.

Meanwhile, in saucepan, combine remaining Mop Sauce with an equal amount of barbecue sauce; bring to boil. Slice pork and serve with sauce mixture.

SAM'S MOP SAUCE

Makes 2¼ cups

1 lemon
1 cup water
1 cup cider vinegar
1 tablespoon butter or margarine
1 tablespoon olive or vegetable oil
½ teaspoon cayenne pepper
1½ to 3 teaspoons hot pepper sauce
1½ to 3 teaspoons Worcestershire sauce
1½ teaspoons black pepper

With vegetable peeler, remove peel from lemon; squeeze juice from lemon. In heavy saucepan, combine lemon peel, juice and remaining ingredients. Bring to boil. Place saucepan on grill to keep warm, if space permits.

SOUTHERN-STYLE SQUASH AND OKRA

Makes 4 to 6 servings

2 small onions, sliced and separated into rings
3 medium crookneck squash, cut into ¼-inch slices
1 package (10 ounces) frozen whole okra, thawed and cut into bite-size pieces
2 tablespoons butter or margarine
1 clove garlic, minced
1 teaspoon salt
⅛ teaspoon pepper
½ teaspoon dried thyme, crushed
1 tablespoon lemon juice
¼ cup grated Cheddar cheese (1 ounce)

Place onion slices, squash and okra on 24×18-inch piece of heavy-duty foil. Dot with butter. Sprinkle with garlic, salt, pepper, thyme and lemon juice. Fold and seal foil edges tightly. Grill packet, on covered grill, over medium-hot **Kingsford®** briquets 25 to 30 minutes or until tender, turning packet over once. To serve, unwrap foil packet and sprinkle with Cheddar cheese.

PEACHES IN PORT

Makes 4 to 6 servings

6 to 8 large fresh peaches, peeled and cut into sixths
2 teaspoons lemon juice
¼ cup tawny port wine
2 tablespoons butter or margarine

Arrange peaches on 24×18-inch piece of heavy-duty foil. Sprinkle with lemon juice and port; dot with butter. Fold foil loosely around fruit and seal edges tightly. Grill packet, on covered grill, over medium-hot **Kingsford®** briquets about 15 minutes or until fruit is hot, turning packet once.

Southeast Pork Barbecue:
Corn Muffins (page 11), Peaches in Port
and Barbecued Pork Leg with Sam's Mop Sauce

SAVOY CABBAGE POCKETS

Makes 4 servings

    8 to 12 savoy cabbage leaves or green cabbage
        leaves
 ¼ cup olive or vegetable oil
 1 pint shucked oysters
 1 tablespoon chopped fresh thyme *or* 1 teaspoon
        dried thyme, crushed
    Salt and pepper

Immerse cabbage leaves in large saucepan of boiling water 3 minutes; drain. Remove center vein. Brush cabbage leaves with 2 tablespoons of the oil. Divide oysters among cabbage leaves; lightly sprinkle with thyme, salt and pepper.

Roll up leaves, jelly-roll style, folding in sides. Brush outer leaves with remaining 2 tablespoons oil. Place in foil pan, seam-side down. Place uncovered foil pan on grill not directly over coals. Cover grill; cook over medium-hot **Kingsford® briquets** 10 to 15 minutes or until oysters are firm and edges curled.

GRILLED SWORDFISH

Makes 4 servings

 4 fresh or frozen swordfish steaks, ½ inch thick
        (about 2 pounds)
 ⅓ cup tomato paste (half of 6-ounce can)
 ¼ cup dry red wine
 6 cloves garlic, sliced
 ⅛ teaspoon cayenne pepper or few dashes hot
        pepper sauce
 3 tablespoons chopped cilantro or parsley
 2 tablespoons olive or vegetable oil

Thaw fish, if frozen. In small saucepan, combine tomato paste, wine, garlic and cayenne. Bring to boil. Reduce heat; simmer, covered, 1 hour, stirring occasionally. Press mixture through sieve; discard garlic. Stir in cilantro and oil. Cool to room temperature.

Place fish in shallow glass dish; brush cooled marinade over fish. Cover and refrigerate 30 minutes.

Drain fish; reserve marinade. Grill fish, on covered grill, over medium-hot **Kingsford® briquets** 4 minutes; brush with marinade. Turn and cook 3 to 5 minutes longer or until fish flakes easily when tested with fork. Brush again with marinade. Transfer to serving platter.

GRILLED TOMATOES

Makes 4 servings

    2 large tomatoes
    2 tablespoons olive or vegetable oil
 1½ teaspoons chopped fresh basil *or* ½ teaspoon
        dried basil, crushed
    Salt and pepper

In covered grill, arrange medium-hot **Kingsford® briquets** on one side of grill. Slice each tomato in half crosswise; remove excess juice and seeds. Drizzle tomato halves with oil. Place in foil pan. Place foil pan on edge of grill not directly over coals. (Swordfish steaks will grill directly over coals.) Cook tomatoes, on covered grill, 10 to 14 minutes or until heated through. Sprinkle cut surfaces with basil, salt and pepper. Garnish with fresh basil, if desired.

East Coast Fish and Oyster Barbecue:
*Grilled Tomatoes, Savoy Cabbage Pockets
and Grilled Swordfish*

Northwest Grilled Cornish Game Hen Dinner

- **Grilled Cornish Game Hens**
- **Rice Pilaf with Sauteed Pecans**
- **Skewered Vegetables**
- **Baked Honey Apples**

To prepare this menu, you'll need to use 65 Kingsford® Charcoal Briquets (about 4 pounds).

RICE PILAF WITH SAUTEED PECANS

Makes 4 servings

⅓ cup wild rice
2⅔ cups water
1 teaspoon instant chicken bouillon granules
1 cup long grain rice
½ cup coarsely chopped pecans
3 tablespoons butter or margarine
2 tablespoons chopped parsley

Wash wild rice under cold running water in strainer about 1 minute, lifting rice to rinse well.

In 2-quart saucepan with tight-fitting lid, combine water, wild rice and chicken bouillon granules. Bring to boil. Reduce heat; cover and simmer 20 minutes. Add long grain rice; return to boil. Reduce heat and simmer, covered, 20 to 25 minutes longer or until rice is tender and water is absorbed.

Meanwhile, in small skillet, saute pecans in butter about 2 minutes or until golden. Add pecans to hot rice mixture; stir in parsley. Toss lightly until combined. Serve immediately.

BAKED HONEY APPLES

Makes 4 servings

2 to 3 apples, cored and sliced into ¾-inch rings
½ cup butter or margarine
⅓ cup honey

Arrange 2 or 3 apple rings on each of four 12×12-inch pieces of heavy-duty foil. Dot with butter; drizzle with honey. Fold foil loosely around apples; seal edges. Grill packets, on covered grill, over medium-hot **Kingsford® briquets** 12 to 15 minutes or until apples are crisp-tender, turning packets once.

GRILLED CORNISH GAME HENS

Makes 4 servings

2 Cornish game hens (1 to 1½ pounds each)
3 tablespoons olive or vegetable oil
⅓ cup lemon juice
1 tablespoon black peppercorns, coarsely crushed
½ teaspoon salt
Sprig fresh rosemary

Split hens lengthwise. Rinse under cold running water; pat dry with paper toweling. Place hens in large plastic bag; set in bowl. In small bowl, combine oil, lemon juice, peppercorns and salt. Pour marinade over hens in bag. Close bag securely and refrigerate several hours or overnight, turning hens occasionally to coat with marinade.

Arrange medium-hot **Kingsford® briquets** around drip pan. Just before grilling, add rosemary sprig to coals. Drain hens; reserve marinade. Place hens, skin-side up, over drip pan. Cover grill and cook 45 minutes or until thigh moves easily and juices run clear. Baste with marinade occasionally. Garnish with fresh rosemary, if desired.

SKEWERED VEGETABLES

Makes 4 servings

2 medium zucchini, cut into 1½-inch slices
8 small boiling onions
8 fresh medium mushrooms
2 tablespoons butter or margarine, melted
4 cherry tomatoes
Salt and pepper

In medium saucepan, cook zucchini and onions, covered, in boiling water to cover for 1 minute. Remove with slotted spoon and drain. Alternately thread zucchini, onions and mushrooms on 4 skewers. Brush with butter.

Grill vegetables, on covered grill, over medium-hot **Kingsford® briquets** 6 minutes or until tender, carefully turning skewers once. Add cherry tomatoes to end of skewers during last minute of grilling. Season to taste with salt and pepper. Serve immediately.

Northwest Grilled Cornish Game Hen Dinner:
*Grilled Cornish Game Hens, Skewered Vegetables,
Rice Pilaf with Sauteed Pecans and Baked Honey Apples*

Southern Spicy Ribs and Fruit Dinner

- Pork Spareribs
- Hot Apple Salad
- Grilled Potato Hash
- Corn Muffins (see page 11)
- Fruit Kabobs with Whiskey Baste

To prepare this menu, you'll need to use 80 Kingsford® Charcoal Briquets (about 5 pounds).

PORK SPARERIBS

Makes 4 servings

4 pounds pork spareribs or pork back ribs
1¼ cups K.C. Masterpiece® Barbecue Sauce

Remove breast section from ribs, if desired. Cut ribs into 4 or 5 rib portions. Arrange medium-hot **Kingsford® briquets** around drip pan. Place ribs over drip pan; cover grill and cook 1¼ hours. Turn; brush with barbecue sauce. Cook, on covered grill, 10 to 15 minutes longer or until ribs are thoroughly cooked, brushing once or twice with barbecue sauce. Bring remaining sauce to boil and serve with ribs, if desired.

HOT APPLE SALAD

Makes 4 servings

2 red cooking apples, cored and thinly sliced (2 cups)
3 cups finely shredded red cabbage
4 teaspoons butter or margarine, cut up
3 tablespoons rice wine vinegar
4 teaspoons sugar
¾ teaspoon salt
¼ teaspoon caraway seed

In bowl, toss together all ingredients. Turn out onto 24×18-inch piece of heavy-duty foil. Fold edges around apple mixture; seal edges tightly. Grill packet, on covered grill, over medium-hot **Kingsford® briquets** 45 minutes or until apples are tender, turning packet every 15 minutes.

Southern Spicy Ribs and Fruit Dinner:
Pork Spareribs, Fruit Kabobs with Whiskey Baste and Hot Apple Salad

GRILLED POTATO HASH

Makes 4 servings

2 tablespoons butter or margarine
2 tablespoons all-purpose flour
¾ teaspoon salt
¼ teaspoon seasoned pepper
⅛ teaspoon celery seed
1 cup milk
4 medium potatoes, peeled and cut into cubes
1 cup chopped onion
½ cup chopped green pepper
¼ teaspoon paprika

In medium saucepan, melt butter. Blend in flour, salt, seasoned pepper and celery seed. Stir in milk all at once. Cook and stir over medium heat until thickened and bubbly. Cook and stir 1 minute longer.

Add potatoes, onion and green pepper. Turn potato mixture out onto 24×18-inch piece of heavy-duty foil; sprinkle with paprika. Fold foil loosely around potato mixture and seal edges tightly.

Grill packet, on covered grill, over medium-hot **Kingsford® briquets** 45 to 50 minutes or until potatoes are tender, turning packet every 15 minutes.

FRUIT KABOBS WITH WHISKEY BASTE

Makes 4 servings

2 tablespoons honey
2 tablespoons whiskey
1 tablespoon lemon juice
1 can (8 ounces) pineapple chunks, drained
1 large banana, diagonally sliced into 1-inch pieces
1 orange, peeled and sectioned
8 maraschino cherries

In large bowl, combine honey, whiskey and lemon juice; add pineapple chunks, banana pieces, orange sections and cherries. Gently toss to coat fruit well. Cover and refrigerate up to 2 hours or until ready to grill.

Remove fruit with slotted spoon, reserving whiskey baste. Alternately thread fruit on skewers. Grill fruit kabobs, on covered grill, over medium-low **Kingsford® briquets** 5 to 10 minutes or until fruit is warmed through, basting frequently with whiskey baste.

ROASTED CHESTNUTS

Makes 8 servings

4 cups chestnuts

Using sharp knife, make an × on flat side of each chestnut. Place nuts in 13×9×2-inch baking pan or in foil pan. Grill chestnuts, on covered grill, over medium-hot **Kingsford® briquets** 10 to 15 minutes or until skin begins to lift away from nuts, stirring once. Peel outer skin while still warm.

GARLIC MUSHROOMS

Makes 8 servings

32 large fresh mushrooms
½ cup olive or vegetable oil
2 cloves garlic, minced

Remove stems from mushrooms; reserve caps. In bowl, combine oil and garlic; add mushroom caps. Gently toss to coat. Remove mushrooms with slotted spoon; place mushroom caps on piece of heavy-duty foil. Seal edges tightly. Grill at side of roast over medium-hot **Kingsford® briquets** 10 to 15 minutes or until tender.

GRILLED TENDERLOIN WITH COGNAC

Makes 8 servings

1 beef tenderloin roast (2 pounds)
¼ cup whole green, white or black peppercorns
   Garlic Mushrooms (recipe follows)
⅓ cup cognac or other brandy
1 cup whipping cream
2 tablespoons Dijon-style mustard
1 tablespoon Worcestershire sauce
2 teaspoons lemon juice

Trim excess fat from roast. Crack peppercorns coarsely with mortar and pestle; sprinkle on roast and press into surface.

Arrange medium-hot **Kingsford® briquets** around drip pan. Place roast over drip pan. Cover grill and cook, turning once, until meat thermometer registers 140°F for rare (about 45 minutes), 150°F for medium-rare (about 55 minutes), or 170°F for well-done (about 60 minutes). While roast is cooking, prepare Garlic Mushrooms. About 15 minutes before meat is done, place mushrooms next to meat.

When roast is grilled to desired doneness, warm cognac in skillet on range-top. Remove from heat. Place roast in heated skillet. Carefully ignite cognac with match; allow flames to subside, carefully spooning cognac over meat. Remove roast to serving platter; reserve juices.

In saucepan, combine cream, mustard and Worcestershire sauce. Bring to boil. Cook and stir, over medium-low heat, 3 minutes or until slightly thickened. Remove from heat; stir in lemon juice and reserved cognac juices. Carve roast and arrange with Garlic Mushrooms. Pour cream sauce over sliced roast and mushrooms. Garnish with fresh rosemary, if desired.

FRESH BLACKBERRY COBBLER

Makes 8 servings

4 cups whole blackberries or blueberries
½ cup sugar
2 tablespoons butter or margarine
1 cup packaged biscuit mix
2 tablespoons sugar
⅓ cup light cream
   Vanilla ice cream

In 10-inch heavy skillet with tight-fitting lid, combine blackberries and ½ cup sugar. Dot with butter. Cook and stir, over medium heat, until bubbly. Keep hot.

For biscuit topper, in medium bowl, combine biscuit mix, 2 tablespoons sugar and cream; mix well. Spoon biscuit batter in 8 mounds over hot berry mixture.

Cover skillet and place on edge of grill over medium-hot **Kingsford® briquets.** Cook, on covered grill, about 15 minutes or until done. Serve warm with vanilla ice cream.

Western Chestnuts and Tenderloin Barbecue:
Roasted Chestnuts, Grilled Tenderloin with Cognac, Garlic Mushrooms and Fresh Blackberry Cobbler

Pacific Coast Salmon Barbecue

- Grilled Oysters
- Pacific Coast Barbecued Salmon
- Marinated Vegetable Salad with Herbed Salad Dressing
- Grill-Baked Sweet Potatoes
- Sour Cream Biscuits
- Sherbet or Ice Cream

To prepare this menu, you'll need to use 70 Kingsford® Charcoal Briquets (about 4½ pounds).

GRILLED OYSTERS

Makes 4 appetizer servings

12 to 16 fresh oysters in shells
½ cup butter or margarine
2 tablespoons lemon juice
2 tablespoons chopped parsley

Thoroughly scrub oysters. Arrange oysters on grid; do not open shells. Grill oysters, on uncovered grill, over medium-hot **Kingsford® briquets** 12 to 15 minutes or until shells steam open. (Discard any oysters that do not open.)

Meanwhile, in saucepan, combine butter, lemon juice and parsley. Heat butter mixture on edge of grill until butter is melted, stirring frequently.

Carefully remove cooked oysters from grill and serve hot with lemon-butter mixture spooned over.

PACIFIC COAST BARBECUED SALMON

Makes 4 servings

4 fresh or frozen salmon steaks, 1 inch thick (about 8 ounces each)
½ cup butter or margarine
2 tablespoons fresh lemon juice
1 tablespoon Worcestershire sauce

Thaw salmon steaks, if frozen. In saucepan, combine butter, lemon juice and Worcestershire sauce; simmer 5 minutes, stirring frequently. Brush salmon steaks with butter mixture. Place steaks in well-greased wire grill basket.

Grill steaks, on uncovered grill, over medium-hot **Kingsford® briquets** 6 to 9 minutes or until lightly browned. Baste steaks with butter mixture and turn; grill 6 to 9 minutes longer, basting often, until fish flakes easily when tested with fork.

SOUR CREAM BISCUITS

Makes 8 biscuits

1¼ cups all-purpose flour
1½ teaspoons baking powder
½ teaspoon salt
¼ teaspoon baking soda
½ cup sour cream
¼ cup light cream or milk

In bowl, stir together flour, baking powder, salt and baking soda. In small bowl, combine sour cream and light cream. Make a well in center of dry ingredients; add sour cream mixture. Stir just until dough clings together and forms a ball.

Knead dough gently on lightly floured surface 10 to 12 strokes. Roll or pat to ½-inch thickness. Cut dough into 2¼-inch rounds. Using metal spatula, carefully transfer cut biscuits to lightly greased baking sheet. Bake in 375°F oven about 15 minutes or until golden. Serve warm.

Pacific Coast Salmon Barbecue:
Grilled Oysters, Pacific Coast Barbecued Salmon, Marinated Vegetable Salad (page 24) and Sour Cream Biscuits

MARINATED VEGETABLE SALAD

Makes 4 servings

6 medium carrots, diagonally sliced into ¼-inch
    pieces
1 medium zucchini, cut into 2-inch julienne strips
1 medium red onion, thinly sliced and slices
    halved
¼ cup chopped red or green pepper
1 tablespoon chopped parsley
    Herbed Salad Dressing (recipe follows)

In large saucepan, cook carrots, covered, in boiling salted water to cover for 2 minutes. Add zucchini; return to boil. Cook, covered, 2 minutes longer or until vegetables are just tender. Drain; rinse under cold running water and drain again. Transfer vegetables to bowl. Add onion, red pepper and parsley. Toss with Herbed Salad Dressing. Cover and refrigerate several hours or overnight.

HERBED SALAD DRESSING

Makes ½ cup

¼ cup olive or vegetable oil
¼ cup vinegar
2 tablespoons grated Parmesan cheese (optional)
¼ teaspoon dried oregano, crushed
¼ teaspoon dried basil, crushed
⅛ teaspoon salt

In screw-top jar, combine all ingredients. Cover and shake well.

GRILL-BAKED SWEET POTATOES

Makes 4 servings

4 medium sweet potatoes
    Vegetable oil
4 tablespoons butter or margarine
4 tablespoons brown sugar

Tear off four 6×9-inch pieces of heavy-duty foil. Brush sweet potatoes with oil. Pierce several times with fork. Wrap potatoes in foil. Grill potatoes, on uncovered grill, over medium-hot **Kingsford®** **briquets** about 1 hour or until tender, turning once. Remove foil. Open potatoes with tines of fork and push ends to fluff. Top each with 1 tablespoon butter and 1 tablespoon brown sugar.

Western Rockies Beef Ribs and Pineapple Barbecue

- Jalapeño Pepper Jelly with Cream Cheese and Assorted Crackers
- Barbecued Beef Short Ribs
- Spicy Rice Molds
- Tossed Green Salad
- Flaming Pineapple
- Cabernet Sauvignon Wine

To prepare this menu, you'll need to use about 100 Kingsford® Charcoal Briquets (about 7 pounds).

BARBECUED BEEF SHORT RIBS

Makes 8 servings

6 pounds beef short ribs, cut into 1-rib pieces
1 cup water
¾ cup soy sauce
⅔ cup dry sherry
½ cup packed dark brown sugar
6 cloves garlic, minced
1 tablespoon cayenne pepper
1 tablespoon grated fresh ginger
2 teaspoons Chinese five-spice powder

Trim excess fat from ribs. In large roasting pan, arrange ribs in single layer. For marinade, in medium saucepan, combine remaining ingredients. Cook over medium heat until sugar is dissolved. Remove from heat; cool slightly. Pour marinade over ribs. Cover and refrigerate 1 hour, turning ribs once.

Cover roasting pan with foil. Arrange medium-hot **Kingsford®** **briquets** around drip pan. Place roasting pan on grill; cover grill and cook ribs 45 minutes. Remove ribs from roasting pan and cook, on covered grill, 45 to 60 minutes longer or until ribs are tender, turning and brushing with marinade occasionally. Brush ribs again with marinade just before serving. Bring remaining marinade to boil; reserve ⅓ cup marinade to spoon over Spicy Rice Molds, if desired.

Western Rockies Beef Ribs and Pineapple Barbecue:
Barbecued Beef Short Ribs with Spicy Rice Molds
and Flaming Pineapple (recipes on page 26)

JALAPEÑO PEPPER JELLY

Makes 6 half-pints

1 large green pepper, cut into quarters
**2 fresh jalapeño peppers, seeds and ribs
   removed**
6½ cups sugar
1½ cups cider vinegar
**½ of 6-ounce package (1 foil pouch) liquid fruit
   pectin**
Several drops green food coloring (optional)

Finely chop green pepper and jalapeño peppers
using food processor or knife. In 4½-quart Dutch
oven, combine chopped peppers, sugar and vinegar.
Bring to boil; reduce heat. Cover and simmer, stirring
often, about 15 minutes or until pepper mixture turns
transparent.

Stir in pectin; add food coloring. Return to full rolling
boil; boil, uncovered, 1 minute, stirring constantly.
Remove from heat. Skim off any foam with metal
spoon. Pour at once into hot sterilized half-pint jars;
seal, using metal lids or paraffin. Serve with cream
cheese and assorted crisp crackers, if desired.

SPICY RICE MOLDS

Makes 8 servings

2⅔ cups water
1⅓ cups long grain rice
2 tablespoons butter or margarine
1½ teaspoons soy sauce
3 tablespoons chopped green onion (optional)
3 tablespoons slivered almonds, toasted
2 tablespoons finely chopped parsley

In 2-quart saucepan with tight-fitting lid, combine
water, rice, butter and soy sauce. Cover. Bring to boil;
reduce heat. Cook 15 minutes; remove from heat. Let
stand 10 minutes.

Pack about ½ cup rice mixture into buttered ½-cup
mold; unmold onto individual serving plate. Repeat
with remaining rice mixture. Sprinkle green onion,
toasted almonds and parsley on top of each. Drizzle
with ⅓ cup reserved boiled marinade from
Barbecued Beef Short Ribs, if desired.

TOSSED GREEN SALAD

Makes 8 servings

2 heads romaine, red leaf or iceberg lettuce
1 cucumber, peeled
4 medium tomatoes, cut into quarters
4 green onions, finely chopped
¼ cup finely chopped fresh basil leaves or parsley
**1 cup prepared Hidden Valley Ranch® Original
   Ranch® Salad Dressing**
Salt and pepper

Tear lettuce into bite-size pieces; place in serving
bowl and refrigerate, covered with damp paper
toweling, to crispen. Slice cucumber in half
lengthwise and scoop out seeds. Coarsely chop
cucumber. Toss chopped cucumber, tomatoes,
onions, basil and lettuce to mix well. Pour dressing on
salad and toss to coat. Season to taste with salt and
pepper.

FLAMING PINEAPPLE

Makes 8 servings

1 fresh pineapple
½ cup packed light brown sugar
½ teaspoon ground cinnamon
⅛ teaspoon freshly ground nutmeg
¼ cup butter or margarine
½ cup light rum
**Ice cream, whipped cream or chilled soft
   custard (optional)**

Cut pineapple in half lengthwise, leaving on green
top. Cut each half lengthwise into four sections.
Carefully cut pineapple away from peel. Remove
core, then cut pineapple into 1-inch chunks;
rearrange pineapple chunks on peel. Place in large
baking pan or foil pan. Sprinkle with brown sugar,
cinnamon and nutmeg; dot with butter. Place pan on
edge of grill. Heat pineapple, on covered grill, over
medium-hot **Kingsford® briquets** 10 minutes; remove
pan from grill.

In small saucepan, heat rum on range-top over low
heat just until hot. Carefully ignite with match; pour
flaming rum over pineapple, stirring sauce and
spooning over pineapple. Serve with ice cream.

MARINATED ARTICHOKE

Makes 4 to 6 appetizer servings

1 large fresh artichoke
  Lemon juice
⅓ cup olive or vegetable oil
3 tablespoons vinegar
1 tablespoon sliced green onion
2 teaspoons chopped parsley
1 clove garlic, minced
1 teaspoon sugar
1 teaspoon lemon juice
¼ teaspoon salt
¼ teaspoon dried thyme, crushed
  Dash cayenne pepper

Trim stem and remove loose outer leaves from artichoke. Cut 1 inch off tops; snip off sharp leaf tips. Brush cut edges with lemon juice. In large saucepan, cook artichoke in boiling water 20 minutes or just until tender and inner leaves can be pulled out easily. Drain and cool slightly. Place artichoke in plastic bag; set bag in bowl.

In screw-top jar, combine oil, vinegar, onion, parsley, garlic, sugar, 1 teaspoon lemon juice, the salt, thyme and cayenne. Cover tightly; shake well. Pour marinade over artichoke in bag. Close bag tightly and refrigerate several hours or overnight. Drain artichoke; place on platter to serve.

ITALIAN-STYLE PEPPERS

Makes 6 servings

4 large red or green peppers
3 tablespoons olive or vegetable oil
1 clove garlic, minced
⅛ teaspoon dried oregano, crushed
  Salt and pepper

Cut peppers into quarters lengthwise; remove seeds and ribs. Grill peppers, skin-side down, on uncovered grill, over medium-hot Kingsford® briquets 6 to 8 minutes or until skins begin to wrinkle and show grill marks. Immediately place under cold running water. Gently pat dry with paper toweling.

Slice peppers into ½-inch-wide strips. Heat oil in foil pan on grill. Add pepper strips, garlic and oregano. Cover pan with foil. Cook, on covered grill, over medium-hot coals 15 minutes or until heated through, stirring once. Season to taste with salt and pepper. Serve immediately.

CREAMY POTATO BAKE

Makes 6 servings

5 medium potatoes, peeled and thinly sliced
1 medium onion, sliced
6 tablespoons butter or margarine
⅓ cup shredded Cheddar cheese
2 tablespoons chopped parsley
1 tablespoon Worcestershire sauce
  Salt and pepper
⅓ cup chicken broth

Place sliced potatoes and onion on 22×18-inch piece of heavy-duty foil. Dot with butter. Sprinkle with cheese, parsley, Worcestershire sauce, salt and pepper. Fold up foil around potatoes; add chicken broth. Seal edges tightly.

Grill packet, on covered grill, over medium-hot Kingsford® briquets about 35 minutes or until potatoes are tender.

GRILLED CAPON

Makes 6 servings

  1 capon or whole roasting chicken (6 to 7 pounds)
    Salt
¼ teaspoon poultry seasoning
1½ medium onions, quartered
  1 tablespoon rubbed sage
  2 stalks celery with leaves, cut into 1-inch pieces
  2 medium carrots, cut into ½-inch pieces
  2 tablespoons butter or margarine, melted
    K.C. Masterpiece® Barbecue Sauce

Wash capon thoroughly under cold running water; pat dry with paper toweling. Rub cavity lightly with salt and poultry seasoning. Insert a few onion quarters in neck and fold neck skin over onion. Fold wings across back with tips touching to secure neck skin. Sprinkle 1 teaspoon of the sage in body cavity and stuff with remaining onion quarters, the celery and carrots. Tie legs and tail together with kitchen twine. Insert meat thermometer in center of thigh muscle, not touching bone. Brush skin with melted butter. Rub with remaining 2 teaspoons sage.

Arrange medium-hot **Kingsford®** briquets around drip pan. Place capon, breast-side up, over drip pan; cover grill and cook 1½ to 2 hours or until thermometer registers 185°F. Tent with heavy-duty foil to prevent overbrowning, if necessary. Brush capon with barbecue sauce during last 10 minutes of cooking. Garnish with parsley; serve with additional heated barbecue sauce, if desired.

HOT FRUIT WITH POUND CAKE

Makes 6 servings

  2 cans (16 ounces each) fruits for salad
¼ cup Madeira or port wine
  2 tablespoons butter or margarine
¾ teaspoon grated fresh ginger
  1 pound cake (10¾ ounces), sliced and lightly toasted
    Vanilla ice cream (optional)

Drain fruit; reserve ½ cup syrup. Cut up any large pieces of fruit. In heavy skillet or foil pan, combine fruit, reserved syrup, wine, butter and ginger; place skillet on grill. Heat fruit mixture, on covered grill, over medium-hot **Kingsford®** briquets 15 to 20 minutes or until heated through, stirring once. Spoon warm fruit mixture over toasted pound cake slices. Top each serving with vanilla ice cream.

Midwest Italian-Style Capon Dinner:
Grilled Capon with Italian-Style Peppers and Creamy Potato Bake (recipes on page 27)

Gulf Coast Shrimp and Mushroom Barbecue

- Sauteed Mushrooms in Garlic Butter
- Bacon-Wrapped Shrimp with Mexican Fried Rice
- Grilled Zucchini
- Cornbread
- Texas Pecan Pralines

To prepare this menu, you'll need to use 50 Kingsford® Charcoal Briquets (about 3 pounds).

SAUTEED MUSHROOMS IN GARLIC BUTTER

Makes 6 servings

¼ cup butter or margarine
¼ cup white wine vinegar
½ teaspoon garlic powder
¼ teaspoon salt
⅛ teaspoon pepper
  6 cups fresh mushrooms (1 pound)
  1 small red onion, thinly sliced and separated into rings
    Chopped parsley

In heavy 10-inch skillet, melt butter, on uncovered grill, directly over medium-hot **Kingsford®** briquets. Stir in vinegar, garlic powder, salt and pepper; add whole mushrooms and onion rings. Cover skillet; cook 10 minutes. Stir vegetables and cook 10 minutes longer. Sprinkle with parsley before serving.

GRILLED ZUCCHINI

Makes 6 servings

3 medium zucchini
  Desired seasonings: basil, oregano, thyme, dill weed, lemon pepper, grated Parmesan cheese, celery salt or garlic salt
2 to 3 tablespoons butter or margarine, softened

Cut zucchini into halves lengthwise. Sprinkle 3 halves with desired seasoning. Spread butter on remaining 3 halves. Place seasoned and buttered halves together; cut crosswise and wrap individual servings in heavy-duty foil. Grill zucchini, on uncovered grill, over medium-hot **Kingsford®** briquets 15 to 20 minutes or until tender, turning often.

BACON-WRAPPED SHRIMP

Makes 6 servings

1 pound fresh or frozen shrimp, shelled and deveined
1 small onion, finely chopped
½ cup olive or vegetable oil
½ teaspoon sugar
½ teaspoon cayenne pepper
¼ teaspoon salt
¼ teaspoon dried oregano, crushed
½ teaspoon garlic powder
½ pound bacon
Mexican Fried Rice (recipe follows)

Thaw shrimp, if frozen. Place shrimp in plastic bag; set in bowl. For marinade, in small bowl, combine onion, oil, sugar, cayenne pepper, salt, oregano and garlic powder. Pour marinade over shrimp; close bag. Marinate shrimp 3 hours in refrigerator, turning occasionally.

Cut bacon slices into halves lengthwise, then crosswise. In large skillet, partially cook bacon. Drain on paper toweling. Drain shrimp; reserve marinade. Wrap bacon strips around shrimp and secure with wooden picks. Place shrimp in wire grill basket or on 12×9-inch piece of heavy-duty foil. (If using foil, puncture foil in several places.)

Grill shrimp, on uncovered grill, over medium-hot **Kingsford® briquets** 6 minutes or until bacon and shrimp are done, turning basket or individual shrimp once and basting with marinade. Serve with Mexican Fried Rice.

MEXICAN FRIED RICE

Makes 6 servings

3 tablespoons vegetable oil
1 cup long grain rice
2 cups water
1 cup chili salsa
½ cup chopped green pepper
1 small onion, chopped
1 clove garlic, minced

In 12-inch skillet, heat oil. Add rice; cook until golden brown, stirring often. Stir in remaining ingredients. Bring mixture to boil; reduce heat. Cover; simmer 15 to 20 minutes or until rice is tender. Season to taste; serve with additional salsa, if desired.

CORNBREAD

Makes 6 to 8 servings

2 cups water
½ cup chopped green onions
1 teaspoon salt
1 teaspoon sugar
1 teaspoon pepper
1 cup yellow cornmeal
1 cup white cornmeal
Vegetable oil

In medium saucepan, bring water to boil with onions, salt, sugar and pepper. Turn off heat. Combine cornmeals and add to water mixture in thin stream, stirring constantly. Cool to room temperature.

Form cornmeal mixture into 3-inch rounds, ½ inch thick. Heat 1 inch oil to 350°F in deep-fryer or heavy, deep skillet. Add cornbread rounds in batches—do not crowd—and cook until golden brown, about 1 minute per side. Using slotted spoon, transfer to paper toweling to drain. Serve immediately.

TEXAS PECAN PRALINES

Makes about 45 pralines

1 cup granulated sugar
1 cup packed light brown sugar
1 cup buttermilk
¼ teaspoon salt
3 tablespoons butter or margarine
2 cups pecan halves

Butter sides of heavy 2-quart saucepan; add sugars, buttermilk and salt. Cook over medium-high heat 6 to 8 minutes until boiling, stirring constantly with wooden spoon to dissolve sugars. (Avoid splashing mixture on sides of pan.)

Cook over medium-low heat, stirring occasionally, 16 to 18 minutes or until mixture reaches soft-ball stage, 234°F on a candy thermometer (or until syrup, when dropped into very cold water, forms a soft ball that flattens when removed from water). Remove pan from heat.

Add butter; *do not stir*. Cool, without stirring, about 20 minutes or until 150°F. Stir in pecans. Beat vigorously with wooden spoon 2 to 3 minutes or until candy begins to thicken but is still glossy. Drop candy by teaspoonfuls onto wax-paper-lined baking sheet. (If candy becomes too stiff, stir in a few drops of hot water.) Let dry until hard. Store in tightly covered container.

Gulf Coast Shrimp and Mushroom Barbecue:
Sauteed Mushrooms in Garlic Butter (page 29) and Bacon-Wrapped Shrimp with Mexican Fried Rice

Heartland Pork Chops and Fruit Barbecue

- Barbecued Pork Chops
- Corn-Pepper-Sausage Skillet
- Apple Slaw
- Strawberries 'n' Cream

To prepare this menu, you'll need to use 50 Kingsford® Charcoal Briquets (about 3 pounds).

BARBECUED PORK CHOPS

Makes 6 servings

    6 pork loin chops, cut 1 inch thick
 ½ teaspoon seasoned salt
    6 slices orange
    6 thin slices onion
    6 thin slices lemon
 ⅓ cup K.C. Masterpiece® Barbecue Sauce

Arrange medium-hot **Kingsford® briquets** to one side of grill with drip pan next to briquets. Sprinkle chops with seasoned salt. Place chops over drip pan; cover grill and cook 40 minutes or until nearly done, turning once after 25 minutes.

Top each chop with slices of orange, onion and lemon and about 1 tablespoon barbecue sauce. Cover grill and cook 5 to 10 minutes longer or until chops are tender and thoroughly cooked.

APPLE SLAW

Makes 6 servings

    2 red apples, chopped
    1 tablespoon lemon juice
    1 small head cabbage, shredded (about 5 cups)
 ¾ cup prepared Hidden Valley Ranch® Original Ranch® Salad Dressing
    Pepper

In bowl, toss chopped apples with lemon juice. Add cabbage and salad dressing; toss to thoroughly coat. Season to taste with pepper. Cover; refrigerate before serving.

Heartland Pork Chops and Fruit Barbecue: Apple Slaw, Corn-Pepper-Sausage Skillet and Barbecued Pork Chops

CORN-PEPPER-SAUSAGE SKILLET

Makes 6 servings

 12 ounces Italian or bulk pork sausage
    1 cup chopped green or red pepper
    1 cup chopped onion
    3 cups fresh whole kernel corn *or* 1 package (16 ounces) frozen whole kernel corn, thawed
 ½ teaspoon garlic salt
 ¼ teaspoon pepper
 ¼ teaspoon chili powder
 ¼ teaspoon ground cumin
    Halved cherry tomatoes (optional)
    Herbed cream cheese, softened (optional)
    Sprig parsley (optional)

Crumble sausage into heavy 10-inch skillet or heavy foil pan. Add green pepper and onion. Place skillet, on covered grill, over medium-hot **Kingsford® briquets** about 15 minutes or until meat is browned, stirring once or twice. Remove from grill; carefully drain off fat.

Stir in corn, garlic salt, pepper, chili powder and cumin; mix well. Cover skillet with foil. Grill, on covered grill, over medium-hot coals, 10 minutes longer or until heated through. Garnish with tomato halves spread with cream cheese; top with parsley sprig.

STRAWBERRIES 'N' CREAM

Makes 6 servings

    2 pints fresh strawberries, hulled and halved (4 cups)
 ¼ cup honey
    2 tablespoons orange-flavored liqueur
    1 quart vanilla ice cream

Arrange strawberries on 20×18-inch piece of heavy-duty foil. In small bowl, combine honey and liqueur. Drizzle over strawberries. Fold foil loosely around berries; seal edges tightly.

Grill packet, on covered grill, over medium-hot **Kingsford® briquets** 10 to 12 minutes or until berries are heated through. (If coals have cooled to medium, grill packet 12 to 15 minutes or until hot.) Serve hot over vanilla ice cream.

Southwest Mexican Chicken Barbecue

- **Over-the-Coals Spiced Popcorn**
- **Mexican Chicken with Spicy Bacon**
- **Charcoal-Grilled Tortillas**
- **Charcoal-Baked Bananas Flambé**
- **Mexican Beer or Iced Tea**

To prepare this menu, you'll need to use 84 Kingsford® Charcoal Briquets (about 5½ pounds).

MEXICAN CHICKEN WITH SPICY BACON

Makes 4 servings

2 serrano chili peppers
2 cloves garlic
　Dash ground cloves
　Dash ground cinnamon
4 slices bacon, partially cooked
1 whole roasting chicken (3½ to 4 pounds)

Remove stems from peppers. Slit open; remove seeds and ribs. Finely chop peppers and garlic. Place in small bowl. Stir in cloves and cinnamon. Cut bacon into 1-inch pieces.

Lift skin layer of chicken at neck cavity. Insert hand, lifting skin from meat along breast, thigh and drumstick. Using small metal spatula, spread pepper mixture evenly over meat under skin. Place layer of bacon pieces over pepper mixture. Skewer neck skin to back. Tie legs securely to tail with kitchen twine; twist wing tips under back of chicken. Insert meat thermometer in center of thigh muscle, not touching bone.

Arrange medium-hot **Kingsford® briquets** around drip pan. Place chicken, breast-side up, over drip pan. Cover grill and cook about 1 hour or until meat thermometer registers 185°F. Garnish with grilled cherry tomatoes and additional serrano chili peppers, if desired.

OVER-THE-COALS SPICED POPCORN

Makes about 8 cups

½ cup popcorn or 8 cups popped popcorn
2 tablespoons butter or margarine
½ teaspoon Worcestershire sauce
½ teaspoon chili powder
½ teaspoon lemon pepper
¼ teaspoon garlic powder
¼ teaspoon onion powder
⅛ teaspoon salt

If desired, pop ½ cup popcorn over coals in long-handled fireplace corn popper. Hold directly over, but not touching, hot **Kingsford® briquets;** shake vigorously until corn is popped, 3 to 4 minutes.

In saucepan, combine remaining ingredients. Set on edge of grill to melt butter. Toss butter mixture with popped popcorn.

CHARCOAL-BAKED BANANAS FLAMBÉ

Makes 4 servings

4 ripe medium bananas
4 tablespoons butter or margarine
½ cup packed brown sugar
¼ teaspoon ground allspice *or* ½ teaspoon ground cinnamon *or* freshly grated nutmeg
¼ cup lime juice
¼ cup dark rum

Grill unpeeled bananas, on covered grill, over medium-hot **Kingsford® briquets** about 8 minutes or until just barely tender and darkened in color. Remove from grill.

In 10-inch oven-proof skillet, combine butter, brown sugar and desired spice. Heat directly over medium-hot coals 2 to 3 minutes or until mixture is bubbly. Stir in lime juice.

Slit bananas lengthwise without removing peel. Arrange bananas in skillet. Grill, on uncovered grill, 6 to 8 minutes or until sauce thickens slightly and bananas are tender, spooning sauce over bananas occasionally. Remove skillet from grill.

In small saucepan, heat rum on range-top over low heat just until hot. Carefully ignite with match and pour flaming rum over bananas in skillet. When flame subsides, serve bananas with sauce spooned over.

Southwest Mexican Chicken Barbecue:
Charcoal-Baked Bananas Flambé and
Mexican Chicken with Spicy Bacon

Rocky Mountain Grilled Lamb Riblets Dinner

- Grilled Cheese
- Western Lamb Riblets
- Fresh Corn on the Grill
- Tossed Green Salad (see page 26)
- Homemade Peach Ice Cream

To prepare this menu, you'll need to use 65 Kingsford® Charcoal Briquets (about 4 pounds).

GRILLED CHEESE

Makes 6 servings

    1 piece raclette cheese* (12 to 16 ounces)
    1 tablespoon olive or vegetable oil
    ½ teaspoon ground oregano
      Sliced crusty French bread or large crackers

Place cheese in 10-inch iron skillet; brush with oil. Sprinkle oregano on top. Place bread slices around cheese in skillet.

Grill cheese, on covered grill, over medium-hot **Kingsford® briquets** 10 minutes or until cheese is very soft. Remove to table; spread cheese on bread slices.

*Raclette cheese is available at specialty cheese shops. You can try another soft cheese, such as Swiss, but cooking time may vary.

FRESH CORN ON THE GRILL

Makes 6 servings

    6 ears corn, with silk and husks intact
      Butter or margarine
      Salt and pepper

Turn back corn husks; do not remove. Remove silks with stiff brush; rinse corn under cold running water. Lay husks back into position. Roast ears, on covered grill, over medium-hot **Kingsford® briquets** about 25 minutes or until tender, turning corn often. Remove husks and serve with butter, salt and pepper, as desired.

Rocky Mountain Grilled Lamb Riblets Dinner:
Grilled Cheese, Fresh Corn on the Grill and
Western Lamb Riblets

WESTERN LAMB RIBLETS

Makes 6 servings

    5 pounds lamb riblets, cut into serving-size
      pieces
    ¾ cup chili sauce
    ½ cup honey
    ½ cup beer
    ¼ cup Worcestershire sauce
    ¼ cup finely chopped onion
    1 clove garlic, minced
    ½ teaspoon red pepper flakes

Trim excess fat from riblets. In saucepan, combine chili sauce, honey, beer, Worcestershire sauce, onion, garlic and red pepper flakes. Heat mixture to boiling. Reduce heat; simmer, covered, 10 minutes. Remove from heat; cool.

Place riblets in plastic bag; set bag in large bowl. Pour marinade over riblets in bag. Close bag securely and refrigerate about 2 hours, turning bag occasionally to distribute marinade evenly.

Drain riblets; reserve marinade. Arrange medium-hot **Kingsford® briquets** around drip pan. Place riblets over drip pan. Cover grill and cook 45 minutes, turning riblets and brushing with marinade twice. Bring remaining marinade to boil and serve with riblets.

HOMEMADE PEACH ICE CREAM

Makes 3 quarts

    1¼ cups sugar
    1 envelope unflavored gelatin
      Dash salt
    4 cups light cream
    1 egg, beaten
    2 teaspoons vanilla
    3 pounds ripe peaches, peeled and mashed
      (4½ cups)
    ¼ teaspoon ground mace *or* ¼ teaspoon almond
      extract

In large saucepan, combine ¾ cup of the sugar, the gelatin and salt. Stir in 2 cups of the cream. Cook and stir over medium heat until gelatin mixture almost boils and sugar dissolves.

Stir about ½ cup hot gelatin mixture into beaten egg; return to saucepan. Cook and stir 2 minutes longer. Cool. Stir in remaining 2 cups cream and the vanilla.

Stir together mashed peaches, remaining ½ cup sugar and the mace. Add to cooled egg mixture; mix well. Freeze in 4- or 5-quart ice cream freezer according to manufacturer's directions.

BEEF

Nothing brings out the flavor of beef better than a charcoal fire, and here you'll find plenty of savory recipes to fire up your appetite: everything from grilled sirloin steak to burgers and kabobs—even a whole brisket for the grill.

GRILLED STEAK WITH HOT SWEET ONIONS

Makes 4 servings

    3 large onions, cut into ¼-inch-thick slices
    2 tablespoons honey
    ½ teaspoon dry mustard
    ½ teaspoon salt
    ½ teaspoon paprika
    ½ teaspoon pepper
    4 beef loin T-bone or porterhouse steaks, cut 1
       inch thick (8 ounces each)

Arrange sliced onions on large square of heavy-duty foil. In small bowl, combine honey and mustard; drizzle over onions. Sprinkle with salt, paprika and pepper. Fold foil loosely around onions and seal edges tightly. Grill packet, on covered grill, over medium-hot **Kingsford® with Mesquite charcoal briquets** 20 minutes or until onions are tender; turn once. Slash any fat around edge of steaks every 4 inches. About 5 minutes after onions start to grill, place steaks on grill with onion packet. Grill 8 to 10 minutes on each side for medium-rare or to desired doneness. Serve onions on top of each steak.

Grilled Steak with Hot Sweet Onions

Stuffed Cheese Burgers

STUFFED CHEESE BURGERS

Makes 6 servings

1½ cups shredded Monterey Jack cheese (about 8 ounces)
1 can (2¼ ounces) chopped black olives
⅛ teaspoon hot pepper sauce
1¾ pounds ground beef
¼ cup finely chopped onion
1 teaspoon salt
½ teaspoon pepper
6 hamburger buns
   Butter or margarine, melted

In large bowl, combine cheese, olives and hot pepper sauce. Divide mixture evenly and shape into 6 balls. Mix ground beef with onion, salt and pepper; shape into 12 thin patties. Place 1 cheese ball in center of each of 6 patties and top each with a second patty. Seal edges to enclose cheese balls. Lightly oil grid. Grill patties, on covered grill, over medium-hot **Kingsford® briquets** 5 to 6 minutes on each side or until done.

Split buns, brush with butter and place, cut-side down, on grill to heat through. Serve Cheese Burgers on buns.

FLANK STEAK WITH GREEN CHILES

Makes 4 servings

1 beef flank steak (about 2 pounds)
5 long green chili peppers,* roasted and peeled, reserving juices
⅓ cup fresh lime juice (about 2 limes)
2 cloves garlic, minced
¼ teaspoon salt

Trim excess fat from steak. Place steak in shallow glass dish. Combine remaining ingredients in food processor or blender. Process until smooth, about 40 seconds. Pour marinade over steak; cover and refrigerate at least 3 hours or overnight. Drain steak; discard marinade. Grill steak, on uncovered grill, over medium-hot **Kingsford® briquets** about 6 minutes on each side for rare or to desired doneness. Carve steak diagonally across grain into thin slices.

*1 can (7 ounces) long green chili peppers can be substituted.

*Recipe courtesy of **California Beef Council***

SPICY BEEF SATAY

Makes 4 servings or 24 appetizer kabobs

1 boneless beef sirloin steak, cut ¾ to 1 inch thick (1 to 1¼ pounds)
¼ cup soy sauce
¼ cup dry sherry
2 tablespoons sesame oil
¼ cup sliced green onion
2 cloves garlic, minced
2 tablespoons brown sugar
1 teaspoon ground ginger
1 teaspoon red pepper flakes
½ cup crunchy peanut butter
¾ cup water

Place steak in freezer 30 minutes to firm; slice into ⅛- to ¼-inch-thick strips. In shallow glass dish, combine soy sauce, sherry, sesame oil, onion, garlic, sugar, ginger and ½ teaspoon of the red pepper flakes. Add beef strips; turn to coat with marinade. Cover and refrigerate 2 to 4 hours.

Soak twenty-four 8-inch bamboo skewers in water 20 minutes. Drain beef; reserve 2 tablespoons marinade. Thread beef strips, accordion-style, on skewers.

Meanwhile, in small saucepan, combine reserved marinade, remaining ½ teaspoon red pepper flakes, the peanut butter and water. Heat over low heat 8 to 10 minutes or until sauce is thick and warm (add more water if necessary). Grill kabobs, on uncovered grill, over medium-hot **Kingsford® briquets** 2 minutes. Turn and cook 2 minutes longer. Serve beef strips with sauce.

Note: Assembled kabobs may be refrigerated, covered, 1 to 2 hours before grilling.

*Recipe courtesy of **National Live Stock & Meat Board***

GRILLED FLANK STEAK SANGRITA

Makes 6 servings

1 beef flank steak (2½ to 3 pounds)
1 teaspoon salt
¼ teaspoon pepper
1 teaspoon dried thyme, crushed
¼ cup orange juice concentrate, thawed and undiluted
3 tablespoons vegetable oil
Fruity Wine Sauce (recipe follows)

Lightly score steak and rub with salt, pepper and thyme. In shallow glass dish, combine orange juice concentrate and oil. Add steak; turn to coat with marinade. Cover and refrigerate at least 30 minutes. Drain meat; reserve marinade. Grill steak, on covered grill, over medium-hot **Kingsford® briquets** 8 to 10 minutes on each side, turning once and basting often with marinade, until done. Cut meat across grain into diagonal slices. Serve with Fruity Wine Sauce.

FRUITY WINE SAUCE

Makes about 2 cups

1½ cups red wine
1 orange, thinly sliced
1 lime, thinly sliced
1 apple, thinly sliced
¾ cup chopped green onion with tops
½ cup butter or margarine
2 tablespoons chopped parsley

In small saucepan, combine red wine, fruit and green onion; bring to boil. Stir in butter and parsley; cook and stir until butter is melted and sauce is hot.

Spicy Beef Satay

CHARCOAL BEEF KABOBS

Makes 4 servings

- ½ **cup vegetable oil**
- ¼ **cup lemon juice**
- ½ **package Hidden Valley Ranch® Original Ranch® Salad Dressing Mix**
- 2 **pounds beef top round steak, cut into 1-inch cubes**
- 2 **medium green peppers, cut into 1-inch squares**
- 1 **medium onion, cut into wedges**
  Cherry tomatoes

In shallow glass dish, combine oil, lemon juice and dry salad dressing mix. Add beef cubes; turn to coat with marinade. Cover and refrigerate 1 hour or longer. Drain beef cubes; reserve marinade. Thread beef cubes, green peppers and onion alternately on skewers. Grill kabobs, on uncovered grill, over medium-hot **Kingsford® briquets** 15 minutes, brushing often with marinade and turning to brown all sides. Add cherry tomatoes to ends of skewers during last 5 minutes of grilling.

Charcoal Beef Kabobs

BACK RIBS

Makes 4 servings

- 4 **pounds beef back ribs**
  Hoisin Barbecue Sauce (recipe follows) *or* **Pantry Barbecue Sauce (recipe follows)**

Grill ribs, on uncovered grill, over medium-hot **Match light® charcoal briquets** 30 minutes; turn every 10 minutes. Brush ribs generously with either Hoisin Barbecue Sauce or Pantry Barbecue Sauce; cook 10 to 15 minutes or until done.

HOISIN BARBECUE SAUCE

Makes 1 cup

- ½ **cup hoisin sauce**
- 2 **tablespoons white wine**
- 2 **tablespoons vegetable oil**
- 2 **tablespoons grated fresh ginger**
- 2 **cloves garlic, minced**

In small bowl, combine all ingredients; mix well.

PANTRY BARBECUE SAUCE

Makes 1 cup

- ¾ **cup catsup**
- ¼ **cup packed brown sugar**
- 2 **tablespoons soy sauce**
- 1 **tablespoon cider vinegar**
- 1 **clove garlic, minced**
- ¼ **teaspoon ground ginger**
- ¼ **teaspoon hot pepper sauce**

In small bowl, combine all ingredients; mix well.

CALIFORNIA-STYLE STEAK

Makes 4 to 6 servings

- 1 **beef sirloin steak, cut 1 to 1½ inches thick (2 pounds)**
- ½ **teaspoon olive or vegetable oil**
- 1 **teaspoon Beau Monde seasoning**
- ½ **teaspoon dried orange peel**
- ½ **teaspoon dried lemon peel**
- 1 **teaspoon pepper**
- 1½ **teaspoons seasoned salt**

Rub both sides of steak with oil. Rub Beau Monde, orange and lemon peels, pepper and seasoned salt thoroughly into both sides of steak. Grill steak, on uncovered grill, over medium-hot **Match light® charcoal briquets** 4 minutes on each side or to desired doneness.

Grilled Porterhouse Steaks with Italian-Style Vegetables

GRILLED PORTERHOUSE STEAKS WITH ITALIAN-STYLE VEGETABLES

Makes 4 servings

2 beef porterhouse steaks, cut 1 to 1½ inches thick (about 2 pounds)
2 cloves garlic, minced
1½ teaspoons dried basil leaves, crushed
½ teaspoon pepper
1 tablespoon olive or vegetable oil
1 large zucchini, cut into 1½-inch pieces
1 small onion, cut into thin wedges
1¼ cups sliced mushrooms
¼ teaspoon salt
6 cherry tomatoes, cut into halves

Season steaks with 1 clove of the garlic, ¾ teaspoon of the basil and the pepper. Grill steaks, on uncovered grill, over medium-hot **Kingsford® briquets,** turning once. Steaks cut 1 inch thick require about 16 minutes for rare, 20 minutes for medium. Steaks cut 1½ inches thick require about 22 minutes for rare, 30 minutes for medium. After turning steaks, heat oil in skillet on grid over coals. Add remaining clove garlic, the zucchini and onion and saute 4 to 5 minutes. Add mushrooms, salt and remaining ¾ teaspoon basil. Cook 2 minutes longer, stirring frequently. Add tomatoes; heat through. Serve vegetables with steaks.

*Recipe courtesy of **National Live Stock & Meat Board***

GIANT BURGER

Makes 8 servings

Giant Bun (recipe follows)
2 pounds lean ground beef
¼ cup catsup
3 tablespoons spicy brown mustard
¼ teaspoon pepper
1 medium onion, thinly sliced and separated into rings
2 ounces Swiss cheese, cut into ½-inch strips
1 large tomato, thinly sliced

Prepare Giant Bun. In large bowl, combine ground beef, catsup, mustard and pepper; mix lightly but thoroughly. Line 9-inch round baking pan with plastic wrap or foil. Shape beef mixture into large patty in pan, pressing lightly but firmly. Remove patty from pan. Lightly oil grid. Cook burger, on covered grill, over medium-hot **Kingsford® briquets** 7 minutes. To turn, slide a flat baking sheet under burger. Hold a flat plate over burger, flip over and carefully slide uncooked side onto grid. Grill, covered, 7 minutes longer or to desired doneness. Arrange onion rings and cheese on top of burger during last minute of cooking. Remove from grill with flat baking sheet.

Toast cut sides of Giant Bun on grid 1 minute. Place burger on bottom half of bun; arrange tomato slices on top. Cover with top half of Giant Bun. Cut into wedges.

GIANT BUN

1 loaf (1 pound) honey cracked wheat frozen bread dough
2 tablespoons butter or margarine, softened

Thaw bread dough as directed on package. Shape into round flat loaf to fit greased 9-inch round baking pan; let rise in warm place until doubled in volume (approximately 4 to 6 hours). Bake in 350°F oven 30 to 35 minutes. Cool. Slice loaf crosswise in half; spread cut sides with butter.

*Recipe courtesy of **National Live Stock & Meat Board***

Giant Burger

VESTFORK BARBECUE

Makes 20 servings

1 whole beef brisket (10 to 13 pounds)
  Garlic powder
  Pepper
6 cups K.C. Masterpiece® Barbecue Sauce
¼ cup wine vinegar
3 tablespoons vegetable oil
1 tablespoon liquid smoke, optional
  French bread rolls
  Sour cream

Trim excess fat from brisket to ¼ inch. Sprinkle brisket with garlic powder and pepper. In large glass dish, combine 2 cups of the barbecue sauce, the vinegar, oil and liquid smoke. Add brisket; turn to coat with marinade. Cover and refrigerate overnight. Drain meat; reserve marinade. Place brisket over very hot **Kingsford® briquets**. Quickly sear both sides (flare-ups will occur). Add one or two handfuls of soaked hickory chips to briquets, if desired. Cover grill and cook brisket 1½ to 2 hours, adding hickory chips as needed to maintain good smoke. Baste with reserved marinade during last ½ hour of grilling. Remove brisket. Carve across grain into thin slices. To make sandwiches, serve on warmed French rolls with remaining barbecue sauce and sour cream.

ORANGE-FLAVORED GRILLED BEEF

Makes 4 servings

1 orange
3 tablespoons soy sauce
2 tablespoons brown sugar
2 tablespoons cider vinegar
½ teaspoon pepper
½ teaspoon chili powder
1 clove garlic, minced
1 teaspoon grated fresh ginger
2 pounds beef round tip roast, cut into 3-inch
    cubes

Grate peel from orange to equal 1 tablespoon. Squeeze juice from orange into large bowl. Stir in remaining ingredients except beef. Add beef cubes; toss to coat with marinade. Cover and refrigerate 8 hours or overnight. Drain meat cubes; reserve marinade. Grill beef cubes, on covered grill, over medium-hot **Kingsford® briquets** 3 minutes. Turn beef cubes, brush with marinade and cook 5 minutes longer or until done.

Honey-Mustard Beef Ribs

HONEY-MUSTARD BEEF RIBS

Makes 4 servings

1 cup butter or margarine
1 bunch green onions with tops, finely chopped
1 small yellow onion, finely chopped
4 cloves garlic, minced
4 tablespoons prepared mustard
4 tablespoons honey
½ teaspoon liquid smoke, optional
1 teaspoon lemon pepper
1 teaspoon brown sugar
5 pounds beef back ribs

In saucepan, combine butter, green onions, yellow onion and garlic. Cook over low heat 15 minutes or until onions are tender. Remove from heat and add remaining ingredients except ribs. Grill ribs, on covered grill, over medium-hot **Kingsford® briquets** 30 to 35 minutes, brushing ribs generously with mustard-honey mixture, until meat is tender.

TERIYAKI STEAK WITH ONIONS

Makes 5 to 6 servings

1 beef flank steak (about 1½ pounds)
½ cup soy sauce
¼ cup dry white wine
2 tablespoons brown sugar
1 teaspoon grated fresh ginger
2 cloves garlic, minced
1 large sweet onion, sliced
1 tablespoon butter or margarine

Place steak in large plastic bag; place bag in large bowl. In 1-quart measure, combine soy sauce, wine, brown sugar, ginger and garlic. Pour marinade over steak in bag; turn to coat with marinade. Close bag securely and refrigerate 6 to 8 hours or overnight, turning occasionally. Drain meat; reserve marinade. Grill steak, on uncovered grill, over medium-hot **Kingsford®** briquets 10 to 15 minutes or to desired doneness, turning once.

Meanwhile, in skillet, cook onion in butter until soft. Stir in ½ cup reserved marinade; cook 4 to 5 minutes. Carve steak diagonally across grain into thin slices. Serve with cooked onion slices.

Recipe courtesy of **National Live Stock & Meat Board**

SUNNY SIRLOIN STEAK

Makes 4 to 5 servings

½ cup fresh orange juice
¼ cup soy sauce
2 tablespoons dry sherry
1 clove garlic, minced
2 dashes ground cloves
1 beef sirloin steak, cut 1¼ inches thick (about 2 pounds)

In small bowl, combine orange juice, soy sauce, sherry, garlic and cloves. Place steak in plastic bag; place bag in large bowl. Pour marinade over steak in bag; turn steak to coat. Close bag securely and refrigerate 2 to 4 hours, turning steak at least once. Drain meat; discard marinade. Place steak over medium-hot **Kingsford®** briquets. Cover grill and cook 7 to 8 minutes on each side or to desired doneness.

Recipe courtesy of **National Live Stock & Meat Board**

TEXAS-STYLE STEAK ON HOT BREAD

Makes 4 to 6 servings

½ cup olive or vegetable oil
¼ cup lime juice
¼ cup red wine vinegar
1 medium onion, finely chopped
1 clove garlic, minced
¼ teaspoon ground cumin
1 teaspoon chili powder
½ teaspoon salt
1 beef skirt or flank steak (about 1½ pounds)
1 round loaf French or sourdough bread
1 cup salsa
1 cup guacamole

In shallow glass dish, combine oil, lime juice, vinegar, onion, garlic, cumin, chili powder and salt. With meat mallet, pound steak to ¼-inch thickness. Place steak in marinade; turn to coat. Cover and refrigerate several hours or overnight, turning several times. Drain steak; discard marinade. Grill steak, on covered grill, over medium-hot **Kingsford® with Mesquite charcoal briquets** 4 to 8 minutes on each side, or until done. Cut bread into 1-inch slices and toast on grill. Heat salsa. Carve steak into ¾-inch diagonal strips. Arrange steak on toasted bread. Top with hot salsa and guacamole.

BARBECUED BUTTERFLIED EYE ROUND ROAST

Makes 4 to 6 servings

1 can (12 ounces) beer
¼ cup vegetable oil
¼ cup cider vinegar
1 medium onion, chopped
2 cloves garlic, minced
½ teaspoon pepper
1 beef eye-of-round roast (about 3 pounds), butterflied
1 cup K.C. Masterpiece® Barbecue Sauce

In shallow glass dish, combine beer, oil, vinegar, onion, garlic and pepper. Add roast; turn to coat with marinade. Cover and refrigerate overnight, turning occasionally. Drain roast; discard marinade. Grill roast, on covered grill, over medium-hot **Kingsford®** briquets 25 minutes, turning and basting often with barbecue sauce. Season with salt, if desired. Carve roast into thin slices. Heat remaining barbecue sauce and serve with beef slices.

Teriyaki Steak with Onions

T-BONE STEAKS WITH POTATO AND ONION KABOBS

Makes 4 servings

**4 beef loin T-bone steaks, cut 1 to 1½ inches thick
(about 8 ounces each)**
Salt and pepper
Potato and Onion Kabobs (recipe follows)

Season steaks with salt and pepper to taste. Grill steaks, on uncovered grill, over medium-hot **Kingsford® briquets,** turning occasionally, about 16 minutes for rare, 20 minutes for medium. (Steaks cut 1½ inches thick require 22 minutes for rare, 30 minutes for medium). Serve with Potato and Onion Kabobs.

POTATO AND ONION KABOBS

2 large all-purpose potatoes (about 1½ pounds)
1 large sweet onion
3 tablespoons butter or margarine, melted
1 teaspoon paprika
½ teaspoon celery salt
¼ teaspoon garlic powder
⅛ teaspoon pepper

In saucepan, cook unpeeled potatoes in boiling water to cover 20 minutes; drain. When cool enough to handle, cut each potato crosswise into four 1-inch-thick slices. Cut onion crosswise into four 1-inch-thick slices. Alternately thread potato and onion slices on each of four 8-inch skewers. In small bowl, combine remaining ingredients. Brush both sides of potatoes and onions with seasoned butter. Grill kabobs, on uncovered grill, over medium-hot **Kingsford® briquets** 20 minutes, turning after 10 minutes and brushing with seasoned butter occasionally.

*Recipe courtesy of **National Live Stock & Meat Board***

ISLANDER'S BEEF BARBECUE

Makes 4 to 6 servings

1 boneless beef chuck roast (3 to 3½ pounds)
¾ cup apricot-pineapple jam
2 tablespoons soy sauce
1 teaspoon ground ginger
1 teaspoon grated lemon peel

Slice roast across grain into ¼-inch-thick slices. In bowl, combine remaining ingredients. Grill beef slices, on uncovered grill, over medium-hot **Kingsford® briquets** 8 to 10 minutes. Turn and baste often with jam mixture.

T-Bone Steaks with Potato and Onion Kabobs

Nutty Burgers

NUTTY BURGERS

Makes 6 servings

1½ pounds ground beef
  1 medium onion, finely chopped
  1 clove garlic, minced
  1 cup dry bread crumbs
⅓ cup grated Parmesan cheese
⅔ cup pine nuts
⅓ cup chopped parsley
  2 eggs
1½ teaspoons salt
  1 teaspoon pepper

In large bowl, combine all ingredients. Shape into 6 thick patties. Grill patties, on covered grill, over medium-hot **Kingsford® briquets** 5 minutes on each side or until done. Serve on French bread and garnish with chopped green onion, if desired.

STEAK KABOBS

Makes 6 servings

  2 pounds beef top round steak
  1 bottle (8 ounces) French salad dressing
  2 tablespoons lemon juice
  1 can (16 ounces) white whole onions, drained
18 cherry tomatoes

Place steak in freezer 30 minutes to firm; slice into ¼-inch-thick strips. Place strips in shallow glass dish. Drizzle with salad dressing and lemon juice. Cover and refrigerate at least 4 hours. Drain beef strips; reserve marinade. Thread beef, onions and tomatoes alternately on 6 skewers. Brush with marinade. Grill kabobs, on uncovered grill, over medium-hot **Match light® charcoal briquets** 7 to 10 minutes, turning and basting often, until beef is cooked to desired doneness.

PEPPER-STUFFED FLANK STEAK

Makes 6 to 8 servings

2 beef flank steaks (about 1 pound each)
1¼ teaspoons garlic powder
¼ teaspoon black pepper
1 green pepper, cut into strips
1 red pepper, cut into strips
1 onion, cut into thin slices
1 can (15 ounces) tomato sauce
½ cup finely chopped onion
¼ cup soy sauce
1 tablespoon sugar
1 teaspoon dry mustard
⅛ teaspoon cayenne pepper
¼ cup vegetable oil

With meat mallet, pound each steak to ¼-inch thickness. Sprinkle steaks with ¼ teaspoon of the garlic powder and the pepper. Arrange green and red pepper strips horizontally on steaks. Cover with onion slices. Starting at narrow end of each steak, roll up jelly-roll fashion; tie with kitchen twine. Set aside. In large jar with screw-top lid, combine remaining ingredients except oil. Shake to blend. Brush outsides of beef rolls with oil. Lightly oil grid. Grill steaks, on covered grill, over hot **Kingsford® briquets** about 30 minutes, turning often, until done. Brush steaks with tomato-soy mixture during last 10 minutes of grilling.

GRILLED STEAK WITH MUSHROOM-WINE SAUCE

Makes 4 servings

4 beef loin T-bone, porterhouse or filet mignon steaks, cut 1 inch thick (8 ounces each)
3 tablespoons butter or margarine
½ pound mushrooms, sliced (about 2 cups)
¼ cup white wine
2 tablespoons minced parsley
½ teaspoon dried tarragon, crushed
1 teaspoon instant beef bouillon granules

Slash any fat around edge of steaks every 4 inches. Lightly oil grid. Grill steaks, on covered grill, over medium-hot **Kingsford® with Mesquite charcoal briquets** 8 to 10 minutes on each side for medium-rare, or to desired doneness. While steak is grilling, heat butter in large skillet until hot. Add mushrooms and saute 1 minute or until tender. Add wine, parsley, tarragon and beef bouillon granules; simmer 4 minutes, stirring often. Serve sauce over steak.

BEEF BRISKET, TEXAS-STYLE

Makes 8 to 10 servings

1 beef brisket (6 to 8 pounds)
¾ cup finely chopped onion
2 teaspoons paprika
½ teaspoon pepper
   Water
1 cup prepared steak sauce
   Special Sauce (recipe follows)

Trim fat covering brisket to ¼ inch. In small bowl, combine onion, paprika and pepper. Rub mixture evenly over surface of brisket. Place brisket, fat-side up, in large foil pan. Cover pan tightly with foil. Place pan in center of grill over low **Kingsford® briquets.** Cover grill and cook 5 hours, turning brisket every 1½ hours. (Remove fat from pan with baster.) Add ½ cup water, as needed, to pan. (Be sure to add briquets as needed to maintain low heat.)

Remove foil from pan. Remove brisket; place on grid directly over coals. Combine pan drippings with steak sauce; reserve 1 cup mixture for Special Sauce. Brush some of remaining mixture over brisket. Cover grill and cook brisket 1 hour longer, brushing occasionally with sauce mixture. Cut brisket into thin slices and serve with Special Sauce.

SPECIAL SAUCE

Makes 2 cups

½ cup finely chopped onion
2 tablespoons butter or margarine
1 cup steak sauce mixture (reserved from recipe above)
1 cup catsup
1 tablespoon brown sugar
¼ teaspoon red pepper flakes

In small saucepan, saute onion in butter until tender. Stir in reserved steak sauce mixture, catsup, brown sugar and red pepper flakes. Simmer 10 minutes.

*Recipe courtesy of **National Live Stock & Meat Board***

Beef Brisket, Texas-Style

HOT & SPICY BEEF BACK RIBS

Makes about 8 servings

7 pounds beef back ribs (two 3½-pound slabs)
¾ cup water
1 cup catsup
2 tablespoons lemon juice
1 teaspoon ground cinnamon
1 teaspoon hot pepper sauce
½ to 1 teaspoon red pepper flakes

Place each slab of ribs, meat-side down, in center of double-thick rectangle of heavy-duty foil. Sprinkle 2 tablespoons of the water over each slab of ribs. To form packets, bring two long sides of foil together over ribs. Fold edges over 3 or 4 times, pressing crease in tightly each time. (Allow room for heat circulation.) Flatten foil at one short end; crease to form triangle and fold edge over several times toward packet, pressing tightly to seal. Repeat with other short end. Place packets directly over low to medium **Kingsford® briquets.** Cover grill and cook 1½ hours, turning packets every ½ hour. Add additional briquets as necessary to maintain heat.

Meanwhile, in small saucepan, combine catsup, remaining ½ cup water, the lemon juice, cinnamon, hot pepper sauce and red pepper flakes. Bring to boil; reduce heat and simmer 10 to 12 minutes. Remove ribs from packets. Place on grid over medium coals and grill 30 to 40 minutes, turning and brushing with sauce occasionally. Bring remaining sauce to boil and serve with ribs.

*Recipe courtesy of **National Live Stock & Meat Board***

BARBECUED ROUND-UP ROAST

Makes 12 servings

1 beef round tip roast or beef chuck cross-rib roast (about 5 pounds)
1 cup strong black coffee
1 cup orange juice
1 cup chopped onion
1 tablespoon dried rosemary, crushed
1 tablespoon dried thyme, crushed
1 teaspoon pepper

Place roast in shallow glass dish. In small bowl, combine remaining ingredients; pour over roast. Cover and refrigerate, turning occasionally, at least 6 hours or overnight.

Arrange medium-hot **Kingsford® briquets** around drip pan. Drain roast; reserve marinade. Place roast over drip pan. Grill roast, on covered grill, 1½ to 2½ hours, turning every 20 minutes and basting with marinade, until meat thermometer registers 140°F for rare, 160°F for medium, or 170°F for well-done. Remove roast when thermometer registers 5°F below the temperature of desired doneness. Roast will continue to cook after removing it from grill. For easier carving, allow roast to stand in warm place 15 to 20 minutes.

*Recipe courtesy of **California Beef Council***

SIRLOIN STEAK WITH VEGETABLE KABOBS

Makes 4 servings

1 beef sirloin steak, cut 1 inch thick (about
   2 pounds)
Salt and pepper
Vegetable Kabobs (recipe follows)

Grill steak, on covered grill, over medium-hot
Kingsford® briquets 7 to 8 minutes. Turn steak;
season with salt and pepper. Cover grill and cook 8 to
9 minutes longer or to desired doneness.

VEGETABLE KABOBS

Makes 4 servings

½ cup butter or margarine
1 tablespoon chopped parsley
1 teaspoon chopped fresh basil
½ teaspoon dried oregano, crushed
½ teaspoon salt
¼ teaspoon pepper
1 medium zucchini, cut into 8 slices
8 large mushrooms
8 large cherry tomatoes

In small saucepan, melt butter; add parsley, basil,
oregano, salt and pepper. Cook over low heat 2 to 3
minutes. Thread 2 slices zucchini crosswise and 2
mushrooms lengthwise on each of four 12-inch
skewers. Brush both sides of vegetables with
seasoned butter. Grill kabobs, on uncovered grill,
over medium-hot Kingsford® briquets 15 minutes,
turning and brushing kabobs occasionally with
seasoned butter. Add 2 cherry tomatoes to ends of
each skewer during last 5 minutes of grilling.

Recipe courtesy of Beef Industry Council

PEPPERY RIB STEAKS

Makes 4 servings

⅓ cup lemon juice
2 tablespoons vegetable oil
1 clove garlic, crushed
1 teaspoon chili powder
1 teaspoon seasoned salt
½ teaspoon seasoned or cracked pepper
4 beef rib eye steaks, cut ¾ to 1 inch thick (about
   6 ounces each)

In shallow glass dish, combine all ingredients except
steaks. Add steaks; turn to coat with marinade. Cover
and refrigerate at least 2 hours or overnight. Drain
steaks; reserve marinade. Grill steaks, on uncovered
grill, over medium-hot Match light® charcoal briquets
about 15 minutes or until cooked, turning and basting
often with marinade.

BARBECUED BEEF TIP ROAST

Makes 8 to 10 servings

1 tablespoon Italian seasoning
1 teaspoon garlic salt
½ teaspoon cayenne pepper
1 beef round tip roast (6 to 8 pounds)

In small bowl, combine Italian seasoning, garlic salt
and cayenne pepper; rub evenly over roast. Arrange
medium-hot Kingsford® briquets around drip pan.
Place roast over drip pan. Insert meat thermometer in
thickest part (make certain bulb does not rest in fat).
Partially close bottom dampers, if necessary, to
control heat. Cover grill (leaving top damper open)
and cook until meat thermometer registers 140°F for
rare, 160°F for medium (allow 30 to 35 minutes per
pound). Remove roast when thermometer registers
5°F below temperature of desired doneness. For
easier carving, allow roast to stand in warm place 15
to 20 minutes.

Recipe courtesy of Weber Grills and Beef Industry Council

BARBECUED MEATBALL AND VEGETABLE PACKETS

Makes 4 servings

1½ pounds lean ground beef
¼ cup finely chopped onion
1 egg
¾ cup catsup
2 teaspoons instant beef bouillon granules
⅛ teaspoon pepper
1 can (8½ ounces) cut green beans, drained
1 can (8¾ ounces) whole kernel corn, drained
1 can (2½ ounces) sliced mushrooms, drained
1 can (10 ounces) pizza sauce
1 cup shredded Cheddar cheese (about 4 ounces)

In large bowl, combine beef, onion, egg, catsup, beef
bouillon granules and pepper. Mix lightly and shape
into 16 balls. Grill meatballs, on uncovered grill, over
medium-hot Kingsford® briquets 15 to 20 minutes,
turning often. Tear off four 12-inch squares of heavy-
duty foil. Place 4 grilled meatballs in center of each
piece. Divide green beans, corn and mushrooms
evenly among foil squares. Spoon pizza sauce over
vegetables. Top with cheese. Fold and seal foil edges
tightly. Grill packets over medium-hot coals 25
minutes, turning packets often. To serve, place
opened packets on plate.

POULTRY

A range of recipes for your grill, from an easy-to-serve grilled chicken to a chili-fired bird for extra zip. Also included are great ways to grill Cornish hens, and, of course, a classic barbecued turkey.

DAN D'S CHICKEN BBQ

Makes 4 servings

⅓ **cup white Zinfandel wine**
⅓ **cup olive or vegetable oil**
1 **tablespoon Dijon-style mustard**
1 **teaspoon dried rosemary, crushed**
1 **clove garlic, minced**
Salt and pepper
1 **broiler-fryer chicken (2 to 3 pounds), quartered**

In shallow glass dish, combine all ingredients except chicken. Add chicken; turn to coat with marinade. Cover and refrigerate several hours or overnight, basting occasionally. Drain chicken; reserve marinade. Grill chicken, on covered grill, over medium-hot **Kingsford® briquets** about 15 minutes on each side or until fork-tender, basting often with marinade.

Dan D's Chicken BBQ

GRILLED CHICKEN RIBBONS

Makes 4 servings

- ¼ cup olive or vegetable oil
- 2 tablespoons lemon or lime juice
- 2 cloves garlic, minced
- 1 teaspoon honey
- ¾ teaspoon dried thyme, crushed
- ½ to 1 teaspoon red pepper flakes
  - Salt and pepper
- 4 chicken breast halves, skinned and boned (about 6 ounces each)

In small bowl, combine all ingredients except chicken; mix well. Cut chicken lengthwise into strips about 1 inch wide. Thread chicken on 8 skewers; brush generously with sauce mixture. Grill chicken, on covered grill, over hot **Kingsford®** briquets 3 to 4 minutes on each side or until chicken is cooked through, basting with sauce once or twice. Serve with green, red, yellow or orange pepper kabobs, if desired.

SPICY SOY-APPLE CHICKEN

Makes 12 servings

- 1 cup soy sauce
- 1 can (6 ounces) frozen apple juice concentrate, thawed and undiluted
- 1½ teaspoons dry mustard
- 1½ teaspoons ground ginger
- ¾ teaspoon ground cloves
- ½ teaspoon garlic powder
- 3 broiler-fryer chickens (2 to 3 pounds each), quartered

In small saucepan, combine soy sauce and apple juice concentrate. In small bowl, combine mustard, ginger, cloves and garlic powder. Add ¼ cup of soy-apple liquid to spice mixture; blend thoroughly. Stir spice mixture into remaining liquid in saucepan and bring to boil over medium heat. Place chicken in large shallow glass dish. Pour marinade over chicken; turn to coat with marinade. Cover and refrigerate at least 8 hours or overnight.

Drain chicken; reserve marinade. Lightly oil grid. Grill chicken, on covered grill, over medium-hot **Kingsford®** briquets 1 to 1½ hours or until fork-tender, turning and brushing with marinade every 15 minutes.

*Recipe courtesy of **National Broiler Council***

ORIENTAL GAME HENS

Makes 4 servings

- 4 Cornish game hens (1 to 1½ pounds each)
  - Salt
- ½ cup peanut or vegetable oil
- ½ cup soy sauce
- 2 tablespoons brown sugar
- 1 tablespoon wine vinegar
- ½ teaspoon grated fresh ginger
  - Dash ground cloves

Remove giblets from hens. Remove fatty portion from neck and tail area of hens. Rinse hens under cold running water. Pat hens dry with paper toweling. Sprinkle cavities with salt. Close neck and body openings with skewers. Tie legs together; tuck wings under back and tie with kitchen twine. Arrange hens in shallow microwaveable dish and cover with vented plastic wrap. Microwave at 50% power 10 minutes. For basting sauce, in small bowl, combine remaining ingredients. Lightly oil grid. Grill hens, on uncovered grill, over medium-hot **Kingsford®** briquets 20 minutes or until thigh moves easily and juices run clear, basting often with sauce.

GLAZED CHICKEN

Makes 4 servings

- 1 jar (16 ounces) orange marmalade
- ⅓ cup soy sauce
- ¼ cup cider vinegar
- 2 cloves garlic, crushed
- 1 broiler-fryer chicken (2 to 3 pounds), quartered
  - Vegetable oil
  - Salt and pepper

In small bowl, combine orange marmalade, soy sauce, vinegar and garlic. Brush both sides of chicken with oil; sprinkle with salt and pepper. Lightly oil grid. Grill chicken, skin-side up, on uncovered grill, over medium-hot **Kingsford®** briquets about 45 minutes or until fork-tender, turning often. Brush chicken with marmalade sauce during last 20 minutes of grilling.

Grilled Chicken Ribbons
served with mixed pepper kabobs

Apricot-Stuffed Chicken

TEXAS-BARBECUED CHICKEN

Makes 4 servings

½ **cup fresh lemon juice**
¼ **cup vegetable oil**
1 **clove garlic, minced**
2 **teaspoons salt**
1 **teaspoon paprika**
1 **teaspoon pepper**
1 **broiler-fryer chicken (2 to 3 pounds), cut into parts**
1 **tablespoon honey**

In small saucepan, combine lemon juice, oil, garlic, salt, paprika and pepper. Heat, stirring constantly, 2 to 3 minutes; cool. Place chicken in shallow glass dish; pour marinade over chicken. Cover and refrigerate at least 1 hour. Drain chicken; reserve marinade. Lightly oil grid. Grill chicken, on covered grill, over medium-hot **Kingsford® with Mesquite charcoal briquets** about 30 minutes, turning every 10 minutes. Stir honey into marinade and brush on chicken. Cook chicken about 20 minutes longer or until fork-tender, turning often and brushing with marinade.

*Recipe courtesy of **National Broiler Council***

APRICOT-STUFFED CHICKEN

Makes 4 servings

2 **tablespoons butter or margarine, melted**
¼ **cup chopped green onion**
½ **teaspoon ground ginger**
½ **cup stuffing mix**
2 **whole chicken breasts, boned, skin on**
4 **fresh California apricots (about ½ pound), halved and pitted**
½ **cup apricot jam**
1 **tablespoon cider vinegar**

In medium bowl, combine butter, onion, ¼ teaspoon of the ginger and the stuffing mix. Place chicken skin-side down and pound with meat mallet to flatten slightly. Spoon half the stuffing mixture in a strip along center of each breast. Place apricot halves on top of stuffing. Roll chicken pieces and tie with kitchen twine to enclose stuffing.

Lightly oil grid. Grill chicken rolls, on uncovered grill, over medium-hot **Kingsford®** briquets 15 minutes, turning once or twice. In small bowl, combine apricot jam, vinegar and remaining ¼ teaspoon ginger. Brush chicken rolls with jam mixture and cook 5 to 10 minutes longer or until chicken is cooked through.

*Recipe courtesy of **California Apricot Advisory Board***

TURKEY FILLETS IN SPICY CILANTRO MARINADE

Makes 4 servings

1 **cup chopped onion**
1 **large tomato, quartered**
⅓ **cup soy sauce**
¼ **cup chopped green pepper**
3 **tablespoons vegetable oil**
3 **tablespoons lime juice**
2 **tablespoons minced cilantro or parsley**
2 **cloves garlic, minced**
¾ **teaspoon pepper**
4 **turkey breast fillets (about ½ pound each)**

Place all ingredients, except turkey, in blender; blend 30 seconds. Place turkey fillets in large plastic bag; place bag in bowl. Pour marinade over turkey in bag. Close bag securely; refrigerate 4 hours, turning occasionally. Drain turkey fillets; reserve marinade. Grill turkey, on uncovered grill, over hot **Kingsford®** briquets 5 minutes on each side or until tender, brushing often with marinade.

GRILLED AND GLAZED GAME HENS

Makes 4 to 6 servings

½ cup K.C. Masterpiece® Barbecue Sauce
¼ cup dry sherry
3 tablespoons frozen orange juice concentrate, thawed and undiluted
4 Cornish game hens (1 to 1½ pounds each)

In saucepan, combine barbecue sauce, sherry and juice concentrate. Bring to boil; simmer 10 minutes. Remove from heat; cool. Remove giblets from hens. Remove fatty portion from neck and tail area of hens. Rinse hens under cold running water. Pat cavities dry with paper toweling; brush with sauce. Grill hens, on covered grill, over medium-hot **Kingsford®** briquets 40 to 50 minutes or until thigh moves easily and juices run clear, turning once. Baste with sauce during last 10 minutes of grilling. Remove from grill; brush generously with additional sauce.

SESAME GRILLED CHICKEN

Makes 4 servings

½ cup white wine
⅓ cup white vinegar
1 tablespoon sesame oil
⅓ cup vegetable oil
2 cloves garlic, sliced
1 tablespoon grated fresh ginger
2 sprigs fresh thyme *or* ¼ teaspoon dried thyme, crushed
1 tablespoon sesame seed
1 broiler-fryer chicken (2 to 3 pounds), quartered

In shallow glass dish, combine all ingredients except chicken. Add chicken; turn to coat with marinade. Cover and refrigerate about 3 hours. Drain chicken; reserve marinade. Grill chicken, skin-side down, on covered grill, over medium-hot **Kingsford®** briquets 15 to 20 minutes, brushing often with marinade. Turn and cook about 20 minutes longer or until fork-tender, brushing often with marinade.

Grilled and Glazed Game Hens

LEMON HERBED CHICKEN

Makes 6 servings

½ cup butter or margarine
½ cup vegetable oil
⅓ cup lemon juice
2 tablespoons finely chopped parsley
2 tablespoons garlic salt
1 teaspoon dried rosemary, crushed
1 teaspoon dried summer savory, crushed
½ teaspoon dried thyme, crushed
¼ teaspoon coarsely cracked black pepper
6 chicken breast quarters with wings attached

In saucepan, combine all ingredients except chicken. Heat until butter melts. Place chicken in shallow glass dish and brush with sauce; let stand 10 to 15 minutes before cooking. Lightly oil grid. Grill chicken, skin-side up, on uncovered grill, over medium-hot **Kingsford®** briquets 30 to 45 minutes or until fork-tender, turning and basting with sauce every 10 minutes.

GRILLED GAME HENS, TEXAS-STYLE

Makes 4 servings

1 can (8 ounces) tomato sauce
¼ cup vegetable oil
1½ teaspoons chili powder
1 teaspoon paprika
¼ teaspoon garlic powder
¼ teaspoon cayenne pepper
4 Cornish game hens (1 to 1½ pounds each), cut into halves

In small bowl, combine all ingredients except game hens. Brush hens generously with tomato mixture. Grill hens, on covered grill, over medium-hot **Kingsford®** with **Mesquite charcoal briquets** 45 to 50 minutes or until fork-tender, brushing frequently with tomato mixture.

GRILLED STUFFED CHICKEN BREASTS

Makes 6 servings

6 chicken breast halves, skinned and boned
6 tablespoons butter or margarine
3 tablespoons Dijon-style mustard
6 slices cooked ham
1 cup shredded Swiss cheese (about 4 ounces)
3 tablespoons vegetable oil
1 tablespoon honey
   Salt and pepper

With meat mallet, pound chicken breasts to ¼-inch thickness. In small bowl, blend butter with 2 tablespoons of the mustard; spread over one side of each chicken breast. Cut ham slices to fit chicken breasts. Place 1 ham slice on each breast; top with shredded cheese. Roll chicken pieces and skewer each to enclose ham and cheese. In small bowl, combine remaining 1 tablespoon mustard, the oil and honey; brush on all sides of each roll. Grill chicken, on covered grill, over medium-hot **Kingsford®** briquets 25 to 35 minutes or until chicken is tender, basting often with mustard-honey mixture.

ZINGY BARBECUED CHICKEN

Makes 4 servings

½ cup grapefruit juice
½ cup apple cider vinegar
½ cup vegetable oil
¼ cup chopped onion
1 egg
½ teaspoon celery salt
½ teaspoon ground ginger
⅛ teaspoon pepper
1 broiler-fryer chicken (2 to 3 pounds), cut into parts

Place all ingredients except chicken in blender or food processor; blend 30 seconds. Pour sauce mixture into small saucepan and heat over low heat about 5 minutes or until slightly thick; remove from heat. Dip chicken in sauce, 1 piece at a time, turning to coat thoroughly. Grill chicken, skin-side up, on covered grill, over medium-hot **Kingsford®** briquets 45 minutes to 1 hour or until fork-tender, turning and brushing with sauce every 15 minutes.

Note: Watch chicken carefully, because egg may cause chicken to become too brown.

*Recipe courtesy of **National Broiler Council***

Lemon Herbed Chicken

LEMON-YOGURT GRILLED CHICKEN

Makes 4 servings

1 cup plain yogurt
¼ cup minced fresh parsley
2 tablespoons lemon juice
2 tablespoons vegetable oil
2 tablespoons grated onion
1 tablespoon honey
3 cloves garlic, minced
1 broiler-fryer chicken (2 to 3 pounds), quartered

In small bowl, combine yogurt, parsley, lemon juice, oil, onion, honey and garlic. Place chicken in shallow glass dish. Brush marinade on all sides. Cover and refrigerate at least 3 hours. Drain chicken; reserve marinade. Lightly oil grid. Grill chicken, on covered grill, over medium-hot **Kingsford® briquets** about 45 to 60 minutes or until fork-tender, turning and basting with marinade every 15 minutes.

*Recipe courtesy of **National Broiler Council***

Lemon-Yogurt Grilled Chicken

GRILLED TURKEY WITH VEGETABLE PIZZAZZ

Makes 6 servings

1½ pounds turkey breast, cut into 2-inch pieces
2 medium zucchini, cut into 1-inch chunks
12 large mushrooms
1 medium red pepper, cut into 1½-inch pieces
12 jumbo pimiento-stuffed olives
1 tablespoon vegetable oil
1 cup pizza sauce
1 tablespoon dried basil, crushed

Thread turkey, zucchini, mushrooms, pepper and olives alternately on skewers; brush thoroughly with oil. In small bowl, combine pizza sauce and basil. Grill kabobs, on uncovered grill, over medium-hot **Match light® charcoal briquets** about 10 minutes, turning occasionally. Baste with pizza sauce and cook about 15 minutes longer or until turkey is tender and vegetables are cooked, turning and basting 2 to 3 times.

OIL-AND-VINEGAR GRILLED CHICKEN

Makes 4 servings

¼ cup olive oil
¼ cup wine vinegar
2 teaspoons sugar
1 clove garlic, minced
1 teaspoon dry mustard
1 teaspoon salt
½ teaspoon pepper
½ teaspoon dried tarragon, crushed
¼ teaspoon dried rosemary, crushed
1 broiler-fryer chicken (2 to 3 pounds), cut into parts

In glass jar with tight-fitting lid, combine oil, vinegar, sugar, garlic, mustard, salt, pepper, tarragon and rosemary; cover and shake well to blend. Place chicken in shallow glass dish; pour marinade over. Turn chicken pieces to coat. Cover and refrigerate at least 3 hours or overnight. Drain chicken; reserve marinade. Lightly oil grid. Grill chicken, on covered grill, over medium-hot **Kingsford® briquets** 45 to 60 minutes* or until fork-tender, turning often and brushing with marinade.

*To shorten grilling time, you can precook the chicken in a microwave oven. Place drained chicken in microwave-safe dish, cover loosely and microwave at 100% power 18 minutes, turning every 6 minutes. Grill over medium-hot coals about 12 to 15 minutes or until fork-tender, brushing with marinade.

*Recipe courtesy of **National Broiler Council***

Chicken Fajitas

CHICKEN FAJITAS

Makes 6 servings

½ cup vegetable oil
⅓ cup lime juice
¼ cup red wine vinegar
¼ cup finely chopped onion
2 cloves garlic, minced
1 teaspoon sugar
1 teaspoon dried oregano, crushed
½ teaspoon salt
½ teaspoon pepper
¼ teaspoon ground cumin
6 chicken breast halves, skinned and boned
  Flour tortillas
  Chopped tomatoes
  Chopped onion
  Sliced avocado
  Salsa

In shallow glass dish, combine first 10 ingredients; mix well. Add chicken breasts; turn to coat with marinade. Cover and refrigerate 4 hours, turning occasionally. Drain chicken; reserve marinade. Grill chicken, on covered grill, over medium-hot **Kingsford® briquets** 8 minutes; turn and cook 5 to 7 minutes longer or until cooked through, basting often with marinade.

While chicken is grilling, wrap tortillas in large piece of heavy-duty foil and place on edge of grill. Heat about 10 minutes, turning packet once. Slice chicken breasts into thin slices. Place slices of chicken and garnishes in warm flour tortillas and roll up.

*Recipe courtesy of **Weber Grills***

BARBECUED TURKEY WITH HERBS

Makes 8 to 10 servings

1 turkey (9 to 13 pounds), fresh or frozen, thawed
¾ cup vegetable oil
½ cup chopped fresh parsley
2 tablespoons chopped fresh sage *or*
    2 teaspoons dried sage, crushed
2 tablespoons chopped fresh rosemary *or*
    2 teaspoons dried rosemary, crushed
1 tablespoon chopped fresh thyme *or* 1 teaspoon
    dried thyme, crushed
Salt and coarsely cracked black pepper

Remove neck and giblets from turkey. Rinse turkey under cold running water; drain and pat dry with paper toweling. In small bowl, combine remaining ingredients. Brush cavities and outer surface of turkey generously with herb mixture. Pull skin over neck and secure with skewer. Fold wings behind back and tie legs and tail together with kitchen twine. Insert meat thermometer into center of thickest part of thigh, not touching bone.

Arrange medium-hot **Kingsford® briquets** around large drip pan. Position turkey directly over drip pan. Cover grill and cook turkey 11 to 13 minutes per pound or until internal temperature reaches 185°F, basting occasionally with herb mixture. Add more briquets as necessary, following guidelines for indirect cooking (page 4) for number of briquets needed. Garnish with additional fresh herbs, if desired.

CHICKEN KYOTO

Makes 4 servings

1 cup apple cider
½ cup soy sauce
½ cup vegetable oil
¼ cup sugar
2 teaspoons ground ginger
1 broiler-fryer chicken (2 to 3 pounds), quartered

In small saucepan, combine all ingredients except chicken. Simmer over medium heat 5 to 8 minutes or until sugar is dissolved. Place chicken in shallow glass dish. Pour marinade over chicken; cover and refrigerate about 6 hours. Drain chicken; reserve marinade. Grill chicken, on uncovered grill, over medium-hot **Kingsford® briquets,** about 25 minutes on each side or until fork-tender, basting often with marinade.

SUPER SIMPLE SURPRISE CHICKEN

Makes 4 servings

¼ butter or margarine
3 tablespoons lemon juice
1 teaspoon crab boil (seafood spice blend)
1 teaspoon garlic salt
1 broiler-fryer chicken (2 to 3 pounds), quartered
Lemon wedges

In saucepan, melt butter. Stir in lemon juice, crab boil and garlic salt. Place chicken in shallow glass dish. Pour marinade over chicken; turn to coat with marinade. Cover and refrigerate at least 3 hours or overnight. Drain chicken; reserve marinade. Lightly oil grid. Grill chicken, on covered grill, over medium-hot **Kingsford® briquets** about 1 hour or until fork-tender, turning and brushing with marinade every 15 minutes. Serve with lemon wedges.

*Recipe courtesy of **National Broiler Council***

BARBECUED CHICKEN

Makes 4 servings

1 cup chicken broth
¼ cup catsup
2 tablespoons vinegar
2 tablespoons Worcestershire sauce
2 tablespoons finely chopped onion
1 teaspoon dry mustard
½ teaspoon garlic salt
½ teaspoon salt
¼ teaspoon pepper
1 broiler-fryer chicken (2 to 3 pounds), quartered

In small saucepan, combine all ingredients except chicken. Bring to boil; cool slightly. Place chicken in shallow glass dish. Pour warm sauce over chicken; cover and refrigerate at least 2 hours. Grill chicken, skin-side up, on uncovered grill, over medium-hot **Kingsford® briquets** 45 to 60 minutes or until chicken is fork-tender, turning frequently and basting with marinade.

Barbecued Turkey with Herbs

Kansas City–Style Barbecued Chicken Legs

TASTY GRILLED CHICKEN

Makes 4 serving

¼ teaspoon pepper
4 broiler-fryer chicken leg-thigh quarters
1 can (10½ ounces) beef broth
3 tablespoons soy sauce
1 lemon, thinly sliced
1 tablespoon olive or vegetable oil
1 tablespoon red wine vinegar
1 tablespoon white wine
1 clove garlic, minced

Rub pepper into chicken quarters. In shallow glass dish, combine beef broth, soy sauce, lemon, oil, vinegar, wine and garlic. Add chicken; turn to coat with marinade. Cover and refrigerate at least 3 hours or overnight. Drain chicken; reserve marinade. Lightly oil grid. Grill chicken, on covered grill, over medium-hot **Kingsford® briquets** about 1 hour or until fork-tender, turning and brushing with marinade every 10 minutes.

*Recipe courtesy of **National Broiler Council***

KANSAS CITY–STYLE BARBECUED CHICKEN LEGS

Makes 6 servings

½ cup butter or margarine, softened
⅓ cup finely chopped parsley
2 cloves garlic, minced
2¾ to 3 pounds chicken legs (about 12 legs)
3 tablespoons olive or vegetable oil
¾ cup K.C. Masterpiece® Barbecue Sauce

In small bowl, blend butter, parsley and garlic. Rinse chicken legs under cold running water; pat dry with paper toweling. Starting at thick end of each leg, work finger between skin and meat to form a pocket. Insert about 2 teaspoons parsley butter into pocket; massage outer skin to spread filling. Rub completed legs with oil. Lightly oil grid. Grill chicken, on covered grill, over medium-hot **Kingsford® briquets** about 45 minutes or until fork-tender. Turn and baste occasionally with remaining oil. Baste thoroughly with barbecue sauce during last 15 minutes of grilling. Baste once more before serving. Serve with additional warmed barbecue sauce, if desired.

BARBECUED TURKEY DRUMSTICKS

Makes 4 to 6 serving

1 medium onion, finely chopped
½ cup celery, finely chopped
1 tablespoon butter or margarine
2 tablespoons brown sugar
1 can (8 ounces) seasoned tomato sauce
½ cup catsup
2 tablespoons prepared mustard
1 tablespoon Worcestershire sauce
1 cup water
4 to 6 turkey drumsticks

In saucepan, saute onion and celery in butter until onion is soft and translucent. Stir in remaining ingredients except drumsticks. Lightly oil grid. Grill drumsticks, on covered grill, over medium-hot **Kingsford® briquets** 1 to 1½ hours, turning occasionally. Baste with sauce during last 15 minutes of grilling. Bring remaining sauce to boil and serve with drumsticks.

*Recipe courtesy of **National Turkey Federation***

CHILI-TOMATO GRILLED CHICKEN

Makes 6 to 8 servings

½ cup finely chopped onion
1 clove garlic, minced
2 tablespoons vegetable oil
1 chicken bouillon cube
½ cup hot water
1 can (8 ounces) taco sauce or tomato sauce
2 tablespoons vinegar
1 tablespoon prepared mustard
1 teaspoon salt
¼ teaspoon dried oregano, crushed
2 broiler-fryer chickens (2 to 3 pounds), quartered
1 tablespoon mild chili powder

In small skillet, saute onion and garlic in oil about 3 minutes or until onion is soft and translucent. Dissolve bouillon cube in hot water. Add bouillon, taco sauce, vinegar, mustard, salt and oregano to skillet. Dip chicken in sauce, turning to coat thoroughly; lightly sprinkle on all sides with chili powder. Refrigerate chicken until ready to grill. Add remaining chili powder to sauce; bring to boil and remove from heat; cool slightly.

Just before grilling, redip each chicken piece in sauce. Lightly oil grid. Grill chicken, on covered grill, over medium-hot **Kingsford® briquets** 25 to 30 minutes, turning often. Brush chicken with sauce and cook 20 to 30 minutes longer or until fork-tender, turning and brushing with sauce every 10 minutes.

*Recipe courtesy **National Broiler Council***

APPLE-STUFFED CHICKEN

Makes 6 servings

1 large roasting chicken (5 to 6 pounds)
   Salt-free seasoning and seasoned pepper
2 Granny Smith apples, cored and quartered
3 large leeks, trimmed, washed and cut into
   2-inch pieces
4 or 5 sprigs fresh tarragon, rosemary *or* parsley
⅓ cup butter or margarine, melted
1 tablespoon Kitchen Bouquet® browning sauce

Remove giblets and neck from chicken. Rinse chicken under cold running water; pat dry with paper toweling. Season inside with salt-free seasoning and pepper. Place apples, leeks and herbs in chicken cavity. Pull skin over neck and body openings; secure with skewers. Fold wing tips under body; secure with kitchen twine wrapped around wings and body. Bring legs together and tie at tip ends.

In small bowl, combine butter and browning sauce; brush on chicken. Grill chicken, breast-side down, on covered grill, over medium-hot **Kingsford® with Mesquite charcoal briquets** 25 minutes, basting once with butter sauce. Turn chicken breast-side up and baste again. Cover grill and cook 15 minutes longer; baste again with butter sauce. Cook 35 minutes longer or until thigh moves easily and juices run clear, adding briquets as necessary to maintain heat.

Chili-Tomato Grilled Chicken

PORK & LAMB

Pork has long been one of America's favorites for barbecue, and the hearty flavor of lamb makes it a natural for outdoor cooking. Enjoy simple chops, spicy ribs, exotic kabobs or a variety of whole roasts.

TERIYAKI PORK CHOPS

Makes 4 servings

¼ cup soy sauce
¼ cup peanut or vegetable oil
¼ cup minced onion
3 tablespoons honey
3 tablespoons dry sherry
2 teaspoons grated fresh ginger *or* ¾ teaspoon ground ginger
1 clove garlic, minced
4 pork loin chops, cut 1 inch thick

In shallow glass dish, combine all ingredients except pork chops. Add pork chops; turn to coat with marinade. Cover and refrigerate several hours or overnight, basting occasionally. Drain chops; reserve marinade. Arrange medium-hot **Kingsford® briquets** to one side of grill with drip pan next to briquets. Place chops over drip pan. Cover grill and cook 30 to 40 minutes or until chops are tender and cooked through, turning once and basting often with marinade.

Teriyaki Pork Chops

68

ITALIANO FRANKABOBS

Makes 4 servings

½ cup vegetable oil
2 teaspoons dried oregano, crushed
½ teaspoon ground nutmeg
⅛ teaspoon dried thyme, crushed
⅛ teaspoon dried marjoram, crushed
1 clove garlic, cut in half
8 medium fresh mushrooms
1 medium green pepper, cut into 1-inch pieces
2 large tomatoes, cut into wedges
1 medium zucchini, peeled and cut into 12 slices
2 pounds hot dogs, cut into bite-size pieces

In large bowl, combine oil, oregano, nutmeg, thyme, marjoram and garlic. Add mushrooms, pepper, tomatoes and zucchini. Cover and refrigerate 1 hour or overnight. Alternately thread vegetables and hot dog pieces on 4 skewers. Grill kabobs, on uncovered grill, over medium-hot **Kingsford® briquets** about 10 minutes or just until hot dogs are heated through and vegetables tender-crisp, turning often and brushing with marinade.

*Recipe courtesy of **National Hot Dog & Sausage Council***

Italiano Frankabobs

HERBED LAMB AND VEGETABLE KABOBS

Makes 6 servings

½ cup olive or vegetable oil
¼ cup fresh lemon juice
1 tablespoon finely chopped onion
2 teaspoons fresh thyme
1 garlic clove, crushed
1 teaspoon salt
½ teaspoon paprika
1½ pounds boneless lamb, cut into 1½-inch pieces
12 cauliflowerettes
12 slices carrot (1 inch each)
12 small white onions
12 slices zucchini (1 inch each)
12 large fresh mushrooms

In large bowl, combine oil, lemon juice, chopped onion, thyme, garlic, salt and paprika. Add lamb pieces; turn to coat with marinade. Cover and refrigerate 6 to 8 hours or overnight, turning occasionally. In saucepan, cook cauliflowerettes, carrot and white onions in boiling water to cover until tender-crisp. Thread lamb and all vegetables alternately on skewers. Grill kabobs, on uncovered grill, over medium-hot **Kingsford® briquets** 13 to 16 minutes, turning often and basting with marinade.

SPICY COUNTRY RIBS

Makes 6 servings

1 medium onion, finely chopped
3 cloves garlic, crushed
2 tablespoons vegetable oil
1 can (15 ounces) tomato sauce
½ cup red wine
¼ cup packed brown sugar
¾ teaspoon salt
½ teaspoon dry mustard
½ teaspoon chili powder
½ teaspoon hot pepper sauce
⅛ teaspoon pepper
5 pounds country-style spareribs

In medium skillet, saute onion and garlic in oil until onion is soft but not brown. Stir in remaining ingredients except spareribs. Bring to boil; reduce heat and simmer, covered, 20 minutes. Trim any excess fat from ribs. Arrange ribs in shallow glass dish. Cover with plastic wrap, vented. Microwave at 50% power 20 minutes, rearranging ribs once. Remove from oven. Brush ribs with sauce. Lightly oil grid. Grill ribs, on covered grill, over medium-hot **Kingsford® briquets** 30 minutes or until cooked through, turning often and basting with sauce.

Butterflied Southern Citrus Barbecue

BUTTERFLIED SOUTHERN CITRUS BARBECUE

Makes 8 servings

1 boneless leg of lamb (6 to 8 pounds), butterflied
1½ cups grapefruit juice
3 tablespoons brown sugar
1 tablespoon grated grapefruit or lemon peel
1 teaspoon ground cloves
2 cloves garlic, minced
½ teaspoon salt
¼ teaspoon pepper
 Few drops hot pepper sauce

Place lamb in large glass or enamel bowl. In small bowl, combine remaining ingredients; pour over lamb. Cover and refrigerate several hours or overnight. Drain lamb; reserve marinade. Grill lamb, on covered grill, over medium-hot **Kingsford® briquets** 1 hour and 15 minutes, adding more briquets as necessary, until meat thermometer registers 140°F for rare, 150°–155°F for medium or 160°F for well-done. Turn lamb once halfway through cooking time. Baste often with marinade.

Recipe courtesy of American Lamb Council, Inc.

SATAY PORK

Makes 4 to 6 servings

½ cup peanut or vegetable oil
¼ cup soy sauce
2 tablespoons chopped peanuts
1 tablespoon Worcestershire sauce
1 tablespoon chopped onion
2 cloves garlic, crushed
2 teaspoons brown sugar
¼ teaspoon curry powder
⅛ teaspoon coriander
3 pounds boneless pork, cut into ½-inch cubes

In shallow glass dish, combine all ingredients except pork. Add pork, turning to coat with marinade. Cover and refrigerate 1 to 2 hours, stirring occasionally. Drain pork; reserve marinade. Thread pork on skewers. Grill kabobs, on uncovered grill, over hot **Kingsford® briquets** 5 to 6 minutes or until cooked through, turning often and basting with marinade.

Sweet & Sour Pork Loin

SWEET & SOUR PORK LOIN

Makes 4 servings

½ cup chicken broth or water
½ cup catsup
2 tablespoons brown sugar
2 tablespoons cider vinegar
2 tablespoons Worcestershire sauce
1 clove garlic, crushed
½ teaspoon salt
¼ teaspoon black pepper
⅛ teaspoon cayenne pepper
1 boneless pork loin roast (2 pounds), tied

In saucepan, combine all ingredients except roast. Heat to boiling. Cut roast crosswise into 4 pieces; arrange in shallow glass dish. Pour sweet and sour mixture over pork. Cover and refrigerate overnight. Drain pork; reserve sweet and sour mixture. Grill pork, on uncovered grill, over medium-hot **Match light® charcoal briquets** 20 to 25 minutes or until pork is cooked through, turning 3 to 4 times and basting often with sweet and sour mixture.

BASQUE LAMB

Makes 4 to 6 servings

¾ cup fresh lemon juice
1 cup dry sherry
½ cup olive or vegetable oil
1 clove garlic, crushed
1 boneless lamb shoulder (3 pounds), left untied
1 bunch chives, chopped
1 clove garlic, chopped
1 bunch parsley, chopped
Salt and pepper

In small bowl, combine lemon juice, sherry, oil and crushed garlic. Let stand 1 hour. Sprinkle inside of roast with an even layer of chives, chopped garlic and parsley. Season with salt and pepper to taste. Roll up meat and tie securely with kitchen twine. Arrange medium-hot **Kingsford® briquets** around drip pan. Fill pan with water. Add hickory chips to coals, if desired. Place roast over drip pan. Cover grill and cook 45 to 60 minutes or until medium-rare, basting often with lemon juice mixture. Remove roast from grill; let stand 15 minutes. Carve into 1-inch-thick slices.

ISLAND LAMB TERIYAKI STICKS

Makes 4 to 6 servings

1 cup soy sauce
½ cup brown sugar
¼ cup vegetable oil
¼ cup vinegar
3 cloves garlic, minced
2 teaspoons sesame seed
2 teaspoons ground ginger
1 teaspoon salt
2 pounds boneless lamb, cut into 1-inch-wide
    strips
    Water chestnuts
    Pineapple chunks
    Cherry tomatoes

In shallow glass dish, combine soy sauce, brown sugar, oil, vinegar, garlic, sesame seed, ginger and salt. Add lamb strips, turning to coat with marinade. Cover and refrigerate several hours or overnight, turning occasionally.

Drain meat; reserve marinade. Alternately thread lamb strips (accordion-style), water chestnuts, pineapple and tomatoes on skewers. Grill, on uncovered grill, over medium-hot **Kingsford® briquets** 5 to 6 minutes or to desired doneness, turning kabobs often and brushing with marinade. Serve with hot cooked rice, if desired.

*Recipe courtesy of **American Lamb Council, Inc.***

MEXICAN PORK STRIPS

Makes 4 servings or 16 appetizer kabobs

1 boneless pork loin roast (about 1¼ pounds)
2 tablespoons fresh lime juice
2 tablespoons vegetable oil
2 cloves garlic, minced
1 tomato, seeded and finely chopped
1 avocado, peeled and finely chopped
3 tablespoons chopped green chili peppers
2 tablespoons chopped cilantro or parsley
1 green onion, thinly sliced
¾ teaspoon ground cumin
½ teaspoon salt

Place roast in freezer 30 minutes to firm; slice across grain into ⅛- to ¼-inch slices. Cut each slice in half lengthwise. In small bowl, combine lime juice, oil and garlic. Place pork in plastic bag; place bag in bowl. Pour marinade over pork in bag. Close bag securely and refrigerate 30 minutes, turning occasionally.

For salsa, in medium bowl, combine tomato, avocado, chili peppers, cilantro, onion, cumin and salt; cover and refrigerate until ready to serve.

Drain pork; discard marinade. Thread strips of pork accordion-style on skewers. Grill kabobs, on covered grill, over medium-hot **Kingsford® briquets** 6 minutes or until pork is cooked through, turning several times. Serve salsa with kabobs.

*Recipe courtesy of **National Live Stock & Meat Board***

Island Lamb Teriyaki Sticks

Lamb Satay

GRILLED SAUSAGE WITH APPLES & ONIONS

Makes 4 servings

1 pound smoked sausage, cut into 1-inch chunks
2 small apples, cored and cut into quarters
2 small onions, cut into quarters
2 tablespoons apple jelly
1 tablespoon butter or margarine

Thread sausage, apples and onions alternately on 4 skewers. In small saucepan, combine jelly and butter; heat until melted. Brush jelly mixture on sausage kabobs. Grill kabobs, on uncovered grill, over medium-hot **Match light® charcoal briquets** 10 to 15 minutes or until cooked through, turning often and basting with jelly mixture.

RASPBERRY-GLAZED LAMB RIBS

Makes 2 servings

2 lamb ribs, about 6 ounces each (8 ribs per slab)
½ teaspoon salt
¼ teaspoon pepper
¼ teaspoon paprika
½ cup red wine vinegar or raspberry vinegar
½ cup white wine
½ cup seedless raspberry jam
1 tablespoon finely chopped shallots
1 tablespoon cornstarch
1 tablespoon water

Sprinkle ribs with salt, pepper and paprika. In medium saucepan, combine vinegar, white wine, raspberry jam and shallots. Stir over medium heat until jam is melted. Stir together cornstarch and water; add to raspberry mixture and stir until sauce is smooth and clear.

Arrange medium-hot **Kingsford® briquets** around drip pan. Place ribs over drip pan. Cover grill and cook 50 to 60 minutes or until ribs are cooked through, turning ribs every 10 minutes. Brush ribs with sauce during last 10 minutes of grilling.

*Recipe courtesy of **American Lamb Council, Inc.***

LAMB SATAY

Makes 4 servings

1¼ pounds boneless leg of lamb, well trimmed
½ cup lime juice
1 can (20 ounces) pineapple chunks in juice
5 tablespoons creamy peanut butter
Hot cooked rice

Cut lamb into 3×¾×½-inch strips. Place strips in shallow glass dish; add lime juice and toss to coat. Cover and refrigerate at least 1 hour or overnight. Drain lamb strips and pat dry. Thread strips, accordion-style, on 6-inch skewers.

Drain pineapple; reserve juice. Place peanut butter in small saucepan; gradually stir in reserved juice. Cook and stir over medium heat 5 to 6 minutes or until thoroughly heated. Grill lamb strips, on uncovered grill, over medium-hot **Kingsford® briquets** 6 to 7 minutes or to desired doneness, turning often. Serve with peanut sauce, pineapple chunks and hot cooked rice. Garnish with lime slices, if desired.

*Recipe courtesy of **American Lamb Council, Inc.***

Raspberry-Glazed Lamb Ribs

Spicy Lamb Burgers

ALL-AMERICAN PORK RIBS

Makes 4 serving

- 1 small onion, coarsely chopped
- 2 tablespoons water
- ⅔ cup catsup
- ⅔ cup chili sauce
- 2 tablespoons lemon juice
- ½ teaspoon dry mustard
- ¼ teaspoon cayenne pepper
- ¼ teaspoon paprika
- ¼ teaspoon Worcestershire sauce
- ½ teaspoon salt
- 3 pounds pork back ribs

For barbecue sauce, in medium saucepan, cook onion in water 3 to 4 minutes. Add catsup, chili sauce, lemon juice, mustard, cayenne, paprika and Worcestershire sauce. Cook over low heat 15 minutes. Sprinkle salt over surface of ribs. Grill ribs, on covered grill, over medium to low **Kingsford®️ briquets** 45 to 60 minutes or until done, turning occasionally. Brush both sides of ribs with sauce during last 10 minutes of cooking. Bring remaining sauce to boil and serve with ribs.

Note: Recipe can be doubled.

*Recipe courtesy of **National Live Stock & Meat Board***

SPICY LAMB BURGERS

Makes 6 servings

- ¼ cup chopped onion
- 1 teaspoon curry powder
- 1 tablespoon butter or margarine, melted
- ¼ cup finely chopped almonds
- ¼ cup crushed pineapple, drained
- 1½ pounds ground lamb
- ½ cup dry bread crumbs
- 2 eggs
- ⅛ teaspoon pepper
- 6 pita breads

In skillet, saute onion and curry powder in butter until onion is tender. Stir in almonds and pineapple. In bowl, combine onion mixture thoroughly with lamb, bread crumbs, eggs and pepper. Shape meat mixture into 6 patties. Grill patties, on uncovered grill, over medium-hot **Match light®️ charcoal briquets** about 5 minutes on each side or until done. Grill pita breads on edge of grill. Serve lamb burgers in pita breads with bean sprouts and plain yogurt, if desired.

GRILLED HERBED ITALIAN SAUSAGE

Makes 6 serving

- 2¼ pounds fresh mild Italian sausage, cut into 6 pieces
- ¾ cup dry white wine
- ¾ teaspoon dried rosemary, crushed
- ¾ teaspoon dried thyme, crushed
- 6 kaiser rolls, split
- Assorted mustards

Form each piece of sausage into a coil. Secure by inserting skewer horizontally through open end of sausage. Place sausages in shallow glass dish; add wine and herbs, turning sausages to coat with marinade. Cover and refrigerate 2 to 3 hours. Drain sausages; reserve marinade. Grill sausages, on uncovered grill, over low **Kingsford®️ briquets** 20 to 25 minutes or until cooked through, basting often with marinade. Serve sausages on rolls with assorted mustards.

*Recipe courtesy of **National Live Stock & Meat Board***

GRILLED SMOKED SAUSAGE

Makes 6 servings

1 cup apricot or pineapple preserves
1 tablespoon lemon juice
1½ pounds smoked sausage

In small saucepan, heat preserves. Strain; reserve fruit pieces. Combine strained preserve liquid with lemon juice. Grill whole sausage, on uncovered grill, over low **Kingsford® briquets** 5 minutes. Brush with glaze; grill sausage about 5 minutes longer, turning and brushing with glaze occasionally. Garnish with fruit pieces.

GRILLED HAM SANDWICHES

Makes 6 servings

1 pound boneless fully cooked ham, in 1 piece
1 cup catsup
⅓ cup butter or margarine
1½ tablespoons Worcestershire sauce
1½ tablespoons prepared mustard
1 teaspoon onion salt
6 buttered hot dog buns

Cut ham lengthwise into 6 slices. In small saucepan, combine catsup, butter, Worcestershire sauce, mustard and onion salt. Cook over low heat until mixture simmers. Remove sauce from heat; cool slightly.

Coat ham slices with sauce. Grill ham slices, on uncovered grill, over medium-hot **Match light® charcoal briquets** 3 to 4 minutes on each side or until meat is browned and hot. Serve sliced ham in hot dog buns.

CIDER-GLAZED PORK ROAST

Makes 6 servings

½ cup apple cider
¼ cup Dijon-style mustard
¼ cup vegetable oil
¼ cup soy sauce
1 boneless pork loin roast (4 to 5 pounds), tied

In small bowl, combine apple cider, mustard, oil and soy sauce. Insert meat thermometer in center of thickest part of roast. Arrange medium-hot **Kingsford® briquets** around drip pan. Place roast over drip pan. Cover grill and cook 2½ to 3 hours or until meat thermometer registers 170°F, adding more briquets as necessary. Brush roast with cider mixture 3 or 4 times during last 30 minutes of cooking.

Apricot-Glazed Lamb Chops

APRICOT-GLAZED LAMB CHOPS

Makes 4 servings

⅓ cup apricot jam
1 tablespoon white vinegar
1 teaspoon Dijon-style mustard
½ teaspoon dried rosemary, crushed
1 clove garlic, minced
½ teaspoon salt
¼ teaspoon pepper
4 lamb shoulder arm or blade chops, cut ¾ inch thick

In small saucepan, combine apricot jam, vinegar, mustard, rosemary, garlic, salt and pepper. Cook over low heat, stirring, until jam is melted. Grill lamb chops, on uncovered grill, over medium-hot **Kingsford® briquets** 14 to 16 minutes for medium, turning once. Brush both sides with glaze several times during grilling.

*Recipe courtesy of **National Live Stock & Meat Board***

FISH & SEAFOOD

The delicate smoky flavor achieved only by cooking over coals brings out the best in fish. Choose from wonderful recipes for tuna, swordfish, salmon or trout. For shellfish lovers, there are recipes for clams, shrimp, scallops—even lobster.

SALMON STEAKS IN ORANGE-HONEY MARINADE

Makes 4 servings

⅓ cup orange juice
⅓ cup soy sauce
3 tablespoons peanut or vegetable oil
3 tablespoons catsup
1 tablespoon honey
½ teaspoon ground ginger
1 clove garlic, sliced
4 salmon steaks (about 6 ounces each)

In shallow glass dish, combine all ingredients except salmon steaks. Add salmon steaks, turning to coat with marinade. Cover and refrigerate 1 hour. Drain salmon; reserve marinade. Grill salmon, on uncovered grill, over hot **Kingsford® briquets** 5 minutes. Carefully turn salmon steaks, brush with marinade and grill 5 minutes longer or until salmon flakes easily when tested with fork.

Salmon Steaks in Orange-Honey Marinade

GRILLED CATFISH

4 farm-raised catfish steaks or fillets*
½ teaspoon garlic salt
¼ teaspoon white pepper
   Grilled vegetables

Sprinkle fish with garlic salt and pepper. Lightly oil grid. Grill fish steaks, on uncovered grill, over medium-hot **Kingsford®** briquets 4 to 5 minutes per side or until fish flakes easily when tested with fork. Garnish as desired. Serve with assorted grilled vegetables.

*If grilling catfish fillets, use a wire grill basket.
*Recipe courtesy of **The Catfish Institute***

FISH FILLETS WITH DILL SAUCE

Makes 2 servings

½ to ¾ pound mackerel, halibut, sablefish, grouper, salmon or catfish fillets
1 tablespoon vegetable oil
1 teaspoon chopped fresh dill *or* ½ teaspoon dried dill weed
   Generous dash hot pepper sauce
   Dill Sauce (recipe follows)

Measure fish at its thickest part to determine cooking time. In small bowl, combine oil, dill and hot pepper sauce; brush fish fillets with dill mixture. Tear off piece of heavy-duty foil large enough to hold fish; puncture foil in several places. Place fillets on perforated foil. Grill fillets on foil, on covered grill, over medium-hot **Kingsford®** briquets about 10 minutes per inch of thickness or until fish flakes easily when tested with fork, basting often with dill mixture. Serve with Dill Sauce.

DILL SAUCE

Makes about ¼ cup

¼ cup sour cream or plain yogurt
1 teaspoon finely chopped fresh dill *or*
   ¼ teaspoon dried dill weed
¾ teaspoon white wine vinegar
   Few drops hot pepper sauce
   Salt and pepper

In small bowl, combine sour cream, dill, vinegar and hot pepper sauce; season to taste with salt and pepper. Cover and refrigerate until ready to serve to blend flavors.

Note: Recipe can be doubled.
*Recipe courtesy of **National Fisheries Institute***

GRILLED FISH WITH SALSA

Makes 4 servings

½ cup quartered cherry tomatoes
½ cup cubed mango or papaya
¼ cup sliced green onion
¼ cup cubed avocado
2 tablespoons chopped cilantro or parsley
1 tablespoon olive or vegetable oil
2 tablespoons lime juice
1 teaspoon minced jalapeño pepper
   Salt and pepper
1¼ pounds white fish fillets (ling cod, red snapper or halibut)

In small bowl, combine tomatoes, mango, onion, avocado, cilantro, oil, 1 tablespoon of the lime juice and the jalapeño pepper. Season with salt and pepper to taste; set aside. Measure fish at its thickest part to determine cooking time. Sprinkle both sides of fish with remaining 1 tablespoon lime juice and additional pepper. Lightly oil grid. Grill fillets, on covered grill, over medium-hot **Kingsford®** briquets 10 minutes per inch of thickness or until fish flakes easily when tested with fork. Garnish with additional mango or papaya slices, if desired. Serve with salsa.

LEMON SWORDFISH

Makes 4 servings

1 tablespoon grated lemon peel
¾ cup fresh lemon juice
¾ cup olive or vegetable oil
¼ to ½ cup parsley, chopped
2 tablespoons prepared horseradish
2 cloves garlic, minced
1 teaspoon dried thyme, crushed
1 teaspoon salt
¼ teaspoon pepper
1 bay leaf
1½ pounds swordfish steaks

In shallow glass dish, combine all ingredients except fish. Add swordfish; turn to coat with marinade. Cover and refrigerate at least 2 hours, turning fish occasionally. Drain fish; reserve marinade. Grill swordfish, on uncovered grill, over medium-hot **Kingsford®** briquets about 7 minutes, basting lightly with marinade. Carefully turn swordfish and grill 5 to 6 minutes longer or until fish flakes easily when tested with fork, basting lightly with marinade.

Grilled Fish with Salsa

Seafood Kabobs

SEAFOOD KABOBS

Makes 6 servings

2 dozen large sea scallops
1 dozen medium shrimp, shelled and deveined
1 can (8½ ounces) whole small artichoke hearts, drained
2 red or yellow peppers, cut into 2-inch pieces
¼ cup olive or vegetable oil
¼ cup lime juice

In large bowl, combine all ingredients and toss gently. Thread scallops, shrimp, artichoke hearts and peppers alternately on skewers; reserve marinade. Lightly oil grid. Grill kabobs, on uncovered grill, over low **Kingsford® briquets** 6 to 8 minutes or until scallops turn opaque and shrimp turn pink. Turn kabobs carefully at least twice during grilling and brush with marinade.

GRILLED LOBSTER WITH SPICY SAUCE

Makes 4 servings

4 whole, live lobsters* (1 to 1½ pounds each)
¼ cup dry sherry
3 tablespoons soy sauce
2 to 3 tablespoons sugar
2 teaspoons grated fresh ginger *or* ½ teaspoon ground ginger
1 teaspoon red pepper flakes
2 cloves garlic, minced
Butter or margarine, melted

Bring large kettle of water to boil. Plunge lobsters into water. Return water to boil; cover and simmer 3 minutes or just until lobsters turn pink. Remove lobsters; rinse under cold running water and drain. Turn lobsters, underside up, and cut through inner shell of tails to expose meat.

For spicy sauce, in small bowl, combine remaining ingredients except butter. Brush lobster shells and meaty underside with sauce, letting sauce soak into meat. Grill lobsters, meat-side up, on covered grill, over medium-hot **Kingsford® with Mesquite charcoal briquets** 13 to 15 minutes or until meat turns opaque, basting often with sauce. When lobsters are cooked, make a deep cut lengthwise in center of underside with sharp knife. Spread halves enough to remove stomach (near head) and black vein. Crack claw shells with hammer. Serve with melted butter and additional spicy sauce.

*2 pounds jumbo fresh shrimp can be substituted for lobster. Leave shell on and thread on skewers. Grill as above, reducing cooking time to 5 minutes or until shrimp turn pink.

CAJUN FISH

Makes 4 servings

1 cup butter or margarine
2 tablespoons paprika
2 teaspoons popcorn butter salt
2 teaspoons onion powder
2 teaspoons garlic powder
2 teaspoons cayenne pepper
1½ teaspoons white pepper
1½ teaspoons black pepper
1 teaspoon dried thyme, crushed
1 teaspoon dried oregano, crushed
2 pounds red snapper fillets

Heat iron skillet directly over medium-hot **Match light® charcoal briquets** at least 15 minutes. Meanwhile, in small saucepan, melt butter. In small bowl, combine remaining ingredients except fish. Brush fillets with butter; sprinkle seasoning mix evenly on both sides of fillets. Place fillets in hot skillet and ladle melted butter over fillets.* Cook about 2 minutes on each side. Serve immediately with additional melted butter for dipping.

*Note: This method of grilling produces heavy smoke.

CITRUS GRILLED WHOLE FISH WITH LIME BUTTER

Makes 6 to 8 servings

1 whole fish (about 4 pounds), such as salmon,
   bluefish, red snapper or trout, cleaned
Vegetable oil
Pepper
1 or 2 limes, thinly sliced
1 or 2 lemons, thinly sliced
Lime Butter (recipe follows)

Rinse inside cavity of fish under cold running water; pat dry with paper toweling. Brush cavity with oil and season with pepper. Overlap alternating lime and lemon slices in cavity of fish. Measure thickness of fish at its thickest part to determine cooking time. Place fish in oiled wire grill basket. Grill fish, on covered grill, over medium-hot **Kingsford® briquets** 10 to 12 minutes per inch of thickness or until fish flakes easily when tested with fork. Turn fish halfway through cooking time. Serve with Lime Butter.

LIME BUTTER

Makes a generous ½ cup

½ cup butter or margarine, softened
1 teaspoon grated lime peel
2 to 3 tablespoons fresh lime juice
   Dash salt

In bowl or food processor, combine all ingredients. Beat or process until soft and light.

*Recipe courtesy of **National Fisheries Institute***

BACON-WRAPPED TUNA

Makes 6 servings

3 pounds fresh tuna
½ cup olive or vegetable oil
¼ cup lime juice
1 cup dry white wine
2 cloves garlic, crushed
1 teaspoon grated fresh ginger
6 slices bacon

Cut tuna into 6 steaks, each about 1 inch thick. Remove any skin or bone. In shallow glass dish, combine oil, lime juice, wine, garlic and ginger. Add tuna; turn to coat with marinade. Cover and refrigerate 2 hours. Drain fish; reserve marinade. Wrap 1 slice of bacon around each steak and secure with wooden pick. Lightly oil grid. Grill fish steaks, on uncovered grill, over medium-hot **Kingsford® briquets** about 10 minutes or until fish flakes easily when tested with fork. Turn once halfway through cooking time; baste often with marinade.

Grilled Shrimp in Peanut Sauce

GRILLED SHRIMP IN PEANUT SAUCE

Makes 4 servings

¼ cup creamy peanut butter
¼ cup soy sauce
¼ cup sugar
3 cloves garlic, minced
2 tablespoons vegetable oil
1 tablespoon water
1½ pounds medium shrimp, shelled and deveined

In saucepan, combine peanut butter and 2 tablespoons of the soy sauce; blend well. Stir in remaining 2 tablespoons soy sauce, the sugar, garlic, oil and water; heat to dissolve sugar. Thread shrimp on skewers; brush with peanut sauce. Grill shrimp, on covered grill, over medium-hot **Kingsford® with Mesquite charcoal briquets** 5 to 6 minutes or until shrimp turn pink; turn once halfway through cooking time. Brush shrimp with peanut sauce before serving.

GRILLED TROUT WITH TWO SAUCES

Makes 4 servings

**4 whole, cleaned trout or other small whole fish
(about 12 ounces each)
Walnut Butter Sauce (recipe follows)** *or*
Tarragon Cream Sauce (recipe follows)

Grill fish on well-oiled grid or in well-oiled wire grill basket, on covered grill, over medium-hot **Kingsford® with Mesquite charcoal briquets** 3 to 5 minutes or until fish flakes easily when tested with fork; turn once. Serve with Walnut Butter Sauce or Tarragon Cream Sauce.

WALNUT BUTTER SAUCE

Makes about ½ cup

**½ cup chopped walnuts
½ cup butter or margarine
3 tablespoons Madeira wine**

In skillet, saute walnuts in 2 tablespoons of the butter until golden and fragrant. Reduce heat and add remaining 6 tablespoons butter; stir until melted. Stir in Madeira. Serve warm.

TARRAGON CREAM SAUCE

Makes about ½ cup

**¼ cup olive or vegetable oil
¼ cup whipping cream
1 tablespoon red wine vinegar
1 tablespoon finely chopped parsley
1 garlic clove, minced
½ teaspoon dried tarragon, crushed
¼ teaspoon pepper**

In medium bowl, combine all ingredients; mix well with wire whisk. Serve cool.

SHELLFISH APPETIZERS

Makes 4 appetizer servings

**24 clams or 32 mussels, scrubbed
4 tablespoons white wine
½ teaspoon dried thyme, crushed**

For each serving, place 6 clams or 8 mussels on each of 4 pieces of heavy-duty foil. Bring up foil around shellfish and add 1 tablespoon white wine and ⅛ teaspoon thyme to each packet. Fold foil loosely around shellfish; seal edges tightly. Grill packets over medium-hot **Kingsford® briquets** about 5 minutes or until shellfish open. (Discard any shellfish that do not open.)

*Recipe courtesy of **National Fisheries Institute***

CANTONESE GRILLED SHRIMP

Makes 4 to 6 servings

**1 cup soy sauce
½ cup dry white or red wine
2 tablespoons vegetable oil
4 green onions, finely chopped
2 tablespoons grated fresh ginger
2 tablespoons brown sugar
2 teaspoons red pepper flakes
2 teaspoons sesame seed
2 pounds medium shrimp, shelled and deveined**

In shallow glass dish, combine all ingredients except shrimp. Add shrimp; turn to coat with marinade. Cover and refrigerate at least 2 hours, stirring occasionally. Thread shrimp on skewers; reserve marinade. Grill shrimp, on covered grill, over medium-hot **Kingsford® briquets** 6 to 8 minutes or until shrimp turn pink, basting frequently with marinade.

BARBECUED ALASKA SALMON

Makes 12 to 16 servings

**2 whole Alaska salmon fillets (about 1½ pounds
each)
Salt and pepper
1 teaspoon grated lemon peel
½ cup butter or margarine, melted
¼ cup fresh lemon juice
4 teaspoons grated onion
½ teaspoon hot pepper sauce**

Measure fish at its thickest part to determine cooking time. Sprinkle both sides of each fillet with salt and pepper to taste. In small bowl, combine remaining ingredients; brush both sides of fillets with butter mixture. Tear off 2 pieces of heavy-duty foil large enough to hold each fillet; puncture foil in several places. Place each fillet, skin-side down, on perforated foil. Grill salmon on foil, on covered grill, over hot **Kingsford® briquets** 10 minutes per inch of thickness or until salmon flakes easily when tested with fork. Baste often with butter mixture.

*Recipe courtesy of **Alaska Seafood Marketing Institute, Salmon Division***

Grilled Trout with Two Sauce

ALL THE EXTRAS

Here you'll find everything you need to round out a great barbecue: salads, side dishes and desserts. Some recipes are traditional favorites, such as potato salad. Others offer innovative ways to grill your favorite fruits and vegetables.

GRILLED BABY VEGETABLES

Makes 4 servings

1 pound assorted baby vegetables (such as pattypan or zucchini squash, carrots, asparagus tips or red peppers)
Prepared Italian salad dressing for basting
Green onion tops (optional)

Cut larger vegetables into halves. Brush vegetables lightly with dressing. Grill vegetables over medium-hot **Kingsford® briquets** 5 to 10 minutes or until crisp-tender, turning once and basting occasionally with dressing.

To tie vegetables into bundles, blanch green onion tops in boiling water 5 seconds or until limp. Use tops as string to tie bundles together.

BARBECUED GARLIC

Makes 4 servings

1 whole head of garlic
Olive or vegetable oil for basting

Peel loose, outermost skin from garlic; brush all over with oil. Grill garlic, on covered grill, not directly over medium-hot **Kingsford® briquets** 30 to 45 minutes or until garlic cloves are very tender, basting frequently with oil. Press individual cloves between thumb and forefinger to squeeze out garlic. Serve with grilled meats or as a spread for hot fresh bread.

Barbecued Garlic, Fresh Fruit Kabobs (page 88) and Grilled Baby Vegetables

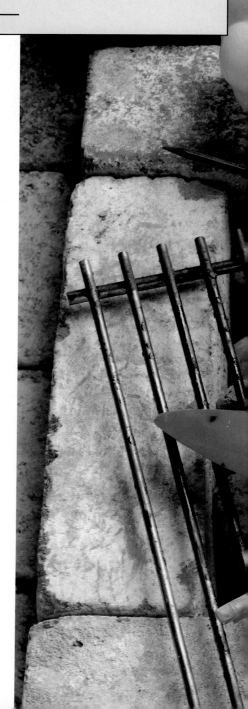

FRESH FRUIT KABOBS

Makes 8 servings

½ cup butter or margarine, softened
⅓ cup honey
1 tablespoon chopped fresh mint *or* 1 teaspoon dried mint, crushed
1 fresh pineapple, cored, peeled and cut into 1-inch cubes
3 fresh nectarines, pears, plums or apples, cut into wedges

In small bowl, combine butter, honey and mint. Thread fruit pieces alternately on skewers. Brush kabobs with butter-honey mixture. Grill kabobs over medium-hot **Kingsford®** briquets 3 to 5 minutes or until fruit is heated through. Turn once or twice and brush with butter-honey mixture. Serve plain or with pound cake, ice cream or whipped topping, if desired.

CHEDDAR CHEESE PEARS

Makes 6 servings

3 fresh pears, peeled, cored and cut into halves *or* 1 can (29 ounces) pear halves, drained
2 teaspoons grated lemon peel
2 tablespoons fresh lemon juice
½ cup shredded Cheddar cheese (about 4 ounces)

Arrange pears on large square of heavy-duty foil. Sprinkle lemon peel and juice over pears. Fill pear halves with cheese. Fold up foil around pears; seal edges tightly. Grill packet over medium-hot **Kingsford®** briquets 15 minutes or until pears are hot and cheese is soft.

Eggplant Parmesan

GRILLED STUFFED RED PEPPER RINGS

Makes 6 servings

4 medium red peppers
1 can (12 ounces) whole kernel corn, drained
½ cup dry bread crumbs
1 egg, beaten
1 tablespoon all-purpose flour
2 tablespoons diced onion
2 tablespoons chopped parsley
1½ cups prepared Hidden Valley Ranch® Original Ranch® Salad Dressing
Salt and pepper
1 bunch fresh spinach, washed and trimmed

Cut 3 thick rings from each pepper; remove seeds. Arrange on lightly oiled piece of heavy-duty foil. In large bowl, combine corn, bread crumbs, egg, flour, onion, parsley and ¾ cup of the salad dressing; season to taste with salt and pepper. Spoon mixture into pepper rings and pack down. Fold up foil around pepper rings into a pyramid shape. Crimp edges together to seal, allowing room for heat circulation. Grill packet over medium-hot **Kingsford®** briquets about 15 minutes. Open foil to allow rings to cool. When ready to serve, line large serving plate with spinach leaves. With wide spatula, carefully transfer stuffed rings to lined plate. Serve with remaining ¾ cup salad dressing.

EGGPLANT PARMESAN

Makes 4 servings

1 eggplant (about 1¼ pounds)
½ cup olive or vegetable oil
½ teaspoon dried oregano, crushed
½ teaspoon dried rosemary, crushed
¼ teaspoon garlic powder
6 ounces sliced mozzarella or Monterey Jack cheese
1 cup freshly grated Parmesan cheese (about 4 ounces)
1 jar (15 ounces) marinara sauce

Slice eggplant crosswise into ½-inch slices. In small bowl, combine oil, oregano, rosemary and garlic powder. Brush sides of eggplant with oil baste. Cut mozzarella cheese into slices to fit eggplant slices. Grill eggplant, on covered grill, over medium-hot **Kingsford® with Mesquite charcoal briquets** 5 minutes, turning often and brushing with baste. Arrange cheese slices on eggplant; spoon Parmesan cheese over each. Grill until cheese melts. Heat marinara sauce in small saucepan on edge of grill. Spoon hot sauce over eggplant slices before serving.

Peach Walnut Spice Cake and Insalata Rustica

PEACH WALNUT SPICE CAKE

Makes 6 to 8 servings

½ cup butter or margarine
½ cup granulated sugar
½ cup packed dark brown sugar
 4 eggs
⅓ cup molasses
 1 large fresh peach, chopped (about 1 cup)
2½ cups all-purpose flour
½ cup walnuts, chopped
 2 teaspoons ground cinnamon
¾ teaspoon baking soda
½ teaspoon ground nutmeg
½ teaspoon salt
 1 large fresh peach, cut into thin slices
    Whipped cream

In large mixer bowl, cream butter and sugars until light and fluffy. Beat in eggs, then molasses. Stir in chopped peach. In medium bowl, combine flour, walnuts, cinnamon, baking soda, nutmeg and salt; stir into creamed mixture. Pour into greased and floured 9-inch square baking pan. Bake in 350°F oven 40 to 50 minutes or until wooden pick inserted in center comes out clean. Cut into squares and top with peach slices and whipped cream.

Recipe courtesy of California Tree Fruit Agreement

INSALATA RUSTICA

Makes 6 servings

1 head iceberg lettuce, torn
1 head romaine lettuce, torn
1 bunch watercress, stems removed, leaves torn
2 tomatoes, sliced
6 radishes, sliced
2 large fresh peaches, cut into wedges (about
   2 cups)
  Mustard Dressing (recipe follows)

Arrange lettuce and watercress leaves in large salad bowl. Arrange tomatoes, radishes and peaches on top. Drizzle with Mustard Dressing.

MUSTARD DRESSING

Makes about 1 cup

½ cup vegetable oil
 6 tablespoons white wine vinegar
 8 teaspoons Dijon-style mustard
 4 teaspoons minced garlic
 1 teaspoon sugar

In small jar with tight-fitting lid, combine all ingredients. Shake to blend well.

Recipe courtesy of California Tree Fruit Agreement

Spicy Quesadillas

SPICY QUESADILLAS

Makes 8 to 10 appetizer servings

½ cup chopped fresh tomatoes
⅓ cup K.C. Masterpiece® Barbecue Sauce (Spicy or Original)
⅔ cup sliced green onions
2 tablespoons lime or lemon juice
1 tablespoon red wine vinegar
1 tablespoon minced jalapeño peppers or
    2 tablespoons diced green chili peppers
Hot pepper sauce
2 cups shredded Muenster or Monterey Jack cheese (about 8 ounces)
8 flour tortillas (6-inch)
Vegetable oil for frying

In small bowl, combine tomatoes, barbecue sauce, 3 tablespoons of the onions, the lime juice, vinegar and jalapeño peppers. Season to taste with hot pepper sauce. Combine cheese with remaining onions. For each quesadilla, sprinkle about ½ cup cheese-onion mixture over 1 tortilla. Spoon 2 tablespoons sauce mixture over cheese; top with another tortilla, pressing gently. Fry in skillet in small amount of hot oil until golden and cheese has melted, turning once. Cut into 6 or 8 wedges. Repeat with remaining ingredients. Garnish with additional green onions, if desired. Heat remaining sauce mixture and serve with quesadillas for dipping.

CALIFORNIA CRAB SALAD

Makes 4 serving

1 package (0.4 ounce) Hidden Valley Ranch® Buttermilk Recipe Original Ranch® Salad Dressing Mix
1 cup buttermilk
1 cup mayonnaise
1 teaspoon prepared horseradish
1 tablespoon grated fresh ginger
2 cups cooked rice, chilled
4 lettuce leaves
½ pound cooked crabmeat, chilled
1 large ripe avocado, peeled and thinly sliced
½ medium cucumber, thinly sliced

In large bowl, combine salad dressing mix, buttermilk and mayonnaise. Whisk in horseradish and ginger. Cover and refrigerate at least 30 minutes. On serving plate, arrange rice on lettuce leaves. Arrange crabmeat, avocado slices and cucumber slices on top of rice. Garnish with lime wedges and cherry tomato, if desired. Serve with salad dressing on the side.

GRILLED DESSERT PEACHES

Makes 4 to 6 serving

3 cups sliced, peeled fresh peaches *or* 1 can (29 ounces) sliced peaches, drained
3 tablespoons almond-flavored liqueur
2 tablespoons brown sugar
Dash ground nutmeg

Arrange peaches in lightly oiled foil pan. Sprinkle remaining ingredients over peaches. Cover pan tightly with foil. Place pan on grill over medium-hot **Kingsford® briquets** about 20 minutes or until hot.

HOT FRUIT COMPOTE

Makes 6 to 8 servings

1 can (16 ounces) pear halves, drained
1 can (20 ounces) pineapple chunks, drained
1 can (16 ounces) peach halves, drained
¼ cup butter or margarine, melted
½ cup packed brown sugar
½ teaspoon ground cinnamon

Combine all ingredients in foil pan. Place pan on grill over medium-hot **Kingsford® briquets** 20 to 25 minutes or until fruit is heated through. Stir often, spooning butter-sugar mixture over fruit while grilling.

California Crab Sala

*Left to right: Potato Salad with Green Beans,
Dutch Potato Salad and Turkish Potato Salad*

TURKISH POTATO SALAD

Makes 8 servings

- 6 medium potatoes (about 2 pounds)
- ¼ cup white wine vinegar
- 1 teaspoon dry sherry
- 1½ cups sliced red onions
  Dill-Mint Dressing (recipe follows)
- ½ cup sliced black olives
  Dill sprigs

In covered saucepan, cook potatoes in 2 inches boiling water until just tender, 20 to 25 minutes. Drain and cool. Peel and cut potatoes into ¼-inch-thick slices. In large bowl, toss potato slices with vinegar and sherry. Add onions; toss. Add Dill-Mint Dressing; toss gently to coat. Sprinkle olives on top; garnish with dill sprigs.

DILL-MINT DRESSING

- ¼ cup olive or vegetable oil
- 2 tablespoons lemon juice
- 1 teaspoon dry mustard
- ¼ teaspoon hot pepper sauce
- 2 tablespoons chopped parsley
- 1 tablespoon chopped fresh dill
- ¼ to ½ teaspoon dried mint, crushed
  Salt and cayenne pepper

In bowl, whisk together oil, lemon juice, dry mustard and hot pepper sauce. Mix in parsley, dill, mint and salt and cayenne pepper to taste.

*Recipe courtesy of **The Potato Board***

DUTCH POTATO SALAD

Makes 8 servings

- 6 medium potatoes (about 2 pounds)
- ½ cup sliced cucumber
- ⅓ cup sliced green onions
- ⅓ cup chopped celery
- 1 tablespoon minced green pepper
  Horseradish-Caraway Dressing (recipe follows)
  Paprika

In covered saucepan, cook potatoes in 2 inches boiling water until just tender, 20 to 25 minutes. Drain and cool. Peel and cut potatoes into ¾-inch cubes. In large bowl, combine potatoes with cucumber, green onions, celery and green pepper. Mix in Horseradish-Caraway Dressing; toss to coat. Refrigerate until ready to serve. Sprinkle with paprika just before serving.

HORSERADISH-CARAWAY DRESSING

- ⅓ cup mayonnaise
- ⅓ cup sour cream
- 4 teaspoons white wine vinegar
- 2 teaspoons prepared horseradish
- 1 teaspoon Worcestershire sauce
- 1 teaspoon caraway seed
- 1 teaspoon salt
- ½ teaspoon dry mustard
- ¼ teaspoon sugar
- ⅛ teaspoon pepper

In bowl, combine all ingredients. Cover and refrigerate until ready to use.

*Recipe courtesy of **The Potato Board***

POTATO SALAD WITH GREEN BEANS

Makes 8 servings

1½ pounds small red potatoes
½ cup sliced green onions
⅓ cup dry white wine
⅓ cup chicken broth
1 tablespoon dry sherry
  Vinaigrette Dressing (recipe follows)
1 pound cooked green beans, cut into halves and chilled
  Salt and pepper

In covered saucepan, cook potatoes in 2 inches boiling water until just tender, 15 to 20 minutes. Drain. While potatoes are still warm, cut into quarters. In large bowl, toss warm potatoes with onions, wine, broth and sherry. Set aside 30 minutes. Toss with Vinaigrette Dressing. Cover and refrigerate at least 2 hours. Just before serving, add green beans and season with salt and pepper to taste.

VINAIGRETTE DRESSING

6 tablespoons vegetable oil
2 tablespoons white wine vinegar
1 teaspoon Dijon-style mustard
¾ teaspoon dried savory, crushed
¾ teaspoon dried basil, crushed
¼ teaspoon dried marjoram, crushed
¼ teaspoon paprika

In bowl, whisk together all ingredients. Refrigerate until ready to serve.

*Recipe courtesy of **The Potato Board***

CORN AU GRATIN

Makes 4 servings

1 can (17 ounces) whole kernel corn, drained*
¼ cup grated Cheddar cheese
2 tablespoons chopped green pepper
2 tablespoons finely chopped onion
½ teaspoon salt
⅛ teaspoon garlic powder
⅛ teaspoon pepper

In large bowl, combine all ingredients; spoon onto large square of heavy-duty foil. Fold up foil around corn; seal edges tightly. Grill packet over medium-hot **Kingsford® briquets** 15 minutes or until corn is hot. Turn packet once.

*Fresh corn-on-the-cob can be substituted for canned corn. Cut 2 cups whole corn from cob. No precooking is necessary.

STRAWBERRY SHORTBREAD SHORTCAKE

Makes 8 servings

1 cup butter or margarine, softened
1 cup confectioners' sugar
2 cups all-purpose flour
1 ounce grated semi-sweet chocolate (about ⅓ cup)
1 cup whipping cream, sweetened and whipped
2 pints fresh strawberries, sliced
  Whole fresh strawberry, for garnish

In large mixer bowl, cream butter and sugar until light and fluffy. On low speed, gradually mix in flour and chocolate. Form dough into 2 balls, one a little larger than the other. On floured surface, roll each ball into a circle about 7 inches in diameter (one should be thicker than the other). Using a broad spatula, gently transfer each circle to greased baking sheet. Prick surfaces with fork. Bake in 350°F oven 20 to 30 minutes or just until golden. While still warm, cut thinner circle into 8 equal wedges. Cool wedges and whole circle completely on wire rack. To serve, place shortbread circle on serving plate. Top with ⅔ of the whipped cream and the sliced strawberries. Set shortbread wedges into cream at an angle, points toward center. Top with remaining whipped cream and whole strawberry. Cut into wedges.

Note: Shortbread can be made ahead and stored, wrapped in plastic wrap, in the refrigerator for several days, or in the freezer for several weeks.

*Recipe courtesy of **California Strawberry Advisory Board***

Strawberry Shortbread Shortcake

INDEX

Barbecue
& More

PUBLICATIONS INTERNATIONAL, LTD.

ISBN: 1-56173-267-2
Library of Congress Catalog Card Number: 91-61023

Pictured on the front cover: Charcoal Beef Kabobs *(page 9)* and Chili Tomato Grilled Chicken
(page 53).

Pictured on the back cover, clockwise from top left: Western Lamb Riblets *(page 28)*, Salmon
Steaks in Orange-Honey Marinade *(page 54)*, Ice Cream Cookie Sandwiches *(page 83)* and
Ranch Picnic Potato Salad *(page 66)*.

8   7   6   5   4   3   2

Contents

Barbecue Basics

CHOOSING A GRILL

Before you purchase a grill, consider where you grill, what you'll be cooking, the seasons you'll be grilling and the size of your budget. A small portable grill is fine if you usually barbecue smaller cuts of meat for a few people. For larger cuts of meat, bigger groups of people and year-round grilling, a large covered grill is worth the expense. Basic types of grills include: gas, brazier, covered cooker, water smoker and portable.

Gas Grill: Fast starts, accurate heat control, even cooking and year-round use make this the most convenient type of grill. Bottled gas is fed into burners under a bed of lava rock or ceramic coals—no charcoal is required.

Brazier: Simple models have hollowed fire bowls set on three or four legs. More elaborate braziers have half-hoods, covers, rotisseries and wheels.

Covered Cooker: Square, rectangular or kettle-shaped, this versatile grill does everything a brazier does. The cover also lets you roast, steam, smoke or cook whole meals in any season of the year. Draft controls on the lid and the base help control temperature.

Water Smoker: This is a heavy, dome-covered grill with two pans—one for charcoal and, above it, one for water. When the grill is covered, steam slowly cooks the food. Hickory chips or other aromatic wood can be added. The water smoker doubles as an open brazier when you remove the water pan and place the charcoal pan directly under the food.

Portable Grills: These include the familiar hibachi and small picnic grills on collapsible legs.

BARBECUE TOOLS AND ACCESSORIES

These tools will help make your barbecue cooking safer and more convenient.

Long-Handled Tongs, Basting Brush and Spatula: Moving hot coals and food around the grill, as well as basting and turning foods, can be dangerous. Select tools with long handles and hang them where you are working. You may want to purchase two pairs of tongs, one for coals and one for food.

Meat Thermometer: There is no better way to judge the doneness of meat than with a good quality meat thermometer that has been kept clean and in working order. Always remember to insert the thermometer into the center of the largest muscle of the meat, with the point away from bone, fat and rotisserie rod.

Heavy-Duty Mitts: You will prevent many burns by safeguarding your hands with big, thick mitts. Keep them close to the barbecue so they are always there when you need them.

Aluminum Foil Drip Pans: A drip pan placed beneath grilling meats will prevent flare-ups. The pan should be 1½ inches deep and extend about 3 inches beyond either end of the meat. The juices that collect in the drip pan may be used for a sauce or gravy.

Water Spritzer: For safety's sake, it's a good idea to keep a water-filled spray bottle near the barbecue for dousing flare-ups.

Other Tools and Accessories: A charcoal chimney or electric charcoal starter is useful for starting the fire without lighter fluid. Hinged wire baskets facilitate the turning of some foods, such as fish fillets. Long skewers made of noncorrosive metal or bamboo are indispensable for kabobs. Bamboo skewers should be soaked in water at least 20 minutes before grilling to prevent the bamboo from flaring up.

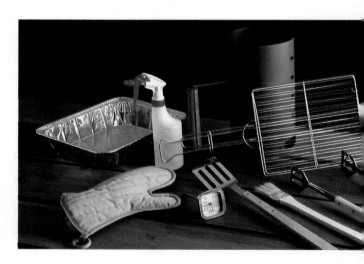

HOW TO LIGHT A CHARCOAL FIRE

The number of coals needed to barbecue foods depends on the size and type of grill and type and amount of food to be cooked. Certain weather conditions, such as wind, cold and high humidity, will require more coals to be used.

Arrange coals in a pyramid shape in center of grill 20 to 30 minutes before cooking. To start with lighter fluid, soak coals with about ½ cup of lighter fluid. Wait 1 minute, then light with a match.

To start with an electric starter, place starter in center of coals. Plug in 8 to 10 minutes or until ash begins to form around edges of coals. Unplug starter and remove. The electric starter will be very hot and should be placed in a safe, heat-resistant place to cool.

To start with a chimney starter, remove grid from grill and place chimney starter in the base of the grill. Crumble a few sheets of newspaper and place in bottom of chimney starter. Place coals on top of newspaper, then light the newspaper. The coals will be ready for grilling in 20 to 30 minutes. Carefully remove chimney starter. Be sure to wear mitts. This method does not use starter fluid.

When coals are ready, they will be ash gray during daylight and will glow at night. Spread coals into a single layer with tongs. To lower cooking temperature, spread coals farther apart or raise the grid, if possible. To make fire hotter, move coals closer together and tap off ash.

ARRANGING COALS FOR COOKING

For **direct cooking,** arrange the coals in a single layer directly under the food. Use this method for quick-cooking foods, such as hamburgers, steaks and fish.

For **indirect cooking,** arrange coals to one side of the grill. Place a drip pan under the food at the other side. For more heat, divide the coals on either side of the drip pan. Use this method for slow-cooking foods, such as roasts and whole chicken.

CHECKING CHARCOAL TEMPERATURE

To check the temperature of the coals, cautiously hold the palm of your hand about 4 inches above the coals. Count the number of seconds you can hold your hand in that position before the heat forces you to pull it away.

Seconds	Coal Temperature
2	hot, 375°F or more
3	medium-hot, 350°F to 375°F
4	medium, 300°F to 350°F
5	low, 200°F to 300°F

MARINATING TIPS

• Marinades add unique flavors to foods and help tenderize less-tender cuts of meat. Turn marinating foods occasionally to let the flavor infuse evenly. Heavy-duty plastic bags are great to hold foods as they marinate.

• After food is removed from a marinade, the marinade may be used as a basting or dipping sauce. When using as a basting sauce, allow food to cook on the grill at least 5 minutes after the last application of marinade. When using as a dipping sauce, place marinade in a small saucepan and bring to a full boil. These precautions are necessary to prevent the cooked food from becoming contaminated with bacteria now present in the marinade from the raw food.

• Basting sauces containing sugar, honey or tomato products should be applied only during the last 15 to 30 minutes of grilling. This will prevent the food from charring. Basting sauces made from seasoned oils and butters may be brushed on throughout grilling.

BARBECUE TIPS

• Cleanup is easier if the grill rack is coated with vegetable oil or vegetable oil cooking spray before grilling.

• For barbecue safety, position the grill on a heat-proof surface, away from trees and bushes that could catch a spark and out of the path of traffic. Also, make sure the grill's vents are not clogged with ashes before starting a fire.

• To avoid flare-ups and charred food when grilling, remove visible fat from meat.

• If you partially cook foods in the microwave or on the range, immediately finish cooking the food on the grill. Do not refrigerate partially cooked foods or let them sit at room temperature before you complete cooking on the grill.

• Always serve cooked food from the grill on a clean plate, not one that held the raw food.

• In hot weather, food should never sit out for over 1 hour. Remember, keep hot foods hot and cold foods cold.

• For the best kabobs, parboil solid or starchy vegetables, such as carrots or potatoes, before using.

• Use long-handled tongs or spatula to turn meat. A fork or knife punctures meat and lets the juices escape.

• Use a meat thermometer to accurately determine the doneness of large cuts of meat or poultry cooked on the rotisserie or covered grill.

• For additional flavor, toss water-soaked wood chips, such as hickory or mesquite, onto hot coals before adding food. Adding wood chips to the coals will create smoke, so make sure the grill is in a well-ventilated area away from any open windows.

• Watch foods carefully during grilling. Total cooking time will vary with the type of food, position on the grill, weather, temperature of the coals and degree of doneness you desire.

• If you plan on grilling for more than 45 minutes, add 10 to 12 new coals around edges of coals just before you begin to cook. When the new coals are ready, move them to the center of the fire.

For the Barbecue Novice

These easy-to-prepare, easy-to-grill recipes will make your guests and family think you're an experienced barbecue chef!

SCANDINAVIAN BURGERS

1 pound lean ground beef
¾ cup shredded zucchini
⅓ cup shredded carrot
2 tablespoons finely minced onion
1 tablespoon fresh chopped dill *or*
    1 teaspoon dried dill weed
½ teaspoon salt
    Dash freshly ground pepper
1 egg, beaten
¼ cup beer
4 whole-wheat buns or rye rolls (optional)

Preheat grill. Combine ground beef, zucchini, carrot, onion and seasonings in medium bowl; mix lightly. Stir in egg and beer. Shape into four patties.

Grill 8 minutes or to desired doneness, turning once. Serve on whole-wheat buns or rye rolls, if desired. *Makes 4 servings*

GRILLED SMOKED SAUSAGE

1 cup apricot or pineapple preserves
1 tablespoon lemon juice
1½ pounds smoked sausage

Heat preserves and strain; reserve fruit pieces. Combine strained preserve liquid with lemon juice. Grill whole sausage, on uncovered grill, over low KINGSFORD® Briquets 5 minutes. Brush with glaze; continue to grill and glaze sausage about 5 minutes longer, turning occasionally. Garnish with fruit pieces.
Makes 6 servings

Top to bottom: Scandinavian Burgers, Grilled Smoked Sausage

BARBECUED ALASKA SALMON

2 whole Alaska salmon fillets (about
    1½ pounds each)
   Salt and pepper
½ cup butter or margarine, melted
¼ cup fresh lemon juice
4 teaspoons grated onion
1 teaspoon grated lemon peel
½ teaspoon hot pepper sauce

Rinse salmon fillets with cold water; pat dry with paper toweling. Sprinkle both sides of each fillet with salt and pepper. Combine remaining ingredients; brush both sides of fillets with butter mixture. Place each fillet, skin side down, on sheet of well-oiled heavy-duty foil. Grill salmon on uncovered grill over hot coals 10 minutes per inch of thickness measured at its thickest part, or until salmon flakes easily when tested with fork. Baste often with butter mixture.

Makes 12 to 16 servings

*Favorite Recipe from **Alaska Seafood Marketing Institute***

Barbecued Alaska Salmon

GRILLED MEXICAN-STYLE BURGERS

1 pound ground beef
2 teaspoons instant minced onion
¾ teaspoon *each* dried oregano leaves,
    ground cumin and salt
¼ teaspoon pepper
1 small tomato, cut into 8 thin slices
4 taco shells or flour tortillas
1 cup shredded lettuce
¼ cup salsa

Combine ground beef, onion, oregano, cumin, salt and pepper, mixing lightly but thoroughly. Divide beef mixture into 4 equal portions; form each into an oval-shaped patty (6×2½ inches). Grill patties on grid over medium coals, turning once. Grill 10 minutes for rare; 12 minutes for medium. To assemble, arrange 2 tomato slices and a grilled burger in each taco shell. Top each with ¼ cup lettuce and 1 tablespoon salsa.   *Makes 4 servings*

*Favorite Recipe from **National Live Stock and Meat Board***

SOUTHWESTERN FRANKFURTERS

1 pound beef frankfurters (8 to 10)
½ cup chopped cucumber
1 medium tomato, chopped
1 can (4 ounces) chopped green chilies,
    undrained
½ teaspoon ground cumin
8 to 10 taco shells
½ avocado, peeled, seeded and cut into
    8 to 10 slices

Place frankfurters on grid over medium coals. Grill 8 to 10 minutes, turning occasionally. Meanwhile, combine cucumber, tomato, chilies and cumin. Place 1 tablespoon cucumber relish in each taco shell; top with grilled frankfurter. Place avocado slice on one side of each frankfurter; top with an additional tablespoon of relish.

Makes 8 to 10 servings

*Favorite Recipe from **National Live Stock and Meat Board***

Charcoal Beef Kabobs

CHARCOAL BEEF KABOBS

½ cup vegetable oil

¼ cup lemon juice

1½ tablespoons (½ package) HIDDEN
    VALLEY RANCH® Salad Dressing Mix

2 pounds beef top round or boneless
    sirloin steak, cut into 1-inch cubes

1 or 2 red, yellow or green peppers, cut
    into 1-inch squares

16 pearl onions *or* 1 medium onion, cut
    into wedges

8 cherry tomatoes

Combine oil, lemon juice and dry salad
dressing mix. Pour over beef cubes in shallow
dish. Cover and refrigerate 1 hour or longer.
Drain beef; reserve marinade. Thread beef
cubes, peppers and onion onto skewers. Grill
kabobs, on uncovered grill, over medium-hot
KINGSFORD® Briquets 15 minutes, brushing
often with reserved marinade and turning to
brown all sides. A few minutes before serving,
add cherry tomatoes to ends of skewers.

Makes 4 servings

Ranch Burgers

RANCH BURGERS

1¼ pounds lean ground beef
 ¾ cup prepared HIDDEN VALLEY
   RANCH® Original Ranch® Salad
   Dressing
 ¾ cup dry bread crumbs
 ¼ cup minced onion
  1 teaspoon salt
 ¼ teaspoon black pepper
   Sesame seed buns
   Lettuce, tomato slices and red onion
     slices (optional)
   HIDDEN VALLEY RANCH® Original
     Ranch® Salad Dressing

In large bowl, combine beef, ¾ cup salad dressing, bread crumbs, onion, salt and pepper. Shape into 6 patties. Grill over medium-hot coals 4 to 5 minutes for medium doneness. Place on sesame seed buns with lettuce, tomatoes and red onions, if desired. Serve with a generous amount of additional salad dressing.   *Makes 6 servings*

PACIFIC COAST BARBECUED SALMON

4 fresh or frozen salmon steaks, 1 inch
  thick (about 8 ounces each)
½ cup butter or margarine
2 tablespoons fresh lemon juice
1 tablespoon Worcestershire sauce

Thaw salmon steaks, if frozen. In saucepan, combine butter, lemon juice and Worcestershire sauce; simmer 5 minutes, stirring frequently. Brush salmon steaks with butter mixture. Place steaks in well-greased wire grill basket.

Grill steaks, on uncovered grill, over medium-hot KINGSFORD® Briquets 6 to 9 minutes or until lightly browned. Baste steaks with butter mixture and turn; grill 6 to 9 minutes longer, basting often, until fish flakes easily when tested with fork.   *Makes 4 servings*

SALSA-MARINATED CHUCK STEAK

1 pound boneless beef chuck shoulder
  steak, cut 1 inch thick
½ cup medium salsa
⅓ cup fresh lime juice
2 tablespoons hoisin sauce*
2 teaspoons grated fresh ginger

Combine salsa, lime juice, hoisin sauce and ginger. Place beef chuck shoulder steak in plastic bag; add ½ salsa mixture, turning to coat steak. Close bag securely; marinate in refrigerator 6 to 8 hours (or overnight, if desired), turning at least once. Remove steak from marinade; discard marinade. Place steak on grid over medium coals. Grill to desired doneness (rare to medium), 14 to 20 minutes, turning once and brushing occasionally with reserved ½ salsa mixture. Carve steak into thin slices.   *Makes 4 servings*

*Hoisin sauce is available in the Oriental section of the supermarket.

*Favorite Recipe from **National Live Stock and Meat Board***

Pacific Coast Barbecued Salmon

GRILLED RAINBOW TROUT WITH ITALIAN BUTTER

    2 tablespoons butter or margarine,
        softened
    1 tablespoon finely chopped red bell
        pepper
    ½ teaspoon dried Italian seasonings
    4 CLEAR SPRINGS® Brand Idaho
        Rainbow Trout fillets (4 ounces each)
    2 tablespoons grated Parmesan cheese
        (optional)

Cream butter, pepper and seasonings; chill and set aside. Over hot coals, place trout fillets, flesh side down, on oiled grid and cook about 2 minutes. Gently turn trout with spatula; continue cooking 2 minutes longer. Serve immediately with a dollop of Italian Butter and a sprinkle of Parmesan cheese.

Makes 4 servings

ISLANDER'S BEEF BARBECUE

    3- to 3½-pound boneless beef chuck roast
    ¾ cup apricot-pineapple jam
    2 tablespoons soy sauce
    1 teaspoon ground ginger
    1 teaspoon grated lemon peel

Slice roast across grain into ¼-inch-thick slices. Combine remaining ingredients in bowl; mix well. Grill beef slices, on uncovered grill, over medium-hot KINGSFORD® Briquets 8 to 10 minutes. Turn and baste often with jam mixture.   *Makes 4 to 6 servings*

Note: If time permits, pierce meat several times with fork and marinate in jam mixture 1 to 4 hours in refrigerator. Drain meat; reserve jam mixture. Continue as directed above.

BEEF KABOBS ITALIANO

    1 (8-ounce) can tomato sauce
    ⅓ cup REALEMON® Lemon Juice from
        Concentrate
    2 tablespoons brown sugar
    2 teaspoons WYLER'S® or STEERO®
        Beef-Flavor Instant Bouillon
    1½ teaspoons thyme leaves
    1 pound beef sirloin steak (about 1½ inch
        thick), cut into cubes
    1 large green bell pepper, cut into bite-size
        pieces
    2 medium onions, quartered and
        separated into bite-size pieces
    8 ounces medium fresh mushrooms (about
        2 cups)
    ½ pint cherry tomatoes

In shallow dish or plastic bag, combine tomato sauce, ReaLemon® brand, sugar, bouillon and thyme; mix well. Add meat. Cover; marinate in refrigerator 6 hours or overnight. Skewer meat with vegetables. Grill or broil as desired, basting frequently with marinade. Refrigerate leftovers.   *Makes 4 servings*

CHICKEN ITALIANO

    ½ cup WISH-BONE® Italian Dressing or
        Herbal Italian Dressing
    2½ to 3 pounds chicken pieces*

In large shallow baking dish, pour Italian dressing over chicken. Cover and marinate in refrigerator, turning occasionally, 4 hours or overnight. Remove chicken; reserve marinade.

Grill or broil chicken, turning and basting frequently with reserved marinade, until done.

Makes about 4 servings

*Use 1 (2½- to 3-pound) beef London broil or beef round steak for chicken pieces.

Grilled Rainbow Trout with Italian Butter

ALL-AMERICAN CHEESEBURGERS

1 pound lean ground beef
1 tablespoon WYLER'S® or STEERO®
    Beef-Flavor Instant Bouillon
¼ cup chopped onion
4 slices BORDEN® Process American
    Cheese Food
4 hamburger buns, split, buttered and
    toasted
    Lettuce
4 slices tomato

In medium bowl, combine beef, bouillon and onion; mix well. Shape into 4 patties. Grill or broil to desired doneness. Top with cheese food slices; heat until cheese food begins to melt. Top bottom halves of buns with lettuce, tomato and meat patties. Serve open-face or with bun tops. Refrigerate leftovers.

Makes 4 servings

VARIATIONS

Santa Fe Burgers: Add 3 tablespoons salsa or taco sauce to ground beef. On warm tortilla, spread refried beans; top with shredded lettuce, cooked burger, cheese food slice, salsa and sour cream.

Kansas City Burgers: Add ½ cup thawed frozen hash browns and 2 tablespoons barbecue sauce to ground beef. Place each cooked burger on bun; top with cheese food slice, cooked, crumbled bacon and sliced green onion.

Manhattan Burgers: Add ¼ cup pizza sauce, 2 tablespoons chopped mushrooms and 3 tablespoons chopped pepperoni to ground beef. Place each cooked burger on grilled Italian bread; top with cheese food slice, pepperoni and green pepper.

Clockwise from left: Santa Fe Burger, Kansas City Burger, Manhattan Burger

Parmesan Seasoned Turkey

PARMESAN SEASONED TURKEY

  2 tablespoons butter or margarine, melted
1½ teaspoons grated Parmesan cheese
    Dash coarsely ground black pepper
    Dash crushed red pepper
    Dash onion powder
  4 slices BUTTERBALL® Slice 'N Serve
    Breast of Turkey, cut ⅜ inch thick

Combine butter, cheese, peppers and onion powder in small dish. Brush both sides of turkey with seasoned butter. Grill over medium coals 6 to 8 minutes or until hot. Turn over halfway through heating.

Makes 4 servings

GRILLED HAKE FILLETS

  2 pounds hake fillets, fresh or frozen
¼ cup French dressing
  1 tablespoon lemon juice
  1 tablespoon grated onion
  2 teaspoons salt
    Dash pepper

Thaw fish, if frozen. Cut into serving-size portions. Mix remaining ingredients in small bowl until blended. Baste fish with sauce. Arrange fish on well-greased grid. Grill, 4 inches from moderately hot coals, 15 to 18 minutes or until fish flakes easily when tested with fork. Turn and baste with remaining sauce halfway through cooking.

Makes 6 servings

*Favorite Recipe from **National Fisheries Institute***

Sizzling Meats

Try your hand with these saucy ribs, tasty burgers, eye-catching kabobs and succulent steaks grilled to flavorful perfection.

HOT AND SPICY SPARERIBS

    1 rack pork spareribs, 3 pounds
    2 tablespoons butter or margarine
    1 medium onion, finely chopped
    2 cloves garlic, minced
    1 can (15 ounces) tomato sauce
    ⅔ cup cider vinegar
    ⅔ cup firmly packed brown sugar
    2 tablespoons chili powder
    1 tablespoon prepared mustard
    ½ teaspoon pepper

Melt butter in large skillet over low heat; add onion and garlic and sauté until tender. Add remaining ingredients, except ribs, and bring to a boil. Reduce heat and simmer 20 minutes, stirring occasionally.

Place large piece of aluminum foil over coals beneath grill to catch drippings. Baste meatiest side of ribs with sauce. Place ribs on grill, meatiest side down, about 6 inches above low coals; baste top side. Close grill hood. Cook about 20 minutes; turn ribs and baste. Cook 45 minutes more or until done, basting every 10 to 15 minutes with sauce.

Makes 3 servings

*Favorite Recipe from **National Pork Producers Council***

ORIENTAL STEAK KABOBS

    1 cup (8 ounces) WISH-BONE® Italian,
        Robusto Italian or Lite Italian Dressing
    ¼ cup soy sauce
    2 tablespoons brown sugar
    ½ teaspoon ground ginger
    1 green onion, thinly sliced
    1 pound boneless beef round, cut into
        1-inch pieces
   12 large mushrooms
    2 cups broccoli florets
    1 medium red pepper, cut into chunks

In large shallow baking dish, combine Italian dressing, soy sauce, brown sugar, ginger and onion. Add beef and vegetables; turn to coat. Cover and marinate in refrigerator, stirring occasionally, 4 hours or overnight. Remove beef and vegetables; reserve marinade.

Onto large skewers, thread beef with vegetables. Grill or broil, turning and basting frequently with reserved marinade, 10 minutes or until beef is done.

Makes about 4 servings

Hot and Spicy Spareribs

HONEY-GARLIC AMERICA'S CUT

4 America's Cut boneless center pork loin
    chops, 1¼ to 1½ inches thick
¼ cup lemon juice
¼ cup honey
2 tablespoons soy sauce
1 tablespoon dry sherry
2 cloves garlic, minced

Place chops in heavy plastic bag. Combine
remaining ingredients in small bowl. Pour over
chops, turning bag to coat. Close bag;
refrigerate 4 to 24 hours.

Prepare covered grill with drip pan in center
banked by medium-hot coals. Remove chops
from marinade; reserve marinade. Grill chops
12 to 15 minutes, turning once and basting
occasionally with reserved marinade.

Makes 4 servings

*Favorite Recipe from **National Pork Producers Council***

SPICY LAMB BURGERS

¼ cup chopped onion
1 teaspoon curry powder
1 tablespoon butter or margarine, melted
¼ cup finely chopped almonds
¼ cup crushed pineapple, drained
1½ pounds ground lamb
½ cup dry bread crumbs
2 eggs
⅛ teaspoon pepper
6 pita breads

Cook onion and curry powder in butter until
onion is tender. Stir in almonds and crushed
pineapple. Mix thoroughly with lamb, bread
crumbs, eggs and pepper. Shape meat mixture
into 6 patties. Grill patties, on uncovered grill,
over medium-hot MATCH LIGHT® Charcoal
Briquets about 5 minutes on each side, or until
done. Grill pita breads on edge of grill. Serve
lamb burgers in pita breads.

Makes 6 servings

Honey-Garlic America's Cut

Greek Burgers

GREEK BURGERS

Yogurt Sauce (recipe follows)
1 pound ground beef
2 tablespoons red wine
2 teaspoons ground cumin
1 tablespoon chopped fresh oregano *or*
    1 teaspoon dried oregano leaves
½ teaspoon salt
    Dash ground red pepper
    Dash ground black pepper
4 pita breads
    Lettuce
    Chopped tomatoes

Prepare Yogurt Sauce. Soak 4 bamboo skewers in water at least 20 minutes before using. Combine meat, wine and seasonings in medium bowl; mix lightly. Divide mixture into eight equal portions; form each portion into an oval, each about 4 inches long. Cover; chill 30 minutes.

Preheat grill. Insert skewers lengthwise through centers of ovals, placing 2 on each skewer. Grill about 8 minutes or to desired doneness, turning once. Fill pita breads with lettuce, meat and chopped tomatoes. Serve with Yogurt Sauce. *Makes 4 servings*

YOGURT SAUCE

2 cups plain yogurt
1 cup chopped red onion
1 cup chopped cucumber
¼ cup chopped fresh mint *or*
    1½ tablespoons dried mint leaves
1 tablespoon chopped fresh marjoram or
    1 teaspoon dried marjoram leaves

Combine ingredients in small bowl. Cover; chill up to 4 hours before serving.

Apricot-Glazed Lamb Chops

GRILLED SAUSAGE WITH SWEET POTATO AND APPLE KABOBS

    1 pound fresh country-style pork sausage
        links, bratwurst or Polish sausage
    ¼ cup apple jelly, melted
    ½ teaspoon orange or lemon juice
        Dash allspice
        Dash nutmeg
    1 large sweet potato, cut crosswise into
        ¾-inch slices (about 12 ounces)
    1 large apple, cored, cut into 8 wedges
    1 tablespoon butter or margarine, melted

Combine jelly, orange juice, allspice and nutmeg. Parboil sweet potatoes in boiling water 7 minutes; drain. Thread sweet potato slices and apple wedges on four 12-inch skewers. Brush lightly with butter. Place sausages on grid over low to medium coals. Grill 5 minutes. Place kabobs on grid and brush sausage and kabobs with apple jelly mixture. Grill 10 minutes, turning and brushing with jelly mixture after 5 minutes. Internal temperature of sausage should register 170°F.   *Makes 4 servings*

*Favorite Recipe from **National Live Stock and Meat Board***

APRICOT-GLAZED LAMB CHOPS

    ⅓ cup apricot jam
    1 tablespoon white vinegar
    1 teaspoon Dijon-style mustard
    ½ teaspoon dried rosemary leaves
    ½ teaspoon salt
    1 clove garlic, minced
    ¼ teaspoon pepper
    4 lamb shoulder or blade chops, cut
        ¾ inch thick

Combine apricot jam, vinegar, mustard, rosemary, salt, garlic and pepper in small saucepan; cook slowly, stirring, until melted. Grill lamb chops, on uncovered grill, over medium coals 14 to 16 minutes for medium, turning once. Brush both sides with glaze several times during grilling.
                    Makes 4 to 5 servings

*Favorite Recipe from **National Live Stock and Meat Board***

Grilled Sausage with Sweet Potato and Apple Kabobs

Fajitas

FAJITAS

    Pico de Gallo Sauce (recipe follows)
2 pounds boneless beef skirt steak or flank steak
¾ cup beer
½ cup lime juice
2 tablespoons Worcestershire sauce
8 (6-inch) flour tortillas

Prepare Pico de Gallo Sauce. Trim excess fat from steak; place in shallow glass dish. Combine beer, lime juice and Worcestershire sauce; pour over steak. Cover and refrigerate overnight, spooning marinade over meat occasionally.

Drain steak; reserve marinade. Pat steak dry with paper toweling. Grill steak, on covered grill, over medium-hot KINGSFORD® Briquets 8 to 10 minutes, basting meat occasionally with reserved marinade. Turn and grill to desired doneness, allowing 8 to 10 minutes longer for medium. Carve meat across grain into thin slices.

Meanwhile, wrap tortillas in heavy-duty foil; place tortillas at edge of grill 5 minutes or until heated through. Wrap steak slices in warmed tortillas; top with chilled Pico de Gallo Sauce.
Makes 8 servings

PICO DE GALLO SAUCE

3 medium tomatoes, peeled and chopped
½ cup chopped green onions
1 large Anaheim chili pepper, chopped
1 fresh jalapeño chili pepper, seeded and chopped
2 teaspoons chopped fresh cilantro or parsley
1 teaspoon salt

In small bowl, combine tomatoes, onions, peppers, cilantro and salt. Cover and refrigerate 5 hours or overnight.
Makes about 1¾ cups

Flank Steak Teriyaki with Savory Rice

FLANK STEAK TERIYAKI WITH SAVORY RICE

½ cup peanut or vegetable oil
¼ cup dry red wine
3 tablespoons teriyaki sauce
1 jar (12 ounces) roasted red peppers, drained and chopped
2 tablespoons light brown sugar
1 tablespoon plus 1 teaspoon finely chopped garlic
⅛ teaspoon crushed red pepper
½ pound beef flank steak, sliced diagonally into ¼-inch strips
2 tablespoons butter or margarine
1 teaspoon finely chopped fresh ginger (optional)
½ cup thinly sliced zucchini
2 cups water
1 package LIPTON® Rice & Sauce – Herb & Butter
Pepper to taste

In large shallow glass baking dish, thoroughly combine oil, wine, teriyaki sauce, 1 cup roasted peppers, brown sugar, 1 tablespoon garlic and crushed red pepper. Add steak and turn to coat. Cover and marinate in refrigerator, turning occasionally, at least 4 hours. Remove steak, reserving marinade.

Onto 4 large skewers, thread steak, weaving back and forth. Grill or broil, turning and basting with reserved marinade, 3 minutes or until done.

Meanwhile, in large skillet, melt butter and cook remaining 1 teaspoon garlic with ginger over medium-high heat 30 seconds. Add zucchini and cook, stirring frequently, 2 minutes or until tender. Stir in water and rice & herb & butter sauce and bring to a boil. Reduce heat and simmer, stirring occasionally, 10 minutes or until rice is tender. Stir in remaining roasted peppers and pepper. Serve rice with steak.   *Makes about 2 servings*

BLUE CHEESE BURGERS

1¼ pounds lean ground beef
  1 tablespoon finely chopped onion
1½ teaspoons chopped fresh thyme *or*
      ½ teaspoon dried thyme leaves
  ¾ teaspoon salt
    Dash ground pepper
  4 ounces blue cheese, crumbled
    Lettuce, tomato slices, Dijon-style
      mustard (optional)
  4 whole-wheat buns, split (optional)

Preheat grill. Combine ground beef, onion and seasonings in medium bowl; mix lightly. Shape into eight patties.

Place cheese in center of four patties to within ½ inch of outer edge; top with remaining burgers. Press edges together to seal.

Grill 8 minutes or to desired doneness, turning once. Serve with lettuce, tomatoes and Dijon-style mustard on whole-wheat buns, if desired.
Makes 4 servings

STEAK PORT ANTONIO

  ¼ cup rum
  1 tablespoon chopped shallots
  4 tablespoons butter or margarine
  1 tablespoon chopped parsley
  2 teaspoons lime juice
  ½ teaspoon TABASCO® Pepper Sauce
  4 beef shell steaks

In saucepan, combine rum and shallots; bring to a boil. Reduce heat; simmer 2 minutes. Stir in butter, parsley, lime juice and Tabasco® sauce.

Brush steaks with rum butter. Grill or broil 6 inches from heat. Cook about 8 minutes, turning steak once. Brush occasionally with rum butter. Heat any remaining rum butter to a boil and serve with steaks. Serve with additional Tabasco® sauce.
Makes 4 servings

BARBECUED PORK CHOPS

  6 pork loin chops, cut 1 inch thick
  ½ teaspoon seasoned salt
  6 slices orange
  6 thin slices onion
  6 thin slices lemon
  ⅓ cup K.C. MASTERPIECE® Barbecue
    Sauce

Arrange medium-hot KINGSFORD® Briquets to one side of grill with drip pan next to briquets. Sprinkle chops with seasoned salt. Place chops over drip pan; cover grill and cook 40 minutes or until nearly done, turning once after 25 minutes.

Top each chop with slices of orange, onion, lemon and about 1 tablespoon barbecue sauce. Cover grill and cook 5 to 10 minutes longer or until chops are tender and thoroughly cooked.
Makes 6 servings

Barbecued Pork Chops

GRILLED LAMB FAJITAS

　3 tablespoons olive oil
　3 tablespoons tequila or orange juice
　2 tablespoons fresh lime juice
　1 teaspoon ground cumin
　1 teaspoon chili powder
　1 teaspoon dried oregano leaves, crushed
　½ teaspoon salt
　¼ teaspoon black pepper
　¼ teaspoon red pepper flakes, crushed
　¼ cup chopped fresh cilantro
1½ pounds lean American lamb leg steaks,
　　　cut 1 inch thick
　6 green onions
　3 fresh poblano or ancho chilies (optional)
　1 red pepper, halved and seeded
　1 green pepper, halved and seeded
　1 yellow pepper, halved and seeded
12 medium flour tortillas, warmed
　　Salsa

For marinade, in small bowl combine oil, tequila, lime juice, cumin, chili powder, oregano, salt, black pepper, red pepper flakes and cilantro. Place lamb in glass dish. Pour marinade over lamb; cover and refrigerate 4 to 6 hours.

Ignite coals in barbecue; allow to burn until bright red and covered with gray ash. Drain lamb; discard marinade. Grill lamb, onions, chilies and red, green and yellow peppers 4 inches from coals. Cook steaks 5 to 6 minutes per side for medium-rare or to desired degree of doneness. Turn vegetables frequently until cooked. Slice lamb steaks and vegetables into ¼-inch-thick slices. Serve on tortillas, top with salsa and roll up.

Makes 12 servings

Favorite Recipe from **American Lamb Council**

Grilled Lamb Fajitas

Barbecued Beef Short Ribs

BARBECUED BEEF SHORT RIBS

6 pounds beef chuck ribs, cut into 1-rib
    pieces
1 cup water
¾ cup soy sauce
⅔ cup dry sherry
½ cup packed dark brown sugar
6 cloves garlic, minced
1 tablespoon ground red pepper
1 tablespoon grated fresh ginger
2 teaspoons Chinese five spice powder

Trim excess fat from ribs. In large roasting pan, arrange ribs in single layer. For marinade, in medium saucepan combine remaining ingredients. Cook over medium heat on range top until sugar is dissolved. Remove from heat; cool slightly. Pour marinade over ribs. Cover and marinate in refrigerator 1 hour, turning ribs once.

Cover roasting pan with foil. Arrange medium-hot KINGSFORD® Briquets around drip pan. Place roasting pan on grid; cover grill and cook ribs 45 minutes. Remove ribs from roasting pan and place directly on grid; reserve marinade. Continue cooking, in covered grill, 45 to 60 minutes longer or until ribs are tender, turning occasionally. Brush ribs again with reserved marinade just before serving.

Makes 8 servings

BUTTERFLIED LEG OF LAMB WITH ORANGE SAUCE

3½- to 4-pound butterflied lamb leg
⅔ cup orange juice
½ cup orange marmalade
1 teaspoon butter or margarine
½ teaspoon grated fresh ginger
¼ teaspoon dry mustard
2 tablespoons lemon juice
1 tablespoon cornstarch

Thread 2 long metal skewers through butterflied lamb leg to secure and facilitate turning the roast. Grill lamb, on covered grill, over medium coals to desired doneness. Allow 40 to 60 minutes total cooking time.

Meanwhile, combine orange juice, marmalade, butter, ginger and mustard in small saucepan. Cook over medium-low heat until marmalade is melted, stirring occasionally. Combine lemon juice and cornstarch; stir into orange juice mixture and cook until thickened. Remove from heat; reserve. Turn leg several times during cooking, brushing with ⅓ cup reserved sauce during last 10 minutes of cooking. Remove skewers and separate leg into three sections along natural seams. Carve each section across grain into thin slices. Serve remaining sauce with carved lamb.

Makes 10 to 12 servings

*Favorite Recipe from **National Live Stock and Meat Board***

TEXAS BARBECUE BEEF BRISKET

  1 boneless beef brisket (6 to 8 pounds)
  2 teaspoons paprika
  1 teaspoon freshly ground black pepper, divided
  1 tablespoon butter or margarine
  1 medium onion, grated
1½ cups catsup
  1 tablespoon fresh lemon juice
  1 tablespoon Worcestershire sauce
  1 teaspoon hot pepper sauce

Trim external fat on beef brisket to ¼ inch. Combine paprika and ½ teaspoon of the black pepper; rub evenly over surface of beef brisket. Place brisket, fat side down, in 11½×9-inch disposable foil pan. Add 1 cup water. Cover pan tightly with aluminum foil. Place in center of grid over very low coals (use a single layer of coals with space in between each); cover cooker. Cook 5 hours, turning brisket over every 1½ hours; use baster to remove fat from pan as it accumulates. Add ½ cup water, if needed, to pan during cooking. (Add just enough briquets during cooking to keep coals at a very low temperature.) Remove brisket from pan; place on grid, fat side down, directly over very low coals. Reserve pan drippings. Cover; continue cooking 30 minutes.

Meanwhile, skim fat from pan drippings; reserve 1 cup drippings. Melt butter in medium saucepan over medium heat. Add onion; cook until tender-crisp. Add reserved pan drippings, remaining ½ teaspoon black pepper, the catsup, lemon juice, Worcestershire sauce and hot pepper sauce; simmer 15 minutes. Carve brisket into thin slices across grain; serve with sauce. Garnish with fresh peppers and lemon and lime slices.   *Makes 18 to 24 servings*

Note: For a smoky flavor, soak oak, pecan, mesquite or hickory chips in water 30 minutes and add to very low coals.

Favorite Recipe from **National Live Stock and Meat Board**

PEANUT PORK SATÉ

  1 cup (8 ounces) WISH-BONE® Sweet 'n Spicy French or Lite Sweet 'n Spicy French Dressing
 ¼ cup peanut butter
  1 tablespoon dry sherry
  2 teaspoons soy sauce
 ½ to 1 teaspoon crushed red pepper
  1 (1-inch) piece fresh ginger, peeled and cut into pieces *or* ½ teaspoon ground ginger
  1 medium clove garlic
 ¼ cup water
1½ pounds pork tenderloin, sliced diagonally into ¼-inch strips*

In blender or food processor, blend sweet 'n spicy French dressing, peanut butter, sherry, soy sauce, pepper, ginger and garlic until smooth.

In large shallow baking dish, blend ½ cup dressing mixture with water; add pork and turn to coat. Cover and marinate in refrigerator, stirring occasionally, 4 hours or overnight. Cover and refrigerate remaining dressing mixture for use as basting sauce. Remove pork from marinade; discard marinade.

Onto 12-inch skewers thread pork strips, weaving back and forth. Grill or broil, turning and basting occasionally with reserved dressing mixture, 12 minutes or until pork is done.   *Makes about 6 servings*

*Use 1½ pounds boneless beef flank or round steak, sliced diagonally into ¼-inch strips for the pork strips.

WESTERN LAMB RIBLETS

   **5 pounds lamb riblets, cut into serving-
       size pieces**
   ¾ cup chili sauce
   ½ cup honey
   ½ cup beer
   ¼ cup Worcestershire sauce
   ¼ cup finely chopped onion
   1 clove garlic, minced
   ½ teaspoon crushed red pepper

Trim excess fat from riblets. In saucepan, combine chili sauce, honey, beer, Worcestershire, onion, garlic and red pepper. On range top, heat mixture to boiling. Reduce heat; simmer, covered, 10 minutes. Remove from heat; cool.

Place riblets in plastic bag; pour marinade over riblets. Close bag; set bag in large bowl. Marinate riblets in refrigerator about 2 hours, turning bag occasionally to distribute marinade evenly.

Drain riblets; reserve marinade. Arrange medium-hot KINGSFORD® Briquets around drip pan. Place riblets over drip pan. Cover grill and cook 45 minutes, turning riblets and brushing with reserved marinade twice. Heat remaining marinade to boiling and serve with riblets.   *Makes 6 servings*

CAROLINA PORK BARBECUE

   **4- to 5-pound boneless pork shoulder
       (Boston Butt)**
   1 quart cider vinegar
   1 to 1½ ounces crushed red pepper
   1 tablespoon black pepper
   Hush puppies (optional)
   Coleslaw (optional)

Stir together vinegar and peppers. Prepare covered grill with drip pan in center banked by medium-hot coals. Place pork on grill over drip pan; close hood. Cook 2½ to 3½ hours until pork is very tender, basting frequently with vinegar marinade. Remove pork from grill; cool slightly. Chop meat and serve with hush puppies and cole slaw, if desired.

Makes about 12 servings

*Favorite Recipe from **National Pork Producers Council***

Western Lamb Riblets

Javanese Pork Saté and Raita (page 71)

JAVANESE PORK SATÉ

    1 pound boneless pork loin
 ½ cup minced onion
    2 tablespoons peanut butter
    2 tablespoons lemon juice
    2 tablespoons soy sauce
    1 tablespoon brown sugar
    1 tablespoon vegetable oil
    1 clove garlic, minced
      Dash hot pepper sauce
      Raita (page 71)

Cut pork into ½-inch cubes; place in shallow
dish. In blender or food processor combine
remaining ingredients. Blend until smooth.
Pour over pork. Cover and marinate in
refrigerator 10 minutes. Thread pork on
skewers (if using bamboo skewers, soak in
water 1 hour to prevent burning).

Grill or broil 10 to 12 minutes, turning
occasionally, until done. Serve with hot cooked
rice, if desired. Serve with Raita.

Makes 4 servings

*Favorite Recipe from **National Pork Producers Council***

TEX-MEX FLANK STEAK

    1 medium onion, thinly sliced
 ½ cup REALEMON® Lemon Juice from
      Concentrate
 ½ cup vegetable oil
    2 tablespoons dry sherry
    2 teaspoons WYLER'S® or STEERO®
      Beef-Flavor Instant Bouillon
    2 teaspoons chili powder
    2 teaspoons ground cumin
    2 cloves garlic, finely chopped
    1 (1- to 1½-pound) beef flank steak, scored

In shallow dish or plastic bag, combine all
ingredients except meat; add meat. Cover;
marinate in refrigerator 6 hours or overnight.
Remove meat from marinade; grill or broil as
desired, basting frequently with marinade.

Makes 4 to 6 servings

Grilled Steaks with Vegetables

GRILLED STEAKS WITH VEGETABLES

2 beef Porterhouse steaks, cut 1 to
    1½ inches thick (about 1 pound each)
2 cloves garlic, finely minced, divided
1½ teaspoons dried basil leaves, divided
  ½ teaspoon coarse ground black pepper
  1 tablespoon olive oil
  1 large zucchini, cut into 2×½-inch pieces
  1 small onion, cut into thin wedges
1¼ cups sliced fresh mushrooms
  ¼ teaspoon salt
  6 cherry tomatoes, cut into halves

Season steaks with 1 clove of the garlic,
¾ teaspoon of the basil and the pepper. Place
steaks on grid over medium coals. Grill to
desired doneness, turning once. (Steaks cut

1 inch thick require about 16 minutes for rare;
20 minutes for medium. Steaks cut 1½ inches
thick require about 22 minutes for rare;
30 minutes for medium.) After turning steaks,
heat oil in large heavy skillet on grid over
coals. Add remaining clove garlic, the zucchini
and onion; cook and stir 4 to 5 minutes. Add
mushrooms, salt and remaining ¾ teaspoon
basil; continue cooking 2 minutes, stirring
frequently. Add tomatoes; heat through.

Makes 4 to 6 servings

*Favorite Recipe from **National Live Stock and Meat Board***

SNAPPY BEEF ROAST

1 boneless beef chuck eye roast or
    boneless chuck cross rib roast (3½ to
    4 pounds)
  ½ cup catsup
  3 tablespoons fresh lemon juice
  2 tablespoons vegetable oil
1½ tablespoons Worcestershire sauce
  2 large cloves garlic, minced
  1 teaspoon ground cumin
  1 teaspoon salt
  ½ teaspoon ground red pepper

Combine catsup, lemon juice, vegetable oil,
Worcestershire sauce, garlic, cumin, salt and
red pepper. Brush mixture evenly over surface
of beef chuck eye roast; place in large plastic
bag. Close bag securely; refrigerate 12 hours
(or overnight, if desired).

Insert meat thermometer in roast so bulb is
centered in thickest part, not resting in fat.
Cook in covered grill using indirect heat.
Arrange coals on lower grid around outside
edges; place drip pan between coals. When
coals are ash-gray (about 30 minutes), place
roast, fat side up, on grid above drip pan.
Cover cooker, leaving all vents open. Cook
roast to desired doneness, about 25 to
30 minutes per pound. Remove from grill when
meat thermometer registers 135°F for rare or
155°F for medium. Allow roast to stand 15 to
20 minutes in warm place before carving.
(Roast will continue to rise about 5°F in
temperature to 140°F for rare and 160°F for
medium.) Carve roast into thin slices.

Makes 12 to 16 servings

*Favorite Recipe from **National Live Stock and Meat Board***

LAMB SHASLEK
(Shish Kebab)

½ cup fresh lemon juice
3 tablespoons virgin olive oil
⅓ cup minced onion
4 cloves garlic, minced
1 tablespoon cracked pepper
1 teaspoon coarse salt
1½- pound fresh American lamb sirloin
　　　roast, cut into 2-inch cubes
1 small red onion, cut into 8 wedges
1 small white onion, cut into 8 wedges
1 lemon, cut into 8 wedges, for garnish

For marinade, in small bowl combine lemon juice, oil, minced onion, garlic, pepper and salt. In glass dish, place lamb and red and white onions. Pour marinade over lamb and onions; cover and refrigerate 6 to 24 hours. Stir lamb occasionally. Drain lamb and onions; discard marinade. Thread red onion, lamb and white onion onto skewers, ending with lemon wedge.

Ignite coals in barbecue; allow to burn until bright red and covered with gray ash. Grill lamb shaslek 4 inches from coals 5 to 6 minutes per side for medium-rare or until desired degree of doneness.

Makes 4 servings

Favorite Recipe from **American Lamb Council**

Lamb Shaslek

Raspberry-Glazed Lamb Ribs

RASPBERRY-GLAZED LAMB RIBS

   2 Denver ribs of American lamb (about
      6 ounces), 8 ribs each
½ teaspoon salt
¼ teaspoon pepper
¼ teaspoon paprika
½ cup red wine vinegar or raspberry
      vinegar
½ cup white wine
½ cup raspberry jam, seedless
   1 tablespoon shallots, minced
   1 tablespoon cornstarch
   1 tablespoon water

One hour before grilling, rub salt, pepper and
paprika into lamb ribs. In medium saucepan,
combine vinegar, white wine, raspberry jam
and shallots. Stir over medium heat until jam is
melted. Stir together cornstarch and water; add
to raspberry mixture and stir sauce until
smooth and clear.

Preheat grill. Move hot white coals to each side
of grill. Place foil drip pan in center. Place
lamb ribs in center of pan. Cover and cook
50 to 60 minutes, turning every 10 minutes.
Brush on glaze during last 10 to 15 minutes of
grilling.   *Makes 2 servings*

Favorite Recipe from American Lamb Council

TEXAS-STYLE STEAK ON HOT BREAD

½ cup olive or vegetable oil
¼ cup lime juice
¼ cup red wine vinegar
   1 medium onion, finely chopped
   1 large clove garlic, minced
   1 teaspoon chili powder
½ teaspoon salt
¼ teaspoon ground cumin
1½ pounds beef skirt or flank steak
   1 round loaf French or sourdough bread
   1 cup Mexican-style salsa
   1 cup guacamole

Combine oil, lime juice, vinegar, onion, garlic,
chili powder, salt and cumin in large glass dish.
Pound steak to ¼-inch thickness. Place steak in
marinade; turn to coat. Cover and refrigerate
overnight or several hours, turning several
times. Drain steak; discard marinade. Grill
steak, on covered grill, over medium-hot
KINGSFORD® with Mesquite Charcoal
Briquets 4 to 8 minutes on each side or until
done. Cut bread into 1-inch slices and toast on
grill. Heat salsa. Arrange steak, sliced into
¾-inch diagonal strips, on toasted bread. Top
with hot salsa and guacamole.

Makes 4 to 6 servings

CAMPERS' PIZZA

¼ pound ground beef (80% lean)
1 medium onion, chopped
½ teaspoon salt
1 can (8 ounces) refrigerated crescent rolls
1 can (8 ounces) pizza sauce
1 can (4 ounces) mushroom stems and
    pieces, drained and chopped
1 can (2½ ounces) sliced pitted ripe
    olives, drained
⅓ cup coarsely chopped green bell pepper
1 cup (4 ounces) shredded mozzarella
    cheese
1 teaspoon dried oregano leaves

Brown ground beef and onion in well-seasoned 11- to 12-inch cast-iron skillet over medium coals. Remove to paper towels; season with salt. Pour off drippings from pan. Separate crescent dough into triangles; place in skillet, points toward center, to form circle. Press edges together to form bottom crust and 1-inch rim up side of pan. Spread half of pizza sauce over dough; spoon ground beef mixture over sauce. Top with mushrooms, olives and green pepper. Pour remaining sauce over all; sprinkle with cheese and oregano. Place pan in center of grid over medium coals. Place cover on grill; cook 20 to 30 minutes or until crust is lightly browned. *Makes 4 servings*

Note: If cooked over open grill or coals, cover pan securely with foil.

*Favorite Recipe from **National Live Stock and Meat Board***

Campers' Pizza

BARBECUED PORK LEG

1 fresh pork leg, skinned, boned, trimmed
   of fat, rolled and tied (14 to
   16 pounds)
Sam's Mop Sauce (recipe follows)
K.C. MASTERPIECE® Hickory
   Barbecue Sauce

Arrange medium-hot KINGSFORD® Briquets
around drip pan. Place prepared pork leg over
drip pan; cover grill and cook pork 4 to
4½ hours or until thermometer inserted into
thickest portion registers 170°F. Baste pork
with Sam's Mop Sauce every 30 minutes,
patting a thin coating of sauce on meat with
cotton swab mop or pastry brush. Let stand,
covered with foil, 10 minutes before serving.

Meanwhile, in saucepan, combine half the
remaining mop sauce with an equal amount of
barbecue sauce. Heat through and serve with
slices of pork.   *Makes about 20 servings*

Note: The final weight of the fresh pork leg for
grilling should be 8 to 10 pounds. To save time,
you can have the butcher prepare the fresh
pork leg for you.

SAM'S MOP SAUCE

1 lemon
1 cup water
1 cup cider vinegar
1 tablespoon butter or margarine
1 tablespoon olive oil
½ teaspoon ground red pepper
1½ to 3 teaspoons hot pepper sauce
1½ to 3 teaspoons Worcestershire sauce
1½ teaspoons black pepper

With vegetable peeler, remove peel from
lemon; squeeze juice from lemon. In heavy
saucepan, combine lemon peel, juice and
remaining ingredients. Bring to boil. Place
saucepan on grill to keep warm, if space
permits.   *Makes 2¼ cups*

Barbecued Pork Leg

Beef Fajitas

BEEF FAJITAS

½ cup REALEMON® Lemon Juice from
    Concentrate
¼ cup vegetable oil
2 cloves garlic, finely chopped
2 teaspoons WYLER'S® or STEERO®
    Beef-Flavor Instant Bouillon
1 (1- to 1½-pound) beef top round steak
10 (6-inch) flour tortillas, warmed
    according to package directions
    Picante sauce, shredded lettuce,
    shredded cheddar cheese, sliced green
    onions for garnish

In shallow dish or plastic bag, combine
ReaLemon® brand, oil, garlic and bouillon; add
meat. Cover; marinate in refrigerator 6 hours
or overnight. Remove meat from marinade;
grill or broil as desired, basting frequently with
marinade. Slice meat diagonally into thin
strips; place on tortillas. Top with one or more
garnishes; fold tortillas. Serve immediately.
Refrigerate leftovers. *Makes 10 fajitas*

HONEY MUSTARD PORK TENDERLOIN

¼ cup vegetable oil
2 tablespoons brown sugar
2 tablespoons honey
2 tablespoons REALEMON® Lemon Juice
    from Concentrate
1 tablespoon Dijon-style mustard
2 teaspoons WYLER'S® or STEERO®
    Beef- or Chicken-Flavor Instant
    Bouillon
1 (¾- to 1-pound) pork tenderloin

In shallow dish or plastic bag, combine all
ingredients except meat; add meat. Cover;
marinate in refrigerator 6 hours or overnight.
Remove meat from marinade; grill or broil as
desired, basting frequently with marinade.
Refrigerate leftovers.

Makes 2 to 4 servings

Kamaaina Spareribs

KAMAAINA SPARERIBS

4 pounds lean pork spareribs
   Salt and pepper
1 can (20 ounces) DOLE® Crushed
      Pineapple in Juice, drained
1 cup catsup
½ cup packed brown sugar
⅓ cup red wine vinegar
¼ cup soy sauce
1 teaspoon ground ginger
½ teaspoon dry mustard
¼ teaspoon garlic powder

Have butcher cut across rib bones to make
strips 1½ inches wide. Preheat oven to 350°F.
Place ribs close together in single layer in
baking pan. Sprinkle with salt and pepper to
taste. Cover tightly with aluminum foil. Bake
1 hour. Uncover; pour off and discard drippings.

In bowl, combine remaining ingredients.
Spoon sauce over ribs. Place ribs over hot
coals. Grill 15 minutes or until ribs are tender
and glazed.   *Makes 6 servings*

BARBECUED SAUSAGE KABOBS

1 pound ECKRICH® Smoked Sausage, cut
      into 1-inch pieces
1 cup dried apricots
1 can (12 ounces) beer
½ red bell pepper, cut into 1¼-inch squares
½ green bell pepper, cut into 1¼-inch
      squares
1 Spanish onion, cut into wedges
¼ pound fresh medium mushrooms
¾ cup apricot preserves
2 tablespoons chili sauce
1 tablespoon prepared mustard
1 teaspoon Worcestershire sauce

Simmer sausage and apricots in beer in large
saucepan over low heat 10 minutes. Add
peppers to sausage mixture; remove from heat.
Let stand 10 minutes. To assemble kabobs,
thread on skewers sausage, onion, red and
green peppers, mushrooms and apricots.
Combine preserves, chili sauce, mustard and
Worcestershire sauce in small saucepan. Heat
over medium heat, stirring until blended.
Brush kabobs with sauce. Grill or broil,
4 inches from heat, 10 minutes, turning and
brushing with more sauce after 5 minutes.
Brush with remaining sauce and serve.
                          Makes 4 servings

CURRIED BEEF AND FRUIT KABOBS

1- to 1¼-pound beef top round or boneless
    beef sirloin steak, cut 1 inch thick
1 cup plain yogurt
2 teaspoons fresh lemon juice
1½ teaspoons curry powder
⅛ to ¼ teaspoon ground red pepper
1 ripe mango* (about 1 pound)
    Salt to taste

Partially freeze beef top round steak to firm; slice into ⅛- to ¼-inch-thick strips. Combine yogurt, lemon juice, curry powder and red pepper. Place beef strips and marinade in plastic bag, turning to coat. Close bag securely and marinate in refrigerator 30 minutes, turning occasionally. Meanwhile, soak eight 12-inch bamboo skewers in water 20 minutes. Peel mango and cut into ¾-inch pieces. Remove beef from marinade; discard marinade. Thread an equal amount of beef strips (weaving back and forth) and mango pieces on each skewer. Place kabobs on grid over medium coals. Grill 4 to 5 minutes, turning once. Season with salt to taste.

Makes 4 servings

*Peaches, nectarines, plums or pineapple may be substituted for mango. Peel and cut fruit into ¾-inch pieces.

Note: Kabobs may also be cooked covered over medium coals. Grill 3 to 4 minutes, turning once.

*Favorite Recipe from **National Live Stock and Meat Board***

BIRTHDAY BURGERS

¾ cup boiling water
¼ cup bulgur (cracked wheat)
⅓ cup whole natural almonds
1 pound lean ground beef or ground turkey
¼ cup chopped green onions
1 teaspoon garlic salt
1 teaspoon dried basil leaves
4 hamburger buns
    Lettuce
    Tomato slices
    Red onion slices

Pour water over bulgur; let stand until cool. Place almonds in single layer on baking sheet. Bake at 350°F, 12 to 15 minutes, stirring occasionally, until lightly toasted. Cool; chop coarsely. Drain bulgur well. Combine bulgur, almonds, ground beef, green onions, garlic salt and basil; mix well. Shape into 4 patties. Grill or broil until desired doneness. Serve on hamburger buns with lettuce, tomatoes and red onions.

Makes 4 servings

*Favorite Recipe from **Almond Board of California***

Birthday Burgers

Fired-Up Poultry

Grilled chicken, Cornish hens and turkey taste great! Kabobs, burgers and boneless pieces cook in minutes. Quarters, halves and whole poultry need a slower heat and longer cooking time.

ZINGY BARBECUED CHICKEN

  1 broiler-fryer chicken, cut into parts
½ cup grapefruit juice
½ cup apple cider vinegar
½ cup vegetable oil
¼ cup chopped onion
  1 egg
½ teaspoon celery salt
½ teaspoon ground ginger
⅛ teaspoon pepper

In blender container, place all ingredients except chicken; blend 30 seconds. In small saucepan, pour blended sauce mixture and heat about 5 minutes, until slightly thick. Remove from heat; dip chicken in sauce one piece at a time, turning to thoroughly coat. Reserve sauce.

Place chicken on prepared grill, skin side up, about 8 inches from heat. Grill, turning every 10 minutes, for about 50 minutes or until fork tender and juices run clear. Brush generously with reserved sauce during last 20 minutes of grilling. Watch chicken carefully as egg in sauce may cause chicken to become too brown.

Makes 4 servings

*Favorite Recipe from **National Broiler Council***

GRILLED TURKEY WITH VEGETABLE PIZZAZZ

1½ pounds turkey breast, cut into 2-inch pieces
  2 medium zucchini, cut into 1-inch chunks
12 large mushrooms
  1 medium red pepper, cut into 1½-inch pieces
12 jumbo pimiento-stuffed olives
  1 tablespoon vegetable oil
  1 cup pizza sauce
  1 tablespoon dried basil leaves

Thread turkey, zucchini, mushrooms, pepper and olives alternately on skewers; brush thoroughly with oil. Mix pizza sauce and basil; reserve. Grill kabobs, on uncovered grill, over medium-hot MATCH LIGHT® Charcoal Briquets about 10 minutes, turning occasionally. Baste with reserved pizza sauce and continue to grill about 15 minutes, basting and turning 2 to 3 times, until turkey is tender and vegetables are cooked.

Makes 6 servings

Zingy Barbecued Chicken

SWEET AND SPICY CHICKEN BARBECUE

1½ cups DOLE® Pineapple Orange Juice
  1 cup orange marmalade
⅔ cup teriyaki sauce
½ cup packed brown sugar
½ teaspoon ground cloves
½ teaspoon ground ginger
  4 frying chickens (about 2 pounds each),
     halved or quartered
     Salt and pepper
     DOLE® Pineapple Slices, drained
  4 teaspoons cornstarch

In saucepan, combine juice, marmalade, teriyaki sauce, brown sugar, cloves and ginger. Heat until sugar dissolves; let cool. Sprinkle chicken with salt and pepper to taste. Place in glass baking dish. Pour juice mixture over chicken; turn to coat all sides. Marinate, covered, 2 hours in refrigerator, turning often.

Preheat oven to 350°F. Light charcoal grill. Drain chicken; reserve marinade. Bake chicken in oven 20 minutes. Arrange chicken on lightly greased grid 4 to 6 inches above glowing coals. Grill, turning and basting often with reserved marinade, 20 to 25 minutes or until meat near bone is no longer pink. Grill pineapple slices 3 minutes or until heated through.

In small saucepan, dissolve cornstarch in remaining marinade. Cook over medium heat until sauce boils and thickens. To serve, arrange chicken and pineapple on plate; spoon sauce over tops.   *Makes 8 servings*

Sweet and Spicy Chicken Barbecue

JALAPENO GRILLED CHICKEN

  1 broiler-fryer chicken, quartered
  2 tablespoons vegetable oil
¼ cup chopped onion
  1 clove garlic, minced
  1 cup catsup
  2 tablespoons vinegar
  1 tablespoon brown sugar
  1 tablespoon minced jalapeño peppers
½ teaspoon salt
½ teaspoon dry mustard

In saucepan, heat oil to medium temperature. Add onion and garlic; cook, stirring occasionally, about 5 minutes or until onion is tender. Add catsup, vinegar, brown sugar, jalapeño peppers, salt and mustard. Cook, stirring occasionally, until mixture is blended. Place chicken, skin side up, on prepared grill about 8 inches from heat. Grill, turning every 8 to 10 minutes, about 50 minutes. Brush chicken with sauce; grill, turning and basting with sauce every 5 minutes, about 25 minutes more or until chicken is fork tender.

Makes 4 servings

Favorite Recipe from **Delmarva Poultry Industry, Inc.**

Turkey Fajitas

TURKEY FAJITAS

⅓ cup REALEMON® Lemon Juice from
    Concentrate
2 tablespoons vegetable oil
1 tablespoon WYLER'S® or STEERO®
    Chicken-Flavor Instant Bouillon
3 cloves garlic, finely chopped
2 fresh turkey breast tenderloins (about
    1 pound), pierced with fork
8 (8-inch) flour tortillas, warmed
    according to package directions
    Shredded lettuce and cheese, sliced ripe
        olives and green onions, salsa,
        guacamole and sour cream for garnish

In shallow dish or plastic bag, combine
ReaLemon® brand, oil, bouillon and garlic; add
turkey. Cover; marinate in refrigerator 4 hours
or overnight, turning occasionally. Remove
turkey from marinade; reserve marinade. Grill
or broil as desired, 6 inches from heat,
10 minutes per side or until no longer pink,
basting frequently with reserved marinade. Let
stand 10 minutes. Slice turkey; place on
tortillas. Top with one or more of the garnishes;
fold tortillas. Serve immediately. Refrigerate
leftovers.   *Makes 4 servings*

STUFFED GRILLED GAME HENS

4 (1 to 1½ pounds each) Cornish game hens, thawed
½ cup orange juice
½ cup vegetable oil
1 garlic clove, minced
⅛ teaspoon pepper
1⅓ cups MINUTE® Rice, uncooked
1 (8-ounce) container PHILADELPHIA BRAND® Soft Cream Cheese
¼ cup golden raisins
¼ cup chopped fresh parsley
2 tablespoons orange juice
1 shallot, minced
1½ teaspoons grated orange peel
½ teaspoon salt
⅛ teaspoon pepper
Whole cooked carrots (optional)

Remove giblets; discard or save for another use. Rinse hens; pat dry.

Marinate hens in combined ½ cup orange juice, oil, garlic and ⅛ teaspoon pepper in refrigerator 30 minutes, basting occasionally.

Prepare coals for grilling.

Prepare rice according to package directions. Mix together rice and remaining ingredients except carrots in medium bowl. Remove hens from marinade, reserving marinade for basting. Stuff hens with rice mixture; close openings with skewers.

Place aluminum drip pan in center of charcoal grate under grilling rack. Arrange hot coals around drip pan.

Place hens, breast side up, on greased grill directly over drip pan. Grill, covered, 1 hour and 15 minutes to 1 hour and 30 minutes or until tender, brushing frequently with reserved marinade.

Serve with whole carrots, if desired.

Makes 4 servings

TASTY TACO CHICKEN GRILL

1 broiler-fryer chicken, cut into parts
1 small onion, minced
1 can (8 ounces) Spanish-style tomato sauce
1 can (4 ounces) taco sauce
¼ cup molasses
2 tablespoons vinegar
1 tablespoon vegetable oil
1 teaspoon salt
½ teaspoon oregano leaves
⅛ teaspoon pepper
½ cup shredded Monterey Jack cheese

In small saucepan, make sauce by mixing together onion, tomato sauce, taco sauce, molasses, vinegar, oil, salt, oregano and pepper; bring sauce to a boil. Remove from heat and cool 2 minutes. In large shallow dish, place chicken; pour sauce over chicken. Cover and marinate in refrigerator at least 1 hour.

Drain chicken; reserve sauce. Place chicken on prepared grill, skin side up, about 8 inches from heat. Grill, turning every 10 minutes, about 50 minutes or until fork tender and juices run clear. Brush generously with reserved sauce during last 20 minutes of grilling. When chicken is done, place on platter; sprinkle with cheese.

Makes 4 servings

Favorite recipe from **National Broiler Council**

TURKEY BURGERS

1 pound ground fresh turkey
¼ cup BENNETT'S® Chili Sauce
1 teaspoon WYLER'S® or STEERO® Chicken-Flavor Instant Bouillon

Combine ingredients; shape into patties. Grill, broil or pan-fry until no longer pink in center. Refrigerate leftovers.

Makes 4 servings

Hot and Spicy Barbecue Drumsticks

HOT AND SPICY BARBECUE DRUMSTICKS

    4 large California-Grown Turkey
        drumsticks, about 1½ pounds each, *or*
        8 small California-Grown Turkey
        drumsticks, about ¾ pound each
    1 can (8 ounces) tomato sauce
      Juice from 1 fresh lemon
    4 large cloves garlic, crushed
    2 tablespoons sugar
    1 teaspoon chili powder
    1 teaspoon salt
    1 teaspoon Worcestershire sauce
    ¼ teaspoon pepper
    ¼ teaspoon hot pepper sauce

Wrap each drumstick in heavy-duty aluminum foil, leaving room for steam expansion and keeping dull side of foil out. Grill over a single layer of slow coals, 1 hour for large drumsticks and 45 minutes for small drumsticks, turning every 15 minutes and adding additional charcoal as needed to maintain temperature.

Meanwhile, prepare barbecue sauce by combining remaining ingredients in small bowl. Remove aluminum foil from drumsticks and continue grilling an additional 30 minutes over slow coals, basting twice on each side with sauce and turning drumsticks after 15 minutes.   *Makes 8 servings (½ large or 1 small drumstick each)*
*Favorite Recipe from **California Turkey Industry Board***

MID-EASTERN TANGY CHICKEN

    1 broiler-fryer chicken, quartered
    1 tablespoon butter or margarine
    ¼ cup minced onion
    1 clove garlic, minced
    1 cup plain yogurt
    1 teaspoon salt
    ½ teaspoon ground turmeric
    ½ teaspoon chili powder
    3 tablespoons white wine

In small saucepan, make sauce by melting butter over medium heat. Add onion and garlic; stir and cook about 3 minutes or until onion is clear and soft. Remove from heat and stir in yogurt, salt, turmeric and chili powder. Let cool 2 minutes; stir in white wine. In large shallow dish, place chicken quarters. Pour sauce over chicken; cover and marinate in refrigerator at least 1 hour.

Remove chicken from sauce; reserve sauce. Place chicken on prepared grill, skin side up, about 8 inches from heat. Grill, turning every 15 minutes, for about 60 minutes or until fork tender and juices run clear. Brush generously with reserved sauce during last 30 minutes of grilling.   *Makes 4 servings*
*Favorite Recipe from **National Broiler Council***

GRILLED TURKEY WITH WALNUT PESTO

1 (4- to 5½-pound) turkey breast
   Walnut Pesto Sauce (recipe follows)

Prepare coals for grilling. Place aluminum drip pan in center of charcoal grate under grilling rack. Arrange hot coals around drip pan. Place turkey on greased grill. Grill, covered, 1½ to 2 hours or until internal temperature reaches 170°F. Slice turkey; serve with Walnut Pesto Sauce. Garnish with red and yellow pear-shaped cherry tomatoes, fresh chives and basil leaves, if desired.   *Makes 12 servings*

WALNUT PESTO SAUCE

1 (8-ounce) container PHILADELPHIA
   BRAND® "Light" Pasteurized Process
   Cream Cheese Product
1 (7-ounce) container refrigerated
   prepared pesto
½ cup finely chopped walnuts, toasted
⅓ cup milk
1 garlic clove, minced
⅛ teaspoon ground red pepper

Stir together all ingredients in small bowl until well blended. Serve chilled or at room temperature.

Grilled Turkey with Walnut Pesto

MEXICAN CHICKEN WITH SPICY BACON

2 serrano chili peppers
2 cloves garlic
    Dash ground cloves
    Dash ground cinnamon
4 slices bacon, partially cooked
1 whole roasting chicken (3½ to 4 pounds)
    Cherry tomatoes and serrano chili
        peppers for garnish (optional)

Remove stems from peppers. Slit open; remove seeds and ribs. Finely chop peppers and garlic. Place in small bowl. Stir in cloves and cinnamon. Cut bacon into 1-inch pieces.

Lift skin layer of chicken at neck cavity. Insert hand, lifting skin from meat along breast, thigh and drumstick. Using small metal spatula, spread pepper mixture evenly over meat, under skin. Place layer of bacon pieces over pepper mixture. Skewer neck skin to back. Tie legs securely to tail and twist wing tips under back of chicken. Insert meat thermometer in center of thigh muscle, not touching bone.

Arrange medium-hot KINGSFORD® Briquets around drip pan. Place chicken, breast side up, over drip pan. Cover grill and cook about 1 hour or until meat thermometer registers 185°F. Garnish with cherry tomatoes and serrano chili peppers, if desired.   *Makes 4 servings*

Mexican Chicken with Spicy Bacon

HERBED LIME CHICKEN

½ cup vegetable oil
⅓ cup lime juice
¼ cup chopped onion
2 cloves garlic, crushed
1 teaspoon TABASCO® Pepper Sauce
¾ teaspoon dried rosemary leaves,
    crumbled
½ teaspoon dried marjoram leaves,
    crumbled
½ teaspoon salt
2 to 3 pounds chicken pieces

In dish, combine oil, lime juice, onion, garlic, Tabasco® sauce, rosemary, marjoram and salt. Place chicken in large shallow dish or plastic bag; pour marinade over chicken. Cover and marinate in refrigerator overnight; turn chicken occasionally.

Drain chicken; reserve marinade. Place chicken on grid about 5 inches from heat. Grill about 20 minutes per side or until done, brushing with reserved marinade several times. *Makes 4 servings*

BEER-BASTED CHICKEN LEGS

4 whole broiler-fryer chicken legs (thigh
    and drumstick attached)
¾ cup chili sauce
½ cup beer
1 tablespoon dark brown sugar
1 tablespoon Worcestershire sauce
2 teaspoons prepared horseradish
½ teaspoon salt

In small bowl, mix together chili sauce, beer, brown sugar, Worcestershire sauce, prepared horseradish and salt. Place chicken, skin side up, on prepared grill about 8 inches from heat. Grill, turning every 10 minutes, about 35 minutes. Brush chicken with sauce; grill, turning and basting with sauce every 5 minutes, about 20 minutes more or until chicken is fork tender. *Makes 4 servings*

*Favorite Recipe from **Delmarva Poultry Industry, Inc.***

California Turkey Skewers

CALIFORNIA TURKEY SKEWERS

California Glaze (recipe follows)
1 California-Grown Turkey breast half,
    about 3 pounds
1 package (9 ounces) frozen artichoke
    hearts, thawed
8 ears of corn, blanched, cut into chunks*

Prepare California Glaze. Cut turkey into 1½-inch cubes. Thread turkey, artichoke hearts and corn chunks on skewers. Barbecue or broil 15 to 20 minutes, brushing frequently with California Glaze; turn often.

Makes 8 to 10 servings

California Glaze: In saucepan combine ½ cup orange juice, 2 tablespoons *each* firmly packed brown sugar, vinegar, lemon juice and honey, 1 tablespoon cornstarch, 1 teaspoon salt, ½ teaspoon *each* dry mustard and grated orange peel and ¼ teaspoon dried tarragon leaves, crushed. Bring to a boil.

*Thawed, frozen ears of corn may be used.

*Favorite Recipe from **California Turkey Industry Board***

BUFFALO TURKEY KABOBS

⅔ cup HELLMANN'S® or BEST FOODS®
    Real, Light or Cholesterol Free
    Reduced Calorie Mayonnaise, divided
1 teaspoon hot pepper sauce
1½ pounds boneless turkey breast, cut into
    1-inch cubes
2 red bell peppers *or* 1 red and 1 yellow
    bell pepper, cut into 1-inch squares
2 medium onions, cut into wedges
¼ cup (1 ounce) crumbed blue cheese
2 tablespoons milk
1 medium stalk celery, minced
1 medium carrot, minced

In medium bowl, combine ⅓ cup of the
mayonnaise and the hot pepper sauce. Stir in
turkey. Cover and marinate in refrigerator
20 minutes. Drain turkey; discard marinade.
On 6 skewers, thread turkey, peppers and
onions. Grill or broil, 5 inches from heat,
brushing with remaining mayonnaise mixture
and turning frequently, 12 to 15 minutes.
Meanwhile, in small bowl blend remaining
⅓ cup mayonnaise with blue cheese and milk.
Stir in celery and carrot. Serve with kabobs.
                                    Makes 6 servings

Note: For best results, use Real Mayonnaise. If
using Light or Cholesterol Free Reduced
Calorie Mayonnaise, use sauce the same day.

SPICY THAI CHICKEN

¾ cup canned cream of coconut
3 tablespoons lime juice
3 tablespoons soy sauce
8 sprigs cilantro
3 large cloves garlic
3 large green onions, cut up
3 anchovy fillets
1 teaspoon TABASCO® Pepper Sauce
2 whole boneless skinless chicken breasts,
    cut into halves (about 1½ pounds)

In blender container or food processor,
combine cream of coconut, lime juice, soy
sauce, cilantro, garlic, green onions, anchovies
and Tabasco® sauce. Cover; process until
smooth. Place chicken in large shallow dish or
plastic bag; add marinade. Cover; refrigerate at
least 2 hours, turning chicken occasionally.

Drain chicken; reserve marinade. Place
chicken on grill about 5 inches from source of
heat. Brush generously with marinade. Grill
5 minutes. Turn chicken; brush with reserved
marinade. Grill 5 minutes longer or until
chicken is cooked. Heat any remaining
marinade to a boil; serve as dipping sauce for
chicken.   *Makes 4 servings*

GRILLED CHICKEN POLYNESIAN TREAT

12 broiler-fryer chicken thighs
2 tablespoons butter or margarine
1 small onion, minced
¾ cup vinegar
¼ cup soy sauce
¼ cup plum jam
¼ teaspoon salt
1 bay leaf
3 large pineapples, cut lengthwise into
    halves
2 large green peppers, sliced into rings

In small saucepan, melt butter over medium
heat; add onion. Stir and cook about 3 minutes
or until onion is clear and soft. Add vinegar,
soy sauce and plum jam. Bring mixture to a
boil, stirring constantly. Remove from heat and
stir in salt and bay leaf. In large shallow dish,
place chicken thighs; pour hot sauce over
chicken. Cover and marinate in refrigerator at
least 1 hour.

Remove chicken from sauce; reserve sauce.
Place chicken thighs on prepared grill, skin
side up, about 8 inches from heat. Grill about
15 minutes or until brown on one side. Turn
and continue grilling 15 minutes longer.
Chicken is done when fork tender and juices
run clear. Brush generously with reserved
sauce during entire grilling time. Serve chicken
thighs in scooped out pineapple halves and top
with green pepper rings.   *Makes 6 servings*
Favorite Recipe from **National Broiler Council**

Buffalo Turkey Kabobs

COOL GRILLED CHICKEN SALAD

  1 pound boneless, skinless chicken breasts
  ¼ cup lemon juice
  2 tablespoons olive or vegetable oil
  1 teaspoon dried tarragon leaves, crushed
  ¾ teaspoon LAWRY'S® Garlic Salt
  1 quart salad greens, torn into bite-size
      pieces
  6 medium red potatoes, cooked, cooled
      and cut into chunks
  1 cup shredded carrot

Rinse chicken and place in resealable plastic bag. In small bowl, combine lemon juice, oil, tarragon and Garlic Salt; blend well. Pour marinade over chicken; seal bag and refrigerate 30 to 45 minutes or overnight. Drain chicken; reserve marinade. Grill or broil chicken 4 minutes on each side, basting with reserved marinade, until golden and cooked through. Cool and cut into strips. Line individual plates with salad greens. Arrange potato chunks, carrot and chicken on top.

Makes 4 main-dish servings

Hint: For a more colorful salad, add sliced tomatoes or shredded red cabbage.

SPICY BARBECUED WINGETTES

  12 PERDUE OVEN STUFFER Wingettes
  ⅔ cup cider vinegar
  ⅓ cup vegetable oil
  ½ teaspoon hot pepper sauce
  ¼ teaspoon crushed dried red pepper
  1 clove garlic, minced or pressed

Rinse wingettes and pat dry; place in shallow dish. In small saucepan over medium heat, stir together remaining ingredients. Cook about 5 minutes or until mixture is hot; pour over wingettes. Cover; refrigerate several hours or overnight.

Prepare outdoor grill for cooking or preheat broiler. Remove wingettes from marinade; reserve marinade. Grill 6 inches from source of heat or broil indoors 25 to 35 minutes, turning and basting frequently with reserved marinade. Let stand 5 minutes before serving.

Makes 6 servings

CHICKEN KABOBS WITH PEANUT SAUCE

  2 whole broiler-fryer chicken breasts,
      halved, boned, skinned, cut into 1-inch
      pieces
  ¼ cup finely chopped onion
  2 tablespoons white wine
  2 tablespoons soy sauce
  1 tablespoon brown sugar
  1 tablespoon vegetable oil
  ½ teaspoon ground coriander
  1 clove garlic, crushed
  2 cans (8 ounces each) pineapple chunks
      in natural juice, drained
  2 red or green peppers, halved, cored, cut
      into 1-inch pieces
  Peanut Sauce (recipe follows)

In shallow, nonmetallic dish, mix together onion, wine, soy sauce, brown sugar, oil, coriander and garlic. Add chicken, stirring to coat. Cover and marinate in refrigerator, stirring occasionally, 1 hour. Drain chicken; reserve marinade. On each of 8 skewers, thread chicken, pineapple and peppers. Place chicken on prepared grill about 8 inches from heat. Grill, turning and basting frequently with reserved marinade, about 20 minutes or until chicken is fork tender. Serve with Peanut Sauce.

Makes 4 servings

Peanut Sauce: In saucepan, place ½ cup chunky peanut butter, ¼ cup finely chopped onion, ¼ cup canned cream of coconut, ¼ cup water, 2 tablespoons soy sauce, 1 tablespoon brown sugar and ¼ tablespoon crushed red pepper flakes. Heat, stirring, until mixture boils.

Makes about 1¼ cups

*Favorite Recipe from **Delmarva Poultry Industry, Inc.***

Cool Grilled Chicken Salad

Grilled Cornish Game Hens

GRILLED CORNISH GAME HENS

   2 Cornish game hens (1 to 1½ pounds
       each)
   3 tablespoons olive oil
   ⅓ cup lemon juice
   1 tablespoon black peppercorns, coarsely
       crushed
   ½ teaspoon salt
       Fresh rosemary sprigs (optional)

Split hens lengthwise. Rinse hen halves; pat dry with paper toweling.

For marinade, in small bowl combine olive oil, lemon juice, peppercorns and salt. Place hen halves in large plastic bag. Set in bowl. Pour marinade over hens. Close bag and refrigerate several hours or overnight, turning hen halves occasionally to coat with marinade.

Arrange medium-hot KINGSFORD® Briquets around drip pan. Just before grilling, add a rosemary sprig to coals. Remove hens from marinade; reserve marinade. Place hens, skin side up, over drip pan. Cover grill and cook 45 minutes or until thigh moves easily and juices run clear. Baste with reserved marinade occasionally. Garnish with rosemary sprigs, if desired. *Makes 4 servings*

BARBECUED CHICKEN

1 cup chicken broth
¼ cup catsup
2 tablespoons vinegar
2 tablespoons Worcestershire sauce
2 tablespoons finely chopped onion
1 teaspoon dry mustard
½ teaspoon garlic salt
½ teaspoon salt
¼ teaspoon pepper
1 broiler-fryer chicken (2 to 3 pounds),
    quartered

Combine all ingredients, except chicken, in small saucepan. Bring to boil; cool slightly. Place chicken in shallow glass dish. Pour warm sauce over chicken; cover and refrigerate at least 2 hours. Drain chicken; reserve marinade. Grill chicken, skin side up, on uncovered grill, over hot KINGSFORD® Briquets 40 to 55 minutes, basting often with reserved marinade and turning frequently, until chicken is fork tender.   *Makes 4 to 5 servings*

CHICKEN VEGETABLE KABOBS

½ cup WISH-BONE® Italian Dressing
¼ cup dry white wine
1 pound boneless chicken breasts, cubed
1 medium zucchini, cut into ½-inch pieces
1 large green pepper, cut into chunks

In large shallow baking dish, blend Italian dressing with wine. Add chicken and vegetables and turn to coat. Cover and marinate in refrigerator, turning occasionally, at least 2 hours. Remove chicken and vegetables; reserve marinade.

Onto skewers; thread chicken and vegetables. Grill or broil, turning and basting frequently with reserved marinade, until chicken is done.
      Makes about 4 servings

CHILI TOMATO GRILLED CHICKEN

6 broiler-fryer chicken quarters
2 tablespoons vegetable oil
½ cup finely chopped onion
1 clove garlic, minced
1 chicken bouillon cube
½ cup hot water
1 bottle (8 ounces) taco sauce *or* 1 can
    (8 ounces) tomato sauce
1 teaspoon salt
¼ teaspoon dried oregano leaves
2 tablespoons vinegar
1 tablespoon prepared mustard
3 teaspoons mild chili powder, divided

In small skillet, place oil and heat to medium temperature. Add onion and garlic; stir and cook about 3 minutes or until clear and soft. Dissolve bouillon cube in hot water; add bouillon to skillet, along with taco sauce, salt, oregano, vinegar and mustard. Dip chicken into sauce mixture; then sprinkle 2 teaspoons of the chili powder on all sides of chicken. Add remaining 1 teaspoon of chili powder to sauce; bring to a boil and remove from heat. Redip each quarter in sauce. Place chicken on prepared grill, skin side up, about 8 inches from heat. Grill, turning every 15 minutes, for about 60 minutes or until fork tender and juices run clear. Brush generously with sauce during last 30 minutes of grilling.
      Makes 6 servings

*Favorite Recipe from **National Broiler Council***

Grilled Seafood

Fish and shellfish cook quickly and deliciously on the grill. In just minutes you can serve your guests fork-tender fish and melt-in-the-mouth scallops or shrimp.

SALMON STEAKS IN ORANGE-HONEY MARINADE

⅓ cup orange juice
⅓ cup soy sauce
3 tablespoons peanut oil
3 tablespoons catsup
1 tablespoon honey
½ teaspoon ground ginger
1 clove garlic, crushed
4 salmon steaks (about 6 ounces each)

In 1-quart measure, mix all ingredients except salmon steaks. Place salmon steaks in shallow glass dish. Pour marinade over salmon steaks; cover and marinate in refrigerator 1 hour. Drain salmon; reserve marinade. Grill salmon, on uncovered grill, 6 inches above hot KINGSFORD® Briquets 5 minutes. Carefully turn salmon steaks. Brush with reserved marinade and grill 5 minutes longer or until salmon flakes easily when tested with fork.

Makes 4 servings

SEAFOOD KABOBS

⅓ cup pineapple juice
⅓ cup REALEMON® Lemon Juice from Concentrate
2 tablespoons vegetable oil
1 to 2 tablespoons brown sugar
1 teaspoon grated orange rind
¼ teaspoon ground cinnamon
¾ pound large raw shrimp, peeled and deveined
½ pound sea scallops
1 cup melon chunks or balls
1 medium avocado, peeled, seeded and cut into chunks

In large shallow dish or plastic bag, combine juices, oil, sugar, rind and cinnamon; add seafood and melon. Cover; marinate in refrigerator 4 hours or overnight. Place shrimp, scallops, melon and avocado on skewers. Grill or broil 3 to 6 minutes or until shrimp are pink and scallops are opaque, basting frequently with marinade. Refrigerate leftovers.

Makes 4 servings

Top to bottom: Salmon Steaks in Orange-Honey Marinade, Seafood Kabobs

MAGIC GRILLED FISH

**6 (½-inch-thick) firm-fleshed fish fillets
(8 to 10 ounces each), such as redfish,
pompano, tilefish, red snapper, or
salmon or tuna steaks**
¾ cup (1½ sticks) unsalted butter, melted
**3 tablespoons plus 2 teaspoons CHEF
PAUL PRUDHOMME 'S BLACKENED
REDFISH MAGIC®**

Heat grill as hot as possible and have flames
reaching above grid before putting fish on grill.
Add dry wood chunks to glowing coals to make
fire hotter.

Dip each fillet in melted butter so that both
sides are well coated, then sprinkle Blackened
Redfish Magic generously and evenly on both
sides of fillets, patting it in by hand. Place
fillets directly over flame on very hot grill and
pour 1 teaspoon of the melted butter on top of
each. (Be careful; butter may flare up.) Cook,
uncovered, directly in flames until underside
looks blackened, about 2 minutes. (Time will
vary according to each fillet's thickness and
heat of grill.) Turn fish over and grill until
cooked through, about 2 minutes more. Serve
piping hot with assorted grilled vegetables.

Makes 6 servings

Note: Do not prepare this recipe indoors.

Magic Grilled Fish

Shrimp and Steak Kabobs

SHRIMP AND STEAK KABOBS

½ cup vegetable oil
¼ cup REALEMON® Lemon Juice from
    Concentrate
1 teaspoon dried oregano leaves
½ teaspoon dried basil leaves
1 clove garlic, finely chopped
½ pound medium raw shrimp, peeled and
    deveined
½ pound boneless beef sirloin, cut into
    cubes
    Zucchini, onion and red or yellow bell
    pepper chunks

In shallow dish or plastic bag, combine oil,
ReaLemon® brand, oregano, basil and garlic;
add shrimp and meat. Cover; marinate in
refrigerator 3 to 4 hours. Skewer shrimp and
meat with vegetables. Grill or broil as desired,
basting frequently with marinade.
    Makes 16 appetizer or 4 main-dish servings

Tip: One-half pound of scallops can be
substituted for sirloin.

LAKESIDE LOBSTER TAILS

4 (1-pound) cleaned lobster tails with shells
    Herb Wine Sauce (recipe follows)
    Lemon wedges (optional)

Prepare coals for grilling. Cut lobster tails
through center of back with knife or kitchen
shears; split open. Place lobster, shell side
down, on greased grill over hot coals (coals will
be glowing). Grill, covered, 5 to 8 minutes on
each side or until shell is bright red and lobster
meat is white. Serve with Herb Wine Sauce.
Garnish with lemon wedges, if desired.
    Makes 4 servings

HERB WINE SAUCE

1 (8-ounce) container PHILADELPHIA
    BRAND® Soft Cream Cheese with
    Herb & Garlic
¼ cup dry white wine
2 green onions, thinly sliced
½ teaspoon salt

Stir together ingredients in small bowl until
well blended.

"Grilled" Tuna with Vegetables in Herb Butter

"GRILLED" TUNA WITH VEGETABLES IN HERB BUTTER

  1 can (12½ ounces) STARKIST® Tuna, drained and broken into chunks
  1 cup slivered red or green bell pepper
  1 cup slivered yellow squash or zucchini
  1 cup slivered carrots
  1 cup pea pods, cut crosswise into halves
  4 green onions, cut into ½-inch slices
  ¼ cup butter or margarine, melted
  1 tablespoon lemon or lime juice
  1 clove garlic, minced
  2 teaspoons dried tarragon leaves, crushed
  1 teaspoon dried dill weed
    Salt and pepper to taste

On four 12×18-inch pieces heavy-duty aluminum foil mound tuna, bell pepper, squash, carrots, pea pods and onions, dividing evenly. For herb butter, in small bowl stir together butter, lemon juice, garlic, tarragon and dill weed. Drizzle mixture over tuna and vegetables. Sprinkle with salt and pepper. Fold edges of each foil square together to make 4 individual packets.

To grill, place foil packets about 4 inches above hot coals. Grill 10 to 12 minutes, or until heated through, turning packet over halfway through grill time.

To bake, place foil packets on baking sheet. Bake in preheated 450°F oven 15 to 20 minutes, or until heated through.

To serve, cut an "X" on top of each packet; peel back foil. Garnish as desired.

Makes 4 servings

SALMON WITH MUSTARD DILL SAUCE

¼ cup mayonnaise or salad dressing
¼ cup BORDEN® or MEADOW GOLD® Sour Cream
1 tablespoon sliced green onion
1 teaspoon Dijon-style mustard
⅓ cup plus 1 teaspoon REALEMON® Lemon Juice from Concentrate
1½ teaspoons dried dill weed
4 (1-inch-thick) salmon steaks (about 1½ pounds)

In small bowl, combine mayonnaise, sour cream, green onion, mustard, *1 teaspoon* ReaLemon® brand and *½ teaspoon* dill weed. Cover; chill. In shallow dish or plastic bag, combine remaining *⅓ cup* ReaLemon® brand and *1 teaspoon* dill weed; add fish. Cover; marinate in refrigerator 1 hour. Grill, broil or bake as desired, brushing frequently with marinade. Serve with mustard dill sauce. Refrigerate leftovers.   *Makes 4 servings*

HOT GRILLED TROUT

¼ cup lemon juice
2 tablespoons butter or margarine, melted
2 tablespoons olive oil
2 tablespoons chopped parsley
2 tablespoons sesame seeds
1 tablespoon TABASCO® Pepper Sauce
½ teaspoon ground ginger
½ teaspoon salt
4 brook trout (about 1 pound each)

In shallow dish, combine lemon juice, butter, oil, parsley, sesame seeds, Tabasco® sauce, ginger and salt. With fork, pierce skin of trout. Coat fish, inside and out, with marinade. Cover and refrigerate 30 to 60 minutes.

Drain fish; reserve marinade. Place fish in oiled grill basket; brush with reserved marinade. Cook 4 inches from hot coals 10 minutes or until fish flakes easily when tested with fork, turning and brushing with marinade once.   *Makes 4 servings*

Salmon with Mustard Dill Sauce

SWORDFISH WITH LEEK CREAM

    4 (1 to 1½ pounds total) swordfish steaks
    2 tablespoons olive oil
      Leek Cream (recipe follows)

Prepare coals for grilling. Brush fish with oil. Place fish on greased grill over hot coals (coals will be glowing). Grill, uncovered, 3 to 4 minutes on each side or until fish flakes easily when tested with fork. Serve with Leek Cream.   *Makes 4 servings*

LEEK CREAM

    1 leek, cut into 1-inch strips
    2 tablespoons PARKAY® Margarine
    1 (3-ounce) package PHILADELPHIA
      BRAND® Cream Cheese, cubed
    3 tablespoons dry white wine
    2 tablespoons chopped fresh parsley
    ½ teaspoon garlic salt
    ¼ teaspoon pepper

Sauté leeks in margarine in medium skillet until tender. Add remaining ingredients; stir over low heat until cream cheese is melted.

DEVILED TROUT FILLETS

    2 pounds trout fillets, fresh or frozen
    ½ cup chili sauce
    2 tablespoons vegetable oil
    2 tablespoons prepared mustard
    2 tablespoons cream-style prepared
      horseradish
    1 tablespoon Worcestershire sauce
    ½ teaspoon salt

Thaw fish, if frozen. Place fish on well-greased grid. Mix remaining ingredients in small bowl until blended. Spread sauce evenly over fish. Grill, 6 inches from medium hot coals, 5 to 8 minutes or until fish begins to flake when tested with a fork.   *Makes 6 servings*

Favorite recipe from **National Fisheries Institute**

SHRIMP IN FOIL

    1 pound medium raw shrimp, peeled and
      deveined
    1 cup sliced fresh mushrooms
    ¼ cup sliced green onions
    2 tablespoons margarine or butter
    ¼ cup REALEMON® Lemon Juice from
      Concentrate
    ½ to 1 teaspoon dried dill weed
    ½ teaspoon salt
    ⅛ teaspoon pepper
    2 tablespoons chopped parsley

On 4 large heavy-duty aluminum foil squares, place equal amounts of shrimp, mushrooms and green onions. Melt margarine; add ReaLemon® brand, dill weed, salt and pepper. Pour equal amounts over shrimp. Sprinkle with parsley. Fold and seal foil securely around shrimp. Grill 8 minutes or until shrimp are pink or bake in preheated 400° oven 12 to 15 minutes. Refrigerate leftovers.

                                        Makes 4 servings

GRILLED SALMON WITH CUCUMBER SAUCE

    ¾ cup HELLMANN'S® or BEST FOODS®
      Real, Light or Cholesterol Free
      Reduced Calorie Mayonnaise
    ¼ cup snipped fresh dill *or* 1 tablespoon
      dried dill weed
    1 tablespoon lemon juice
    6 salmon steaks (4 ounces each),
      ¾ inch thick
    1 small cucumber, seeded and chopped
    ½ cup chopped radishes
      Lemon wedges

In medium bowl combine mayonnaise, dill and lemon juice; reserve ½ cup for sauce. Brush fish steaks with remaining mayonnaise mixture. Grill 6 inches from heat, turning and brushing frequently with mayonnaise mixture, 6 to 8 minutes or until fish is firm but moist. Stir cucumber and radishes into reserved mayonnaise mixture. Serve fish with cucumber sauce and lemon wedges.

                                        Makes 6 servings

Swordfish with Leek Cream

SEAFOOD-VEGETABLE KABOBS

2 dozen large sea scallops
1 dozen medium shrimp, shelled and
    deveined
2 red or yellow peppers, cut into 2-inch
    pieces
1 can (8½ ounces) artichoke hearts,
    drained
¼ cup olive or vegetable oil
¼ cup lime juice

Combine all ingredients in bowl; toss gently. Thread scallops, shrimp, peppers and artichokes onto skewers; reserve marinade. Lightly oil grid. Grill kabobs, on uncovered grill, over low KINGSFORD® Briquets 6 to 8 minutes or until scallops turn opaque and shrimp turn pink. Turn kabobs twice during grilling; brush with reserved marinade.

Makes 6 servings

EASY BROILED ALBACORE

1 tablespoon vegetable oil
2 tablespoons lime juice
1 teaspoon Worcestershire sauce
1½ teaspoons dry mustard
1½ pounds skinned albacore tuna steaks or
    loin cuts, 1 inch thick
2 tablespoons grated lime peel

Combine oil, lime juice, Worcestershire sauce and mustard in small bowl to make basting sauce. Arrange albacore on well-greased grid. Baste with sauce. Grill, 4 to 5 inches from medium-hot coals, 6 to 8 minutes, turning fish halfway through cooking time and basting frequently. Albacore should be pink in center when removed from heat. Top with lime peel.

Makes 4 servings

Favorite Recipe from **National Fisheries Institute**

Seafood-Vegetable Kabobs

Grilled Rainbow Trout with Caponata Relish

GRILLED RAINBOW TROUT WITH CAPONATA RELISH

  2 tablespoons olive oil
  1 to 2 cloves garlic, crushed
  1 cup peeled and chopped eggplant or
      sliced mushrooms
  ½ cup chopped bell peppers (mix of green
      and yellow peppers)
  ½ cup chopped tomatoes
  2 tablespoons sliced ripe olives
  1 tablespoon capers
  1 teaspoon balsamic or red wine vinegar
  4 CLEAR SPRINGS® Brand Idaho
      Rainbow Trout fillets (4 ounces each)

In small saucepan, heat oil over medium heat; sauté garlic 1 minute. Add eggplant and peppers; stir quickly to coat. Sauté 5 minutes until softened. Add tomatoes, olives, capers and vinegar. Continue cooking 5 minutes longer; hold on very low heat. Over hot coals, place trout fillets, flesh side down, on oiled grid and cook about 2 minutes. Gently turn trout with spatula; continue cooking 2 minutes longer or until fish flakes easily with fork. Serve immediately topped with 2 tablespoons of caponata relish. *Makes 4 servings*

TERIYAKI FISH FILLETS

  1 can (20 ounces) DOLE® Pineapple
      Chunks in Juice
  1 clove garlic, pressed
  2 tablespoons slivered fresh ginger root
  1 tablespoon minced green onion
  5 teaspoons teriyaki sauce
  1 teaspoon white vinegar
  1 pound sole fillets
  2 teaspoons cornstarch
  1 teaspoon minced fresh ginger root
  1 teaspoon sesame oil

Measure 2 tablespoons juice from pineapple can; mix with garlic, slivered ginger, onion, 3 teaspoons teriyaki sauce and the vinegar. Arrange fish in shallow dish. Pour marinade over fish. Refrigerate 10 minutes. Drain fish; reserve marinade. Arrange fish on oiled grid. Brush with reserved marinade. Grill or broil 6 inches from heat 5 to 6 minutes or until fish flakes easily with fork.

In saucepan, combine remaining 2 teaspoons teriyaki sauce, undrained pineapple and remaining ingredients. Cook, stirring, until sauce boils and thickens. Serve with fish.
Makes 4 servings

Shark Steaks in Beer Marinade

SHARK STEAKS IN BEER MARINADE

2 pounds shark steaks or fillets, fresh or frozen
⅔ cup beer
⅓ cup vegetable oil
1 teaspoon salt
¼ teaspoon garlic powder
¼ teaspoon pepper
1 teaspoon prepared mustard
2 tablespoons butter or margarine
½ teaspoon paprika
4 cups sliced onions
1 cup sour cream, warmed
½ teaspoon prepared horseradish

Thaw fish, if frozen. Combine beer, oil, salt, garlic powder, pepper and mustard in shallow dish. Add fish. Marinate in refrigerator, covered, at least 30 minutes. Remove fish from marinade; discard marinade. Arrange fish on well-greased grid. Grill, 4 inches from medium-hot coals, 8 to 10 minutes or until fish flakes easily when tested with fork, turning fish over halfway through cooking.

Melt butter in medium saucepan over medium-high heat. Stir in paprika; add onions. Sauté until onions are tender but not brown. Combine warm sour cream and horseradish in small bowl. To serve, top each fish steak with onions and a spoonful of sour cream mixture.

Makes 6 servings

*Favorite Recipe from **Florida Department of National Resources***

CITRUS GRILLED WHOLE FISH WITH LIME BUTTER

1 whole fish (3 to 8 pounds), such as
  salmon, bluefish, red snapper or
  trout, with head and tail removed, if
  desired
  Vegetable oil
  Freshly ground black pepper
1 teaspoon grated lemon peel
1 or 2 limes, thinly sliced
1 or 2 lemons, thinly sliced
  Lime wedges
  Lime Butter (recipe follows)

Brush fish cavity with oil and season with
pepper and lemon peel. Overlap alternating
lime and lemon slices; place in cavity of fish.
Oil outside of fish thoroughly. Measure
thickness of fish at its thickest part. Place fish
in oiled fish basket. Or, make fish-turning
handles: Fold two 18×12-inch pieces of
heavy-duty foil in half 3 times to make two
18×1½-inch strips. Place fish on its side on foil
strips; wrap strips around fish and twist each at
the belly sides.

Bank hot coals on both sides of grill. Oil grid
and place 4 to 6 inches above coals. Place fish
on grid; grill 10 to 12 minutes per inch of
thickness. Baste with oil and turn fish over
halfway through cooking time (re-oil grid).
Fish is cooked when it flakes easily when
tested with fork and internal temperature is
140°F.

Place fish on warm serving platter. Lift off top
layer of skin, if desired. Cut top of fish
lengthwise along backbone. Slide wide spatula
between flesh and ribs and lift off each serving.
When top half of fish has been served, lift and
remove backbone. Cut down to skin to serve
remaining half. Serve with lime wedges and
Lime Butter.   *Makes 6 to 8 servings
for a 4-pound round fish*

Lime Butter: Combine ½ cup softened butter
or margarine, 2 to 3 tablespoons fresh lime
juice, 1 teaspoon grated lime peel and a dash of
salt in bowl or food processor. Beat or process
until soft and light.   *Makes about ½ cup*

*Favorite Recipe from **National Fisheries Institute***

GRILLED LEMON-MUSTARD TROUT

¼ cup fresh lemon juice
1 tablespoon Dijon-style mustard
2 cloves garlic, minced
⅛ teaspoon salt
⅛ teaspoon freshly ground white pepper
2 tablespoons olive oil
2 tablespoons chopped fresh chives
6 to 8 CLEAR SPRINGS® Brand Idaho
  Rainbow Trout fillets (4 ounces each)

Combine lemon juice, mustard, garlic, salt and
pepper; gradually whisk in oil. Stir in chives
and pour marinade over trout. Marinate trout
in refrigerator about 30 minutes.

Drain trout; reserve marinade. Over hot coals,
place trout, flesh side down, on oiled grill and
cook about 2 minutes. Use 2 spatulas to gently
turn trout; cook about 2 minutes longer until
done. Serve immediately. If desired, bring
reserved marinade to a boil and cook 1 minute;
serve with grilled trout.
          Makes 4 to 6 servings

ORIENTAL BARBECUED SCALLOPS

½ cup soy sauce
1 tablespoon sugar
2 tablespoons white wine
2 teaspoons lemon juice
1 teaspoon sesame oil
1 clove garlic, crushed
3 to 4 pounds large sea scallops

Mix all ingredients, except scallops, in large
bowl. Add scallops; cover and refrigerate
1 hour. Thread scallops on skewers; reserve
marinade. Grill scallops, on uncovered grill,
over medium-hot KINGSFORD® Briquets
10 minutes or until scallops turn opaque,
turning and brushing with reserved marinade.
          Makes 6 to 8 servings

Salads & Extras

Potato, vegetable, fruit and gelatin—all the great salad combinations for outdoor eating are here. The extras are the sauces and marinades that add flavor to barbecued foods.

RANCH PICNIC POTATO SALAD

    6 medium potatoes (about 3½ pounds),
        cooked, peeled and sliced
    ½ cup chopped celery
    ¼ cup sliced green onions
    2 tablespoons chopped parsley
    ¼ teaspoon salt
    ⅛ teaspoon black pepper
    1 tablespoon Dijon-style mustard
    1 cup prepared HIDDEN VALLEY
        RANCH® Original Ranch® Salad
        Dressing
    2 hard-cooked eggs, finely chopped
      Paprika
      Lettuce (optional)

In large bowl, combine potatoes, celery, onions, parsley, salt and pepper. In small bowl, stir mustard into salad dressing; pour over potatoes and toss lightly. Cover and refrigerate several hours. Sprinkle with eggs and paprika. Serve in lettuce-lined bowl, if desired.

Makes 8 servings

CALIFORNIA SALAD

    1 DOLE® Fresh Pineapple
    1 head DOLE® Iceberg Lettuce
    2 DOLE® Bananas, peeled, sliced
    8 ounces seedless DOLE® Grapes
    2 DOLE® Carrots, sliced
    1 tomato, cut into wedges
    ½ cucumber, sliced
    2 stalks DOLE® Celery, sliced
    ¼ cup DOLE® Whole Natural Almonds,
        toasted
      Date Dressing (recipe follows)

Twist crown from pineapple. Cut pineapple lengthwise into quarters. Remove fruit with curved knife. Trim off core and cut fruit into thin wedges. Line serving platter with lettuce leaves. Arrange half the pineapple and remaining fruits and vegetables on lettuce. Reserve remaining pineapple for another use. Sprinkle with almonds. Serve with Date Dressing. *Makes 6 servings*

Date Dressing: In 1-quart measure, combine ⅔ cup vegetable oil, ¼ cup raspberry vinegar, 1 tablespoon sugar, 2 teaspoons soy sauce, 1 teaspoon *each* curry powder and dry mustard and ½ teaspoon garlic salt. Stir in ⅓ cup DOLE® Chopped Dates.

Top to bottom: Ranch Picnic Potato Salad, California Salad

FRUIT SALAD WITH ORANGE-ALMOND DRESSING

1 head DOLE® Leaf Lettuce
½ DOLE® Cantaloupe, cut into chunks
2 cups DOLE® Fresh Pineapple chunks
1 cup sliced DOLE® Strawberries
1 cup seedless DOLE® Grapes
1 DOLE® Orange, peeled and sectioned
1 DOLE® Peach, sliced
½ cup DOLE® Whole Natural Almonds, toasted
   Orange-Almond Dressing (recipe follows)

Line large salad bowl with lettuce leaves. Arrange fruit on top; sprinkle with almonds. Serve with Orange-Almond Dressing.

Makes 6 to 8 servings

Orange-Almond Dressing: In 1-quart measure, combine 1 cup dairy sour cream, ½ cup mayonnaise, ¼ cup toasted DOLE® Chopped Natural Almonds, 2 tablespoons lemon juice and 2 teaspoons grated DOLE® Orange peel. Refrigerate, covered, until ready to serve.

COOL AND CREAMY FRUIT SALAD

1 (8-ounce) package PHILADELPHIA BRAND® Cream Cheese, softened
2 tablespoons lemon juice
1 teaspoon grated lemon peel
1 cup thawed COOL WHIP® Whipped Topping
2 cups peach slices
2 cups blueberries
2 cups strawberry slices
2 cups grapes
2 tablespoons chopped nuts

Combine cream cheese, juice and peel, mixing until well blended. Fold in whipped topping; chill. Layer fruit in 2½-quart serving bowl. Top with cream cheese mixture and nuts. Chill.

Makes 8 servings

Variation: Substitute Light PHILADELPHIA BRAND® Neufchâtel Cheese for Cream Cheese.

SPARKLING BERRY SALAD

2 envelopes KNOX® Unflavored Gelatine
2 cups cranberry-raspberry juice, divided
⅓ cup sugar
1 cup club soda
¼ cup creme de cassis (black currant) liqueur (optional)
1 teaspoon lemon juice
1 teaspoon fresh grated orange peel (optional)
3 cups assorted blueberries, raspberries or strawberries
   Sour cream (optional)

In medium saucepan, sprinkle unflavored gelatine over 1 cup cranberry-raspberry juice; let stand 1 minute. Stir over low heat until gelatine is completely dissolved, about 5 minutes. Stir in sugar until dissolved.

In large bowl, blend remaining 1 cup cranberry-raspberry juice, soda, gelatine mixture, liqueur, lemon juice and orange peel. Chill, stirring occasionally, until mixture is consistency of unbeaten egg whites, about 60 minutes. Fold in berries. Pour into 6-cup mold or bowl; chill until firm, about 3 hours. Unmold and serve, if desired, with sour cream.

Makes about 8 servings

Fruit Salad with Orange-Almond Dressing

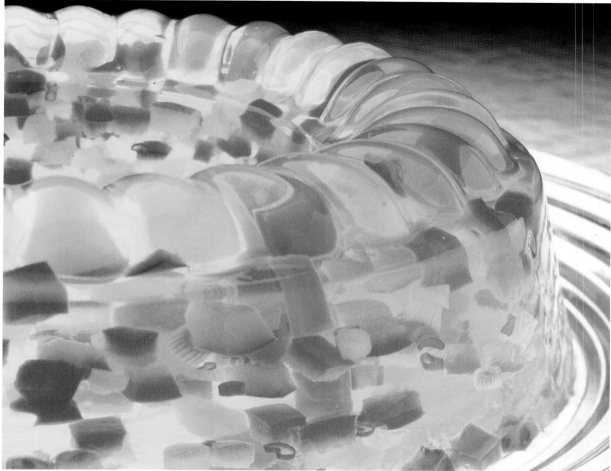

Three Pepper Salad

THREE PEPPER SALAD

---

  2 packages (4-serving size each) *or*
      1 package (8-serving size) JELL-O®
      Brand Gelatin, Lemon Flavor
  2 cups boiling water
1½ cups cold water
  2 tablespoons lemon juice
  2 cups chopped red, green and/or yellow
      peppers
  2 tablespoons sliced scallions
     Salsa Dressing (recipe follows) (optional)

Dissolve gelatin in boiling water. Stir in cold
water and lemon juice. Chill until thickened.
Fold in peppers and scallions. Pour gelatin
mixture into 5-cup mold. Chill until firm,
about 4 hours. Unmold. Cut into slices; serve
with Salsa Dressing, if desired.

Makes 10 servings

SALSA DRESSING
  ½ cup MIRACLE WHIP® Salad Dressing
  ½ cup sour cream
  ½ cup prepared salsa

Mix together ingredients until well blended.
Chill.   *Makes 1½ cups*

TANGY HONEY SAUCE

---

  1 cup catsup
  ¼ cup honey
  1 tablespoon prepared mustard
  ½ teaspoon ground nutmeg

Combine all ingredients; mix thoroughly.
Makes 1¼ cups

Serving Tip: Spread on meatloaf, pork loin,
ribs or chicken pieces during last 15 minutes of
baking or serve as dipping sauce.

*Favorite Recipe from **National Honey Board***

Classic Spinach Salad

CLASSIC SPINACH SALAD

½ pound fresh spinach leaves (about
    10 cups)
1 cup sliced mushrooms
1 medium tomato, cut into wedges
⅓ cup seasoned croutons
¼ cup chopped red onion
4 slices bacon, crisp-cooked and crumbled
½ cup WISH-BONE® Lite Classic Dijon
    Vinaigrette Dressing
1 hard-cooked egg, sliced

In large salad bowl, combine spinach,
mushrooms, tomato, croutons, red onion and
bacon. Add lite classic Dijon vinaigrette
dressing and toss gently. Garnish with egg.
Makes about 6 side-dish servings

DOLE® SUMMER VEGETABLE SALAD

1 head DOLE® Lettuce
2 tomatoes
1 cucumber
½ DOLE® Red Bell Pepper
¼ DOLE® Red Onion
1 cup sliced DOLE® Celery
1 cup snow peas, ends and strings removed
1 cup sliced DOLE® Cauliflower
    Dill Dressing (recipe follows)

Tear lettuce into bite-size pieces. Cut tomatoes
into wedges. Slice cucumber, red pepper and
red onion. Toss all vegetables in salad bowl
with Dill Dressing.   *Makes 4 servings*

Dill Dressing: In 1-quart measure, combine
½ cup *each* dairy sour cream and mayonnaise,
1 tablespoon vinegar, 1 teaspoon *each* dried
dill weed and onion powder, 1 teaspoon Dijon-
style mustard, ¾ teaspoon garlic salt and
cracked pepper to taste. Refrigerate, covered,
until ready to serve.

BARLEY WITH CORN AND RED PEPPER

½ cup WISH-BONE® Italian Dressing*
1 medium red pepper, chopped
½ cup chopped onion
1 cup uncooked pearled barley
1¾ cups chicken broth
1¼ cups water
2 tablespoons finely chopped coriander (cilantro) or parsley
1 tablespoon lime juice
½ teaspoon ground cumin
⅛ teaspoon pepper
1 can (7 ounces) whole kernel corn, drained

In large saucepan, heat Italian dressing; add red pepper and onion. Cook over medium heat, stirring occasionally, 5 minutes or until tender. Stir in barley and cook, stirring constantly, 1 minute. Stir in broth, water, coriander, lime juice, cumin and pepper. Simmer covered 50 minutes or until barley is done. (Do not stir while simmering.) Stir in corn.   *Makes about 6 servings*

*Also terrific with WISH-BONE® Robusto Italian, Herbal Italian, Lite Italian, Blended Italian or Lite Classic Dijon Vinaigrette Dressing.

Country Cole Slaw

COUNTRY COLE SLAW

1 cup HELLMANN'S® or BEST FOODS® Real, Light or Cholesterol Free Reduced Calorie Mayonnaise
3 tablespoons lemon juice
2 tablespoons sugar
1 teaspoon salt
6 cups shredded cabbage
1 cup shredded carrots
½ cup chopped or thinly sliced green pepper

In medium bowl, combine mayonnaise, lemon juice, sugar and salt. Stir in cabbage, carrots and green pepper. Cover; chill.
                    Makes about 10 servings

RAITA
(Cucumber and Yogurt Salad)

3 medium cucumbers, peeled, seeded and thinly sliced
1 tablespoon minced onion
2 cups plain yogurt
½ teaspoon pepper
¼ teaspoon cumin
2 tablespoons cilantro, chopped

Mix together all ingredients. Chill for 2 to 24 hours to develop flavors.
                    Makes 4 to 6 servings
*Favorite Recipe from the **National Pork Producers Council***

Barley with Corn and Red Pepper

EASY MACARONI SALAD

    1 cup HELLMANN'S® or BEST FOODS®
        Real, Light or Cholesterol Free
        Reduced Calorie Mayonnaise
    2 tablespoons vinegar
    1 tablespoon prepared yellow mustard
    1 teaspoon sugar
    1 teaspoon salt
    ¼ teaspoon freshly ground black pepper
    8 ounces elbow macaroni, cooked, rinsed
        with cold water and drained
    1 cup sliced celery
    1 cup chopped green or red bell pepper
    ¼ cup chopped onion

In large bowl, combine mayonnaise, vinegar, mustard, sugar, salt and black pepper. Add macaroni, celery, green pepper and onion; toss to coat well. Cover; chill. Garnish as desired.

Makes about 8 servings

Note: If desired, stir in milk for a creamier salad.

CREAMY ITALIAN PASTA SALAD

    1 cup HELLMANN'S® or BEST FOODS®
        Real, Light or Cholesterol Free
        Reduced Calorie Mayonnaise
    2 tablespoons red wine vinegar
    1 clove garlic, minced
    1 tablespoon chopped fresh basil *or*
        1 teaspoon dried basil leaves
    1 teaspoon salt
    ¼ teaspoon freshly ground black pepper
    1½ cups twist or spiral pasta, cooked, rinsed
        with cold water and drained
    1 cup quartered cherry tomatoes
    ½ cup coarsely chopped green pepper
    ½ cup slivered pitted ripe olives

In large bowl, combine mayonnaise, vinegar, garlic, basil, salt and pepper. Stir in pasta, cherry tomatoes, green pepper and olives. Cover; chill.

Makes about 6 servings

CRANBERRY-APPLE WALDORF

    2 envelopes KNOX® Unflavored Gelatine
    ⅓ cup sugar
    ½ cup boiling water
    3½ cups cranberry juice cocktail
    1 cup chopped apple
    ½ cup chopped celery
    ⅓ cup chopped walnuts
    Lettuce (optional)

In large bowl, mix unflavored gelatine with sugar; add boiling water and stir until gelatine is completely dissolved, about 5 minutes. Stir in cranberry juice. Chill, stirring occasionally, until mixture is consistency of unbeaten egg whites, about 45 minutes. Fold in remaining ingredients. Pour into 8-inch square baking pan; chill until firm, about 3 hours. To serve, cut into 4-inch squares and serve, if desired, on lettuce-lined plates.

Makes about 4 servings

GRAPES AND SPINACH SALAD

    Chutney Dressing (recipe follows)
    1 pound spinach, washed, drained
    1 cup California seedless grapes
    1 apple, cored and diced
    ⅓ cup dry roasted peanuts
    2 tablespoons chopped green onion
    1 tablespoon toasted sesame seeds

Prepare Chutney Dressing. Tear spinach into bite-size pieces. Toss with grapes, apple, peanuts, green onion and sesame seeds in bowl. Toss with Chutney Dressing to coat well.

Makes 6 servings

Chutney Dressing: Combine 3 tablespoons vegetable oil, 2 tablespoons white wine vinegar, 1 tablespoon chopped chutney, ¼ teaspoon curry powder, ¼ teaspoon salt, ¼ teaspoon dry mustard and dash bottled hot pepper sauce in small bowl; mix well.

Makes about ⅓ cup

Favorite Recipe from California Table Grape Commission

Top to bottom: Easy Macaroni Salad,
Creamy Italian Pasta Salad

In small saucepan over medium heat, melt 3 tablespoons of the butter. Whisk in flour until smooth, about 1 minute. Reserve.

In 10-inch skillet over high heat, melt remaining 8 tablespoons butter. When it comes to a hard sizzle, add almonds, Seafood Magic and celery. Cook, stirring frequently at first and constantly near end of cooking time, about 8 minutes or until almonds are browned. Stir in honey and cook, stirring frequently, about 1 minute. Stir in lemon peel and stock. Cook, stirring occasionally, about 8 minutes. Add nutmeg; cook 3 minutes, stirring occasionally. Whisk in reserved butter mixture until it is incorporated and sauce is slightly thickened, 30 to 60 seconds. Remove from heat.

Makes about 2½ cups

Note: This glaze is wonderful on grilled seafood, chicken and pork. Brush it on right before meat is ready to come off the grill and bring some to the table for dipping.

ONION-MOLASSES BARBECUE SAUCE

    4 tablespoons margarine
    2 tablespoons walnut or vegetable oil
    2 tablespoons olive oil
    3 cups chopped onions
    3 tablespoons CHEF PAUL
        PRUDHOMME'S POULTRY MAGIC®
    ¾ cup light molasses
    1 cup cider vinegar
    ¼ cup freshly squeezed orange juice
    ½ teaspoon dried dill weed
    ½ cup chicken stock or water

In 10-inch skillet over high heat, melt margarine with walnut oil and olive oil. When it comes to a hard sizzle, add onions and Poultry Magic. Stir to mix well and cook, stirring frequently, about 8 minutes or until onions are browned. Stir in molasses, mixing well. Add vinegar, orange juice and dill weed. Stir well and cook about 12 minutes, stirring frequently. Stir in stock and cook about 2 minutes more for flavors to blend.

Makes about 3 cups

Note: This sauce was created for anything that can be grilled. Just mop it on generously near the end of cooking time.

Top to bottom: Honey Almond Grilling Glaze, Onion-Molasses Barbecue Sauce

HONEY ALMOND GRILLING GLAZE

    11 tablespoons unsalted butter, in all
    2 tablespoons all-purpose flour
    1 cup slivered almonds
    2 tablespoons CHEF PAUL
        PRUDHOMME'S SEAFOOD MAGIC®
    1 cup chopped celery
    1 cup honey
    1 teaspoon grated fresh lemon peel
    1 cup chicken stock or water
    ⅛ teaspoon ground nutmeg

ORANGE-BERRY SALAD

½ cup prepared HIDDEN VALLEY
RANCH® Original Ranch® Salad
Dressing
2 tablespoons orange juice
1 teaspoon grated orange peel
½ cup heavy cream, whipped
1 can (11 ounces) mandarin orange
segments
2 packages (3 ounces each) strawberry- or
raspberry-flavored gelatin
1 can (16 ounces) whole-berry cranberry
sauce
½ cup walnut pieces
Mint sprigs
Whole fresh strawberries and
raspberries

In large bowl, whisk together salad dressing, orange juice and peel. Fold in whipped cream; cover and refrigerate. Drain oranges, reserving juice. Add water to juice to measure 3 cups; pour into large saucepan and bring to boil. Stir in gelatin until dissolved. Cover and refrigerate until partially set. Fold orange segments, cranberry sauce and walnuts into gelatin. Pour into lightly oiled 6-cup ring mold. Cover and refrigerate until firm; unmold. Garnish with mint and fresh strawberries and raspberries. Serve with chilled dressing.

Makes 8 servings

Orange-Berry Salad

THREE BEAN RICE SALAD

1 can (16 ounces) cut wax beans, drained
1 can (16 ounces) French-style green
beans, drained
1 can (8¾ ounces) red kidney beans,
drained
½ cup prepared GOOD SEASONS® Italian
Salad Dressing
¼ cup thinly sliced onion rings
1 teaspoon salt
⅛ teaspoon pepper
1½ cups water
1½ cups Original MINUTE® Rice or
MINUTE® Premium Long Grain Rice
Lettuce

Mix beans, salad dressing, onion, ½ teaspoon
of the salt and the pepper in large bowl; set
aside to allow flavors to blend.

Meanwhile, bring water and remaining
½ teaspoon salt to a full boil in medium
saucepan. Stir in rice. Cover; remove from
heat. Let stand 5 minutes. Fold rice into bean
mixture. Cover and chill thoroughly. Serve on
lettuce. *Makes 6 servings*

Three Bean Rice Salad

VERSATILE BARBECUE SAUCE

¼ cup chopped onion
1 clove garlic, finely chopped
2 tablespoons margarine or butter
1 cup ketchup
⅓ cup firmly packed brown sugar
¼ cup REALEMON® Lemon Juice from
Concentrate
1 tablespoon Worcestershire sauce
2 teaspoons WYLER'S® or STEERO®
Beef- or Chicken-Flavor Instant
Bouillon *or* 2 Beef- or Chicken-Flavor
Bouillon Cubes
1 teaspoon prepared mustard

In small saucepan, cook onion and garlic in
margarine until tender. Add remaining
ingredients; bring to a boil. Reduce heat;
simmer uncovered 20 minutes, stirring
occasionally. Use as a basting sauce for beef,
chicken or pork. Refrigerate leftovers.
Makes about 1½ cups

To microwave: In 1-quart glass measure, melt
margarine on 100% power (high) 30 to
45 seconds. Add onion and garlic; cook on
100% power (high) 1½ to 2 minutes or until
tender. Add remaining ingredients. Cook
loosely covered on 100% power (high) 3 to
5 minutes or until mixture boils; stir. Reduce
to 50% power (medium); cook covered 4 to
5 minutes to blend flavors.

CLASSIC WALDORF SALAD

½ cup HELLMANN'S® or BEST FOODS®
Real, Light or Cholesterol Free
Reduced Calorie Mayonnaise
1 tablespoon sugar
1 tablespoon lemon juice
⅛ teaspoon salt
3 medium-size red apples, cored and diced
1 cup sliced celery
½ cup chopped walnuts

In medium bowl, combine mayonnaise, sugar,
lemon juice and salt. Add apples and celery;
toss to coat well. Cover; chill. Just before
serving, sprinkle with walnuts.
Makes about 8 servings

VINAIGRETTE MARINADE

⅓ cup vegetable oil
⅓ cup sliced green onions
¼ cup REALEMON® Lemon Juice from Concentrate
5 teaspoons Dijon-style mustard
1½ teaspoons WYLER'S® or STEERO® Chicken- or Beef-Flavor Instant Bouillon
1 teaspoon sugar
¼ teaspoon garlic powder

In shallow dish or plastic bag, combine ingredients; add chicken, beef, pork or fish. Cover; marinate in refrigerator 4 hours or overnight, turning occasionally. Remove meat from marinade; grill or broil as desired, basting frequently with marinade. Refrigerate leftover meat. *Makes about ¾ cup*

MEXICAN COLESLAW SALAD

1 envelope KNOX® Unflavored Gelatine
1 cup cold water
1 pint (16 ounces) sour cream
½ cup mayonnaise
2 cups shredded and coarsely chopped red or green cabbage
1 medium tomato, seeded and coarsely chopped
2 green onions, chopped (about ¼ cup)
2 tablespoons finely chopped coriander (cilantro) or parsley
1 tablespoon chili powder
1 tablespoon lime juice
1 teaspoon salt
½ teaspoon ground cumin
⅛ teaspoon pepper
Red or green cabbage leaves

In medium saucepan, sprinkle unflavored gelatine over cold water; let stand 1 minute. Stir over low heat until gelatine is completely dissolved, about 5 minutes.

In large bowl, with wire whisk or rotary beater, thoroughly blend gelatine mixture, sour cream and mayonnaise. Stir in remaining ingredients except cabbage leaves. Turn into 6-cup bowl lined with cabbage leaves or 6-cup mold; chill until firm, about 3 hours. Unmold onto serving platter. *Makes about 12 servings*

California Fruit Salad

CALIFORNIA FRUIT SALAD

¼ cup HELLMANN'S® or BEST FOODS® Real, Light or Cholesterol Free Reduced Calorie Mayonnaise
¼ cup sour cream
1 tablespoon honey
1 teaspoon lime juice
½ teaspoon grated lime peel
2 cantaloupes, cut into half crosswise and seeded
4 cups assorted fresh fruit (strawberries, blueberries, honeydew melon and cantaloupe)
½ cup (2 ounces) crumbled blue cheese

In medium bowl, combine mayonnaise, sour cream, honey, lime juice and lime peel. Cover; chill. To serve, fill each cantaloupe half with 1 cup mixed fresh fruit. Sprinkle each with 2 tablespoons blue cheese; top with 2 tablespoon dressing. Garnish as desired. *Makes 4 servings*

Tempting Treats

These desserts are a delightful ending to an outdoor meal—they also make terrific indoor snacks!

GIANT RAISIN-CHIP FRISBEES

    1 cup butter or margarine, softened
    1 cup packed brown sugar
    ½ cup granulated sugar
    2 eggs
    1 teaspoon vanilla
1½ cups all-purpose flour
    ¼ cup unsweetened cocoa
    1 teaspoon baking soda
    1 cup (6 ounces) semisweet chocolate chips
    ¾ cup raisins
    ¾ cup chopped walnuts

Preheat oven to 350°F. Line cookie sheets with parchment paper or lightly grease and dust with flour. Cream butter with sugars in large bowl. Add eggs and vanilla; beat until light. Combine flour, cocoa and baking soda in small bowl. Add to creamed mixture with chocolate chips, raisins and walnuts; stir until well blended. Scoop out about ½ cupful of dough for each cookie. Place on prepared cookie sheets, spacing about 5 inches apart. Using knife dipped in water, smooth balls of dough out to 3½ inches in diameter. Bake 10 to 12 minutes or until golden. Remove to wire rack to cool.   *Makes about 16 cookies*

RICH AND CREAMY PEACH ICE CREAM

    2 eggs*
    2 cups sugar
    ½ cup milk
    3 cups whipping cream
    6 large *or* 10 medium fresh California
        peaches, pitted, quartered

Beat eggs until foamy. Gradually beat in sugar until thick and lemon colored. Mix in milk and cream. Purée peaches in blender to measure 5 cups. Combine with egg mixture in ice cream container. Prepare in ice cream maker according to manufacturer's directions. Ice cream will not be solid but should be just holding its shape. Pack into freezing containers and freeze solid.   *Makes about 3 quarts*
*Favorite Recipe from **California Tree Fruit Agreement***

*Use clean, uncracked eggs.

Left to right: Giant Raisin-Chip Frisbees, Rich and Creamy Peach Ice Cream

Hershey's Syrup Pie

HERSHEY'S SYRUP PIE

9-inch baked pastry shell *or* 8-inch
    (6 ounces) packaged graham cracker
    crumb crust
2 egg yolks
⅓ cup cornstarch
¼ teaspoon salt
1¾ cups milk
1 cup HERSHEY'S Syrup
1 teaspoon vanilla extract
    Syrup Whipped Topping (recipe follows)
    Fresh fruit

In medium microwave-safe bowl beat egg
yolks. Add cornstarch, salt, milk and syrup;
blend well. Microwave at MEDIUM-HIGH
(70%) 6 to 8 minutes, stirring every 2 minutes
with whisk, or until mixture is smooth and
very thick. Stir in vanilla. Pour into crust. Press
plastic wrap directly onto surface; chill several
hours or overnight. Garnish with Syrup
Whipped Topping and fresh fruit.

Makes 6 to 8 servings

Syrup Whipped Topping: In small mixer bowl
combine 1 cup chilled whipping cream, ½ cup
HERSHEY'S Syrup, 2 tablespoons powdered
sugar and ½ teaspoon vanilla extract. Beat just
until cream holds definite shape; do not
overbeat. *Makes about 2¼ cups topping*

BROWNIE FRUIT PIZZA

1 (12.9- *or* 15-ounce) package fudge
    brownie mix
1 (8-ounce) package cream cheese,
    softened
1 (14-ounce) can EAGLE® Brand
    Sweetened Condensed Milk (NOT
    evaporated milk)
½ cup frozen pineapple or orange juice
    concentrate, thawed
1 teaspoon vanilla extract
    Assorted fresh or canned fruit
    (strawberries, bananas, kiwifruit,
    orange, pineapple, etc.)

Preheat oven to 350°. Prepare brownie mix as
package directs. On greased pizza pan or
baking sheet, spread batter into 12-inch circle.
Bake 15 to 20 minutes. Meanwhile, in small
mixer bowl, beat cheese until fluffy. Gradually
beat in sweetened condensed milk until
smooth. Stir in juice concentrate and vanilla.
Chill thoroughly. Just before serving, spoon
filling over cooled brownie crust. Arrange fruit
on top. Refrigerate leftovers.

Makes one 12-inch pizza

GRAPE YOGURT POPS

2 cups (1 pint) plain low-fat yogurt
1 can (6 ounces) frozen orange juice
    concentrate, partially thawed
⅓ cup sugar
8 (4 ounces each) waxed paper cups
2 cups red, green or blue/black California
    grapes, halved and seeded, if
    necessary
8 popsicle sticks

Combine yogurt, orange concentrate and sugar;
stir until concentrate melts and sugar is
dissolved. Pour into paper cups, dividing
evenly. Drop ¼ cup grapes into each cup.
Freeze until almost firm. Insert stick in center
of cup. Freeze until firm. If made ahead, wrap
each in plastic wrap to prevent dehydration. To
serve, peel off paper cup.

Makes 8 servings

*Favorite Recipe from **California Table Grape Commission***

Beat-the-Heat Cheesecake

BEAT-THE-HEAT CHEESECAKE

Graham Cracker-Almond Crust (recipe
  follows)
2 envelopes KNOX® Unflavored Gelatine
¾ cup sugar
1 cup boiling water
2 packages (8 ounces each) cream cheese,
  softened
1 cup (8 ounces) creamed cottage cheese
1 cup (½ pint) whipping or heavy cream
1 tablespoon vanilla extract
1 tablespoon fresh grated lemon peel
  (optional)
Fruit for garnish (optional)

Prepare Graham Cracker-Almond Crust. In
large bowl, mix unflavored gelatine with ¼ cup
sugar; add boiling water and stir until gelatine
is completely dissolved, about 5 minutes. With
electric mixer, add remaining ½ cup sugar,
cream cheese, cottage cheese, cream, vanilla
and lemon peel, one at a time, beating well
after each addition. Continue beating an
additional 5 minutes or until mixture is
smooth. Turn into Graham Cracker-Almond
Crust; chill until firm, about 5 hours. Garnish
with fruit, if desired.

Makes about 12 servings

Graham Cracker-Almond Crust: In small
bowl, combine 1 cup graham cracker crumbs,
½ cup ground almonds, 2 tablespoons sugar,
¼ cup melted butter or margarine and
½ teaspoon almond extract. Press onto bottom
and side of 9-inch springform pan; chill.

PEACH MELBA DESSERT

1 package (4-serving size) JELL-O® Brand
    Gelatin, Peach Flavor
2 cups boiling water
¾ cup cold water
1 package (4-serving size) JELL-O® Brand
    Gelatin, Raspberry Flavor
1 pint vanilla ice cream, softened
1 can (8¾ ounces) sliced peaches,
    drained*
½ cup fresh raspberries
    Mint leaves (optional)

Dissolve peach flavor gelatin in 1 cup of the
boiling water. Add cold water. Chill until
slightly thickened.

Dissolve raspberry flavor gelatin in remaining
1 cup boiling water. Spoon in ice cream,
stirring until melted and smooth. Pour into
serving bowl. Chill until set but not firm.

Arrange peach slices and raspberries on ice
cream mixture in bowl. Add mint leaves, if
desired. Spoon peach gelatin over fruit. Chill
until firm, about 3 hours.

Makes 10 servings

*1 fresh peach, peeled and sliced, may be
substituted for canned peaches.

Peach Melba Dessert

HONEY BERRY SAUCE

1 cup *each* frozen blackberries,
    blueberries and raspberries
¾ cup cranberry juice
¼ cup honey
1½ teaspoons grated orange peel

Combine berries and thaw; drain and reserve
½ cup liquid. Combine cranberry juice,
reserved liquid and honey in small saucepan;
bring to boil over high heat. Reduce heat to
medium; simmer about 10 minutes or until
mixture is reduced to 1 cup. Remove from
heat; stir in orange peel. Cool; pour over
berries. Chill until serving time. Spoon over
ice cream or fruit sherbet.   *Makes 3 cups*

Storage Tip: Refrigerate in covered container
up to 1 week.

Favorite Recipe from **National Honey Board**

BANANA FUDGE POPS

1 ripe, medium banana
1½ cups orange-banana juice
½ cup sugar
¼ cup HERSHEY'S Cocoa
1 can (5 ounces) evaporated milk
6 paper cold drink cups (5 ounces each)
6 wooden popsicle sticks

Slice banana into blender container; add juice.
Cover; blend until smooth. Add sugar and
cocoa; cover and blend well. Add evaporated
milk; cover and blend. Pour mixture into cups.
Freeze about 1 hour; insert popsicle sticks into
fudge pops. Cover; freeze until firm. Peel off
cups to serve.   *Makes 6 pops*

ICE CREAM COOKIES

2 squares (1 ounce each) unsweetened
    chocolate
1 cup butter, softened
1 cup powdered sugar
4 egg yolks
1 teaspoon vanilla
3 cups all-purpose flour
    Powdered sugar

Ice Cream Cookie Sandwiches

Melt chocolate in top of double boiler over hot,
not boiling, water. Remove from heat; cool.
Cream butter and 1 cup sugar in large bowl
until blended. Add egg yolks, vanilla and
melted chocolate; beat until light. Blend in
flour to make stiff dough. Divide dough into
4 parts. Shape each part into a roll, about
1½ inches in diameter. Wrap in plastic wrap;
refrigerate until firm, at least 30 minutes or up
to 2 weeks. (For longer storage, freeze up to
6 weeks.)

Preheat oven to 350°F. Line cookie sheets with
parchment paper or leave ungreased. Cut rolls
into ⅛-inch-thick slices; place 2 inches apart
on ungreased cookie sheets. Bake 8 to
10 minutes or just until set, but not browned.
Remove to wire racks to cool. Dust with
powdered sugar.

Makes about 8 dozen cookies

Ice Cream Cookie Sandwiches: Prepare and
bake cookies as directed; cool completely.
Spread desired amount of softened ice cream
on bottoms of half the cookies. Top with
remaining cookies, bottom sides down,
forming sandwiches. Dust tops with powdered
sugar; serve immediately.

Makes about 4 dozen sandwich cookies

Berried Delight

BERRIED DELIGHT

1½ cups graham cracker crumbs
 ½ cup sugar
 ⅓ cup PARKAY® Margarine, melted
 1 package (8 ounces) PHILADELPHIA
     BRAND® Cream Cheese, softened
2⅔ cups cold milk
3½ cups (8 ounces) COOL WHIP® Whipped
     Topping, thawed
 2 pints strawberries, hulled and halved
 1 package (6-serving size) JELL-O®
     Instant Pudding and Pie Filling,
     French Vanilla or Vanilla Flavor

Combine crumbs and ¼ cup of the sugar. Mix
in margarine. Press mixture evenly onto
bottom of 13×9-inch pan. (If desired, bake at
375°F for 8 minutes. Cool on rack.)

Beat cream cheese with remaining ¼ cup
sugar and 2 tablespoons of the milk until
smooth. Fold in ½ of the whipped topping.
Spread over crust. Arrange strawberries in
even layer on cream cheese mixture.

Pour remaining milk into medium bowl. Add
pudding mix. Beat with wire whisk until well
blended, 1 to 2 minutes. Pour over
strawberries. Chill 4 hours or overnight.

Spread remaining whipped topping over
pudding just before serving. Garnish with
additional strawberries, if desired.
                            Makes 18 servings

FRESH STRAWBERRY PIE

 1 (9-inch) baked pastry shell
1¼ cups sugar
 1 tablespoon cornstarch
1½ cups water
 3 tablespoons REALEMON® Lemon Juice
     from Concentrate
 1 (4-serving size) package strawberry
     flavor gelatin
 1 quart fresh strawberries, cleaned and
     hulled (about 1½ pounds)

In medium saucepan, combine sugar and
cornstarch; add water and ReaLemon® brand.
Over high heat, bring to a boil. Reduce heat;
cook, stirring occasionally, until slightly
thickened and clear, 4 to 5 minutes. Add
gelatin; stir until dissolved. Chill until
thickened but not set, about 1 hour. Stir in
strawberries; spoon into prepared pastry shell.
Chill 4 to 6 hours or until set. Refrigerate
leftovers.   *Makes one 9-inch pie*

To microwave: In 2-quart glass measure,
combine sugar and cornstarch; add water and
ReaLemon® brand. Cook on 100% power (high)
6 to 8 minutes, or until slightly thickened and
bubbly, stirring every 2 minutes. Proceed as
above.

Fresh Strawberry Pie

PEACH SURPRISE PIE

2 (8-ounce) packages PHILADELPHIA
    BRAND® "Light" Neufchâtel Cheese,
    softened
¼ cup sugar
½ teaspoon vanilla
    Pastry for 1-crust 9-inch pie, baked
1 (16-ounce) can peach slices, drained
¼ cup KRAFT® Red Raspberry Preserves
1 teaspoon lemon juice
    Fresh mint (optional)

Combine neufchâtel cheese, sugar and vanilla,
mixing until well blended. Spread onto bottom
of crust; chill several hours or overnight. Top
with peaches just before serving. Combine
preserves and juice, mixing until well blended.
Spoon over peaches. Garnish with fresh mint,
if desired.   *Makes 6 to 8 servings*

AMBROSIA

1 can (20 ounces) DOLE® Pineapple
    Chunks in Juice
1 can (11 ounces) DOLE® Mandarin
    Orange Segments in Syrup
1 firm, large DOLE® Banana, peeled,
    sliced (optional)
1½ cups seedless DOLE® Grapes
1 cup miniature marshmallows
1 cup flaked coconut
½ cup pecan halves or coarsely chopped
    nuts
1 cup dairy sour cream or plain yogurt
1 tablespoon brown sugar

Drain pineapple and orange segments. In large
bowl, combine pineapple, orange segments,
banana, grapes, marshmallows, coconut and
nuts. In 1-quart measure, combine sour cream
and brown sugar. Stir into fruit mixture.
Refrigerate, covered, 1 hour or overnight.
                              Makes 4 servings

Creamy Orange Mold

CREAMY ORANGE MOLD

2 packages (4-serving size each) *or*
    1 package (8-serving size)
    JELL-O® Brand Gelatin, Orange
    Flavor
2 cups boiling water
1 pint vanilla ice cream, softened
¾ cup orange juice
    Orange slices (optional)
    Strawberry halves (optional)
    Mint leaves (optional)

Dissolve gelatin in boiling water. Spoon in ice
cream, stirring until melted and smooth. Stir in
orange juice. Pour into 5-cup mold. Chill until
firm, about 4 hours. Unmold. Garnish with
orange slices, strawberry halves and mint
leaves, if desired.   *Makes 10 servings*

Refreshing Coolers

The coolers, mocktails and cocktails featured here are wonderful for sipping during a relaxing summer afternoon or evening.

THE MAIDEN MARY

2½ cups Florida grapefruit juice
2 cups tomato juice
1 cup clam juice
2 teaspoons Worcestershire sauce
Dash hot pepper sauce
Ice cubes

In 2-quart pitcher, combine grapefruit juice, tomato juice, clam juice, Worcestershire and hot pepper sauce; blend well. Add ice cubes. Pour into serving glasses. Garnish as desired.

Makes 4 servings
Favorite Recipe from Florida Department of Citrus

ORANGE FANTASIA

1½ cups Florida orange juice
1 cup (½ pint) orange sherbet
Cracked ice (optional)

Pour orange juice into blender container; add orange sherbet. Cover and process at medium speed until smooth. Or, sherbet may be softened slightly, added to orange juice and beaten with rotary beater until smooth. If desired, pour over cracked ice. Garnish as desired. *Makes 2½ cups or 2 servings*
Favorite Recipe from Florida Department of Citrus

LEMONADE

½ cup sugar
½ cup REALEMON® Lemon Juice from Concentrate
3¼ cups cold water
Ice cubes

In large pitcher, dissolve sugar in ReaLemon® brand; add water. Serve over ice. Garnish as desired. *Makes about 1 quart*

Sparkling Lemonade: Substitute club soda for cold water.

Slushy Lemonade: In blender container, combine ReaLemon® brand and sugar with ½ cup water. Gradually add 4 cups ice cubes, blending until smooth. Serve immediately.

Pink Lemonade: Stir in 1 to 2 teaspoons grenadine syrup *or* 1 to 2 drops red food coloring.

Minted Lemonade: Stir in 2 to 3 drops peppermint extract.

Low Calorie: Omit sugar. Add 4 to 8 envelopes sugar substitute *or* 1½ teaspoons liquid sugar substitute.

Left to right: The Maiden Mary, Orange Fantasia, Lemonade

Top to bottom: Strawberry-Banana Shake, Banana Shake

BANANA SHAKE

2 ripe bananas, cut up (about 2 cups)
⅓ cup REALEMON® Lemon Juice from Concentrate
1 cup cold water
1 (14-ounce) can EAGLE® Brand Sweetened Condensed Milk (NOT evaporated milk)
2 cups ice cubes

In blender container, combine all ingredients except ice; blend well. Gradually add ice; blend until smooth. Garnish as desired. Refrigerate leftovers. (Mixture stays thick and creamy in refrigerator.)

Makes about 5 cups

Strawberry-Banana Shake: Reduce bananas to ½ cup; add 1½ cups fresh strawberries *or* 1 cup frozen unsweetened strawberries, partially thawed. Proceed as above.

Mixer Method: Omit ice cubes. In large mixer bowl, mash bananas; gradually beat in ReaLemon® brand, sweetened condensed milk and 2½ cups cold water. Chill before serving.

PINA COLADA MOCKTAIL

1 can (6 ounces) frozen limeade concentrate, thawed
6 cups DOLE® Pine-Passion-Banana Juice, chilled
2 bottles (28 ounces each) mineral water, chilled
1 can (15 ounces) real cream of coconut
Lime slices for garnish
DOLE® Orange slices for garnish
Mint sprigs for garnish

Reconstitute limeade according to label directions in large punch bowl. Add remaining ingredients. *Makes 24 servings*

MAI TAI SLUSH

1½ cups DOLE® Pineapple Juice
1 pint lemon sherbet
2 ounces rum
2 tablespoons triple sec
1 cup crushed ice
Lime slices for garnish (optional)

Combine pineapple juice, sherbet, rum and triple sec in blender. Add ice; blend until slushy. Garnish with lime slices, if desired.

Makes 2 servings

Mai Tai Slush

Double Berry Coco Punch

DOUBLE BERRY COCO PUNCH

    Ice Ring (recipe follows) (optional) *or*
       block of ice
2 (10-ounce) packages frozen strawberries
    in syrup, thawed
1 (15-ounce) can COCO LOPEZ® Cream
    of Coconut
1 (48-ounce) bottle cranberry juice
    cocktail, chilled
2 cups light rum (optional)
1 (32-ounce) bottle club soda, chilled

Prepare ice ring in advance, if desired. In
blender container, purée strawberries and
cream of coconut until smooth. In large punch
bowl, combine strawberry mixture, cranberry
juice and rum, if desired. Just before serving,
add club soda and ice ring.

Ice Ring: Fill ring mold with water to within
1 inch of top rim; freeze. Arrange strawberries,
cranberries, mint leaves, lime slices or other
fruits on top of ice. Carefully pour small
amount of cold water over fruits; freeze.
Makes about 4 quarts

ORANGE AND SPICE ICED TEA

6 cups cold water, divided
3 cinnamon sticks (2 inches each)
½ teaspoon whole cloves
10 tea bags
1 can (6 ounces) Florida frozen
    concentrated orange juice, thawed,
    undiluted
¼ cup sugar
1 Florida orange, sliced

In medium saucepan, combine 3 cups cold
water, cinnamon sticks and cloves. Bring to
boiling; remove from heat. Add tea bags. Brew
5 minutes. Remove tea bags; discard. Strain
mixture. Add remaining 3 cups cold water,
orange juice concentrate and sugar; mix well.
Chill. Serve in tall glasses over ice cubes.

Garnish with fresh orange slices.
Makes six 8-ounce servings

*Favorite Recipe from **Florida Department of Citrus***

LEMONY LIGHT COOLER

　3 cups dry white wine or white grape juice,
　　chilled
½ to ¾ cup sugar
½ cup REALEMON® Lemon Juice from
　　Concentrate
　1 (32-ounce) bottle club soda, chilled
　　Strawberry, plum, peach or orange slices
　　or other fresh fruit

In pitcher, combine wine, sugar and
ReaLemon® brand; stir until sugar dissolves.
Just before serving, add club soda and fruit;
serve over ice.　　　　*Makes about 7 cups*

Tip: Recipe can be doubled.

Left to right: City Slicker, The Rattlesnake

CITY SLICKER

¾ cup DOLE® Pineapple Juice
　　Ice cubes
　　Ginger ale
　　Dash ground ginger
　　Cucumber slice, cherry tomato and
　　　lemon slice for garnish

Pour pineapple juice over ice cubes in glass.
Fill with ginger ale. Add ginger and stir.
Garnish with cucumber slice, cherry tomato
and lemon slice.　　　　*Makes 1 serving*

THE RATTLESNAKE

　3 cups DOLE® Pineapple Juice
⅓ cup tomato juice
　1 tablespoon powdered sugar
½ to 1 teaspoon liquid hot pepper sauce
　8 ice cubes
　　Lime wedges or slices (optional)
　　Dried red pepper, ripe olive and lime
　　　peel for garnish

In pitcher, combine pineapple juice, tomato
juice, sugar and hot pepper sauce; blend well.
Pour over ice cubes in glass. Squeeze lime
juice into each drink, if desired. Garnish with
dried red pepper, ripe olive and lime peel.
　　　　Makes 4 servings

Lemony Light Cooler

LITE QUENCHER

3 cups DOLE® Pineapple Juice, chilled
3 cups mineral water, chilled
1 cup assorted sliced DOLE® fresh fruit
½ cup mint sprigs
1 lime, sliced, for garnish

Combine all ingredients in pitcher.

Makes 8 servings

APPLE GRAPE PUNCH

Ice Ring (recipe follows) (optional) *or*
    block of ice
1 quart apple juice, chilled
3 cups red grape juice, chilled
1 (8-ounce) bottle REALIME® Lime Juice
    from Concentrate, chilled
1 cup vodka (optional)
½ cup sugar

Prepare ice ring in advance, if desired. In punch bowl, combine juices, vodka, if desired, and sugar; stir until sugar dissolves. Just before serving, add ice ring.

Ice Ring: Combine 1 (8-ounce) bottle ReaLime® brand and ¾ cup sugar; stir until sugar dissolves. Add 3 cups water; mix well. Pour 3 cups mixture into ring mold; freeze. Arrange apple slices and grapes on top of ice. Carefully pour remaining mixture over fruits; freeze.   *Makes about 2 quarts*

Bloody Marys

BLOODY MARY

3 cups tomato juice, chilled
¾ cup vodka
4 teaspoons REALEMON® Lemon Juice
    from Concentrate
2 teaspoons Worcestershire sauce
½ teaspoon celery salt
⅛ teaspoon hot pepper sauce
    Dash pepper

In pitcher, combine ingredients; stir. Serve over ice; garnish as desired.

Makes about 1 quart

Tip: For nonalcoholic Bloody Mary, omit vodka. Proceed as above.

BLOODY MARY GARNISHES
Onion & Olive Pick: Dip cocktail onions in chopped parsley; alternate on toothpick with pimiento-stuffed olives.

Green Onion Firecracker: With small scissors or very sharp knife, cut tips of green onion to end of dark green onion portion. Chill in ice water until curled.

Apple Grape Punch

Top to bottom: Strawberry Margaritas, Frozen Margaritas

STRAWBERRY MARGARITAS

 1 (10-ounce) package frozen strawberries
   in syrup, partially thawed
¼ cup REALIME® Lime Juice from
   Concentrate
¼ cup tequila
¼ cup confectioners' sugar
 2 tablespoons triple sec or other orange-
   flavored liqueur
 3 cups ice cubes

In blender container, combine all ingredients
except ice; blend well. Gradually add ice,
blending until smooth. Garnish as desired.
Serve immediately.   *Makes about 1 quart*

FROZEN MARGARITAS

½ cup REALIME® Lime Juice from
   Concentrate
½ cup tequila
¼ cup triple sec or other orange-flavored
   liqueur
 1 cup confectioners' sugar
 4 cups ice cubes

In blender container, combine all ingredients
except ice; blend well. Gradually add ice,
blending until smooth. Garnish as desired.
Serve immediately.   *Makes about 1 quart*

PACIFIC SUNSET

 1 can (6 ounces) or ¾ cup DOLE®
   Pineapple Juice, chilled
⅓ cup orange juice, chilled
   Ice cubes
 1 tablespoon grenadine syrup
   Lime wedge for garnish

Combine juices in tall glass. Add ice. Slowly
add grenadine. Garnish with lime wedge.
                    Makes 1 serving

STRAWBERRY LEMONADE

 1 quart fresh strawberries, cleaned and
   hulled (about 1½ pounds)
 3 cups cold water
¾ cup REALEMON® Lemon Juice from
   Concentrate
¾ to 1 cup sugar
 2 cups club soda, chilled
   Ice

In blender container, purée strawberries. In
pitcher, combine puréed strawberries, water,
ReaLemon® brand and sugar; stir until sugar
dissolves. Add club soda. Serve over ice;
garnish as desired.   *Makes about 2 quarts*

Strawberry Lemonade

Acknowledgments

The publishers would like to thank the companies and organizations listed below for the use of their recipes in this book.

Alaska Seafood Marketing Institute
Almond Board of California
American Lamb Council
Best Foods
Borden Kitchens, Borden, Inc.
California Table Grape Commission
California Tree Fruit Agreement
California Turkey Industry Board
Chef Paul Prudhomme's Magic Seasoning Blends™
Clear Springs Trout Company
Delmarva Poultry Industry, Inc.
Dole Food Company
Florida Department of Citrus
Florida Department of Natural Resources

©Hershey Foods Corporation
The HVR Company
The Kingsford Products Company
Kraft General Foods, Inc.
Lawry's Foods, Inc.
The Lipton Kitchens
McIlhenny Company, Avery Island, LA 70013
National Broiler Council
National Fisheries Institute
National Honey Board
National Live Stock and Meat Board
National Pork Producers Council
Perdue Farms Incorporated
StarKist Seafood Company
Swift-Eckrich, Inc.

Photo Credits

The publishers would like to thank the companies and organizations listed below for the use of their photographs in this book.

Alaska Seafood Marketing Institute
Almond Board of California
American Lamb Council
Best Foods
Borden Kitchens, Borden, Inc.
California Turkey Industry Board
Chef Paul Prudhomme's Magic Seasoning Blends™
Clear Springs Trout Company
Dole Food Company
Florida Department of Natural Resources

©Hershey Foods Corporation
The HVR Company
The Kingsford Products Company
Kraft General Foods, Inc.
Lawry's Foods, Inc.
The Lipton Kitchens
National Live Stock and Meat Board
National Pork Producers Council
StarKist Seafood Company
Swift-Eckrich, Inc.

Index

Outdoor Fare

Fresh • Light • Quick • Easy

PUBLICATIONS INTERNATIONAL, LTD.

California Summer Fruits

This edition was prepared by the Consumer Services Department, California Tree Fruit Agreement, 701 Fulton, Sacramento, CA 95825.

Editor: Deborah Lane Beall, R.D.
Food Consultant: Madsen/O'Brien Innovations
Assistant: Frances Cook
Cover Photograph: Alan Ross

This edition published by Publications International, Ltd., 7373 North Cicero Avenue, Lincolnwood, IL 60646.

ISBN: 1-56173-657-0

Pictured on the front cover *(clockwise from bottom left):* Marinated Picnic Salad *(page 23),* Pear Zinfandel Ice *(page 34)* and Summer Angel Cake *(page 39).*

First published in the United States.

Manufactured in U.S.A.

8   7   6   5   4   3   2

MICROWAVE COOKING
Microwave ovens vary in wattage and power output; cooking times given with microwave directions in this cookbook may need to be adjusted. All recipes tested at 600 watts of power.

Outdoor Fare

Fresh • Light • Quick • Easy

Summer Fruits You Love

California Summer Fruits®,
"It wouldn't be summer without them!"

When miners rushed to the West in the 1850s in search of gold, they found that the real gold was not in the mines but in the perfect climate and growing conditions to produce bountiful harvests of sweet, juicy, fresh peaches, nectarines and Bartlett pears. Later, when the transcontinental railroad was completed in 1869, California fruit began moving to Eastern cities and, as they say, the rest is history.

Over 2,000 growers farm more than 70,000 acres of nectarines, peaches and Bartlett pears. California produces 97% of the U.S. production of fresh nectarines, 60% of Bartlett pears and 40% of fresh peaches.

Nectarines

Fresh California nectarines are crimson and red with golden yellow background and are as pretty and tasty as peaches. Nectarines, however, are a distinct fruit all their own; they are neither a cross of other fruits nor a fuzzless peach. Juicy, colorful nectarines have only 65 calories each and provide vitamins A and C, potassium, fiber and other essential nutrients.

Nectarines are picked mature, yet firm. Closeness is the key to softening and ripening fruit. Place nectarines in a paper bag; loosely close bag and check their progress daily. Fragrant, ripe nectarines give slightly to gentle palm pressure. Refrigeration will slow down the ripening process. Nectarines are most flavorful when eaten at room temperature.

The goodness and refreshing taste of fresh California nectarines is available late April through September. The summer's peak season for nectarines is late June through early September.

Bartlett Pears

Delicious fresh California Bartlett pears are an excellent source of dietary fiber and potassium and provide a variety of other minerals and vitamins for only 95 calories each.

Bartlett pears are picked mature but still green in color. For sunshine yellow pears, complete ripening at home. Place several pears at room temperature in a paper bag and loosely close bag. Check pears daily by looking for a change of color—from green to a sunny yellow. Ripe Bartletts are at their best when stored in the refrigerator and eaten slightly chilled.

Add refreshing variety to summer and autumn diets with one of California's most important summer fruits — the Bartlett pear. Bartletts are available mid-July through December. Peak supplies are early August through mid-October.

Peaches

Quotes such as "you're a real peach" and "peachy keen" exemplify the goodness of peaches and rightfully so. For 50 calories per fruit, peaches are packed with carbohydrates and a variety of vitamins and minerals, including potassium.

When purchasing peaches, look for creamy or golden background color and smooth, plump skin. A red blush is a varietal characteristic and not necessarily an indication of maturity. Ready-to-eat ripened peaches will give to gentle palm pressure. Closeness is the key to ripening fruit. Place several peaches in a paper bag; loosely close and check daily. Store ripened peaches in the refrigerator and eat at room temperature for additional juiciness and sweetness.

Spring, summer and autumn are peach seasons. Peaches are picked from California orchards in late April through October but are most abundant during the summer months of June, July and August.

Do The Ripe Thing

To assure sweet, juicy fruit all summer long, purchase fruit two or three times each week.

1. Place California peaches, nectarines and Bartlett pears in a paper bag. Close bag loosely and leave at room temperature. This speeds up and improves the natural ripening process of fruit.

2. Check for ripeness daily by placing peaches and nectarines in palm of hand and squeezing gently. If it gives to light pressure and smells sweet and delicious, it's ready to eat. For Bartlett pears, look for a change of color — from green to a sunny yellow color.

3. Remove ripened fruit from bag. Enjoy it right away or store in the refrigerator.

A paper bag — that's the secret to ripening. The paper allows the air to circulate around the fruit and also traps the natural gases given off by the fruit, which in turn continues to ripen the fruit.

DO
• Store on the counter at room temperature until ripe.
• Check the fruit daily. When it gives to gentle palm pressure, it is ripe.
• Select fruit that is free of cuts or bruises and has plump, firm skin.
• Enjoy five or more servings of fruit and vegetables each day.

DON'T
• Store fruit in plastic bags.
• Refrigerate fruit until after it is ripe, unless you don't want it to ripen right away.
• Store fruit in window sill or direct sunlight.

The Ripe Fruit for the Right Job

Perfectly ripened fresh California fruits are delicious eaten out of hand or sliced and used as a flavor-packed ingredient for salads and desserts.

Fruit that is still quite firm is good for baking, sautéing, poaching, broiling or grilling, or for use in dishes such as chutney and chunky cooked salsas and sauces. Very soft fruit is good in recipes calling for purée or for beverages, ice creams, smooth sauces and preserves such as jelly and jam. For recipes calling for fruit purée, place ripe, pitted, chopped fruit and a small amount of lemon juice in blender or food processor. Blend on high until mixture is smooth.

Color

To maintain fresh fruits' vibrant colors and to prevent browning, dip cut fruit in a mixture of 1 tablespoon lemon juice and 1 cup water.

NUTRITION INFORMATION

	Nectarine	Peach	Bartlett Pear
Serving	1 medium (5 oz.)	1 medium (5 oz.)	1 medium (6 oz.)
Calories	65	50	95
Protein	1 g	Trace	Trace
Fat	Trace	Trace	Trace
Carbohydrate	15 g	12 g	23 g
Sodium	Trace	Trace	Trace
Potassium	271 mg	210 mg	194 mg
Dietary Fiber	3 g	3 g	6 g

g = grams
mg = milligrams
Trace = less than 1 gram

PER POUND EQUIVALENTS*

Fruit	One Pound	Sliced	Diced	Puréed
Nectarine	3 medium	2 cups	1¾ cups	1½ cups
Peach	3 medium	2 cups	1⅔ cups	1½ cups
Bartlett Pear	3 medium	2½ cups	2⅓ cups	1¾ cups

*Fruit measurements called for in recipes may vary slightly. See recipe for specific measurements.

Portable Picnics
& Fine Feasts

Cooling Coolers and Splashing Waves (clockwise from left): Fruit Cubes (see page 12), Peachy Beach Daiquiris (see page 10), Fruitful Cooler (see page 11), Nectarine Lemonade (see page 10) and Frostie Nectarine Smoothie (see page 10)

Peachy Beach Daiquiris

   3 fresh California peaches,
       quartered
3½ ounces dark rum
   ⅓ cup lime juice
   ⅓ cup sugar
   10 ice cubes
   4 fresh California peach slices
       (optional garnish)
   4 lime slices (optional garnish)

In blender or food processor, combine all ingredients except ice and peach and lime slices. Blend until smooth. Gradually add ice. Blend until smooth. Serve immediately. Garnish with peach and lime slices, if desired.

Makes 4 servings

Tip: For non-alcoholic version, substitute pineapple juice for rum and decrease sugar to 3 tablespoons.

Picnic Pointers: Store in thermos bottle. Shake well before serving.

Nectarine Lemonade

A flavorful sparkling alternative to plain lemonade.

   2 fresh California nectarines,
       sliced
   1 plum, sliced
   1 can (6 ounces) frozen lemonade
       concentrate
   1 can (6 ounces) cold water
       Fruit Cubes (see page 12)
   2 bottles (10 ounces *each*) soda
       water or sparkling mineral
       water, chilled

Reserve 4 nectarine slices for garnish, if desired. In blender or food processor, combine nectarines, plum, lemonade concentrate and water. Blend until smooth. Divide Fruit Cubes and nectarine mixture among 4 glasses. Fill with sparkling water. Float nectarine slice in lemonade for garnish.

Makes 4 servings

Tip: Substitute 2 peaches or Bartlett pears for the nectarines.

Picnic Pointers: Prepare nectarine-lemonade-water mixture and place in thermos bottle. Place Fruit Cubes in unbreakable container. Pack fruit cubes and sparkling water bottle together in insulated bag.

Frostie Nectarine Smoothie

Almost like dessert but without all the calories.

   2 fresh California nectarines,
       quartered
1½ cups diced cantaloupe
   1 cup low-fat plain yogurt
   1 tablespoon honey
   10 ice cubes
   4 fresh California nectarine slices
       (optional garnish)

In blender or food processor, combine all ingredients except ice and sliced nectarines. Blend until smooth. Gradually add ice. Blend until smooth. Serve immediately. Garnish with nectarine slices, if desired. *Makes 4 servings*

Tip: For a thinner consistency, fill glasses half full with sparkling mineral water before adding purée.

Picnic Pointers: Store in thermos bottle. Shake well before serving.

Cream Cheese Swirl Brownies

A lusciously different brownie.

BROWNIE
    3 tablespoons margarine or butter
    1 cup semi-sweet chocolate chips
    2 eggs
    ¾ cup sugar
    ¾ cup all-purpose flour
    ¾ teaspoon baking powder
    ½ teaspoon salt
    ½ cup chopped walnuts (optional)
    1 teaspoon vanilla extract
    ¼ teaspoon almond extract
        (optional)

CREAM CHEESE SWIRL
    2 tablespoons margarine or
        butter, softened
    3 ounces light cream cheese
        (Neufchatel), softened
    ¼ cup sugar
    1 egg
    1 tablespoon all-purpose flour
    1 teaspoon vanilla extract

NECTARINE SWIRL
    3 fresh California nectarines,
        puréed (about 1¼ cups)
    2 tablespoons all-purpose flour

For Brownie, in small microwave-safe bowl, melt margarine and chocolate on HIGH about 1 minute; set aside. In medium bowl, beat eggs and sugar. Combine flour, baking powder and salt. Beat flour mixture into egg mixture, ½ at a time. Stir in chocolate mixture, nuts, vanilla and almond extract. Spread ½ of brownie mixture into greased 9-inch square baking pan. Set remaining batter aside. Preheat oven to 350°F.

For Cream Cheese Swirl, in medium bowl, combine all ingredients until smooth. Spread on top of chocolate batter.

For Nectarine Swirl, combine nectarine purée and flour. Drop by spoonfuls on top of cream cheese mixture.

Drop remaining chocolate batter into pan by spoonfuls. Using table knife, swirl top of batter to give a marbled effect. Bake 45 minutes or until brownies begin to pull away from sides of pan and top is set. Cool slightly; cut into squares. Refrigerate leftovers.   *Makes 16 servings*

Fruitful Cooler

Refreshing on a sunny day.

    4 fresh California Bartlett pears,
        cored and quartered
    ½ cup halved strawberries
    1 cup low-fat plain or vanilla
        yogurt
    ½ teaspoon vanilla extract
        (optional)
    10 ice cubes

In blender or food processor, combine all ingredients except ice. Blend until smooth. Gradually add ice. Blend until smooth. Serve immediately.   *Makes 4 servings*

Tip: For a thinner consistency, fill individual glasses half full of sparkling mineral water before adding fruit mixture.

Picnic Pointers: Store in thermos bottle. Shake well before pouring.

Sunny-Honey Fruit-Wich

Serve open-faced or closed.

½ cup margarine or butter,
  softened *or* ½ cup light
  cream cheese (Neufchatel),
  softened
¼ cup honey
¼ cup hulled sunflower seeds
4 or 8 slices whole grain whole
  wheat bread
3 fresh California peaches,
  nectarines or Bartlett pears,
  sliced

In small bowl, combine margarine,
honey and sunflower seeds; spread
on bread. Top with fruit and
remaining bread, if desired.
Makes 4 servings

*Picnic Pointers: To keep fruit colors
bright and prevent browning, dip
fruit slices in a mixture of 1
tablespoon lemon juice and 1 cup
water. Or, wait and slice pears at the
picnic site.*

Peachy Peanut Butter
Pita Pockets

*This new twist to a peanut butter
and jelly sandwich is easy to pack
and carry.*

4 pita pocket breads
¾ cup chunky peanut butter
2 fresh California peaches, thinly
  sliced

Cut about 3 inches off of one edge
of pita bread to get inside. Carefully
open pocket and spread a thin layer
of peanut butter on both inside
walls. Fill with peach slices.
Makes 4 servings

*Tip: Warm pita bread slightly to
make it more pliable.*

Frostie Fruit Iced Tea

*Thirst quenching and refreshingly
different.*

4 to 6 tea bags
2 cups boiling water
16 Fruit Cubes (recipe follows)
1 can (12 ounces) citrus soda or
  soda water, chilled
4 slices fresh California nectarine
4 fresh mint sprigs (optional
  garnish)

Place tea bags in heatproof glass
measure. Pour boiling water over tea
bags; let steep 4 to 6 minutes.
Remove tea bags and refrigerate tea
until chilled. Fill 4 tall glasses with
Fruit Cubes and divide tea equally.
Add soda. Serve with nectarine
slices and garnish with mint sprigs,
if desired. *Makes 4 servings*

*Picnic Pointers: Place chilled tea in
individual thermos bottles. Place
Fruit Cubes in container with tight-
fitting lid. Pack Fruit Cubes and
soda bottle together in insulated
bag. Omit garnish.*

Fruit Cubes

*Keep a supply in the freezer to perk
up any beverage.*

4 fresh California nectarines,
  peaches or Bartlett pears,
  quartered
1 tablespoon lemon juice

In blender or food processor, blend
fruit with lemon juice until smooth.
Pour into ice cube trays; freeze until
firm. *Makes about 21 cubes*

*From top to bottom: Frostie Fruit Iced Tea
with Fruit Cubes, Peachy Peanut Butter
Pita Pocket and Sunny-Honey Fruit-Wich*

Ham-Peach Empanada

A nice change from everyday sandwiches.

2½ pie crust sticks
½ pound thinly sliced ham
2 fresh California peaches, thinly sliced
1 cup grated Monterey Jack cheese
2 teaspoons dried basil
Pear Mustard (recipe follows)

Preheat oven to 450°F. Prepare pastry according to package directions. Divide into 4 parts. On lightly floured surface, roll each into an 8-inch circle. Layer ¼ of ham, peaches, cheese and basil on half of each circle. Moisten edge; fold plain half over and crimp edges to seal. Place on baking sheet. Bake 15 minutes or until golden brown. Serve hot or cold with Pear Mustard.

Makes 8 servings

Tip: *For ease in handling dough, after mixing pastry sticks and water, form into ball, wrap in waxed paper and refrigerate 30 minutes.*

Picnic Pointers: *Can be baked early in the day or up to 6 hours ahead and refrigerated or place in cooler until ready to serve.*

Pear Mustard

A mustard with personality.

1 fresh California Bartlett pear, peach or nectarine, quartered
3 tablespoons Dijon-style mustard
2 tablespoons light sour cream

Combine pear, mustard and sour cream in blender or food processor; blend until smooth. Refrigerate. Store in tightly sealed container in refrigerator for up to 1 week.

Makes about 1 cup

Serving Suggestions: *Use as a spread with your favorite sandwich or burger. Serve as a condiment with roast beef or ham.*

Greek Pear Salad

A new flavor twist to a classic salad.

GREEK VINAIGRETTE
¼ cup olive or vegetable oil
4 tablespoons white wine vinegar
2 teaspoons sugar
½ teaspoon dried oregano

SALAD
2 fresh California Bartlett pears, cored and sliced
1 cucumber, thinly sliced
1 tomato, cut into wedges
½ cup pitted ripe or Greek-style olives, drained
4 ounces feta or Monterey Jack cheese, sliced

In medium bowl, combine oil, vinegar, sugar and oregano. Add pears and spoon dressing over to cover all surfaces. In salad bowl, combine cucumber, tomato, olives and cheese. Arrange pears on salad. Pour remaining dressing over top.

Makes 4 servings

Tip: *May be prepared up to 4 hours ahead.*

Picnic Pointers: *Store in container with tight-fitting lid. Before serving, invert container to mix well.*

From left to right: Ham-Peach Empanada, Greek Pear Salad and Pear Mustard

Elegant Country Fruit-Cheese Tart

A lovely summer tart with a zesty citrus cream filling.

TART
   1 unbaked single 9-inch pie crust
   1 package (8 ounces) light cream cheese (Neufchatel), softened
   1/4 cup sugar
   1/4 teaspoon ground nutmeg
   1 tablespoon finely grated orange peel
   1 egg
   2 fresh California nectarines, sliced
   1 fresh California peach, thinly sliced

BLUSH SAUCE
   1/3 cup blush wine
   1 teaspoon cornstarch

For Tart, preheat oven to 325°F. Fit crust into 9-inch removable bottom tart pan. Bake 10 minutes. In medium bowl, beat cheese, sugar, nutmeg, orange peel and egg until smooth. Spread over crust. Bake 20 to 25 minutes or until set. Refrigerate until chilled. Fan nectarine slices around outer edge. Overlap peach slices in a swirl in the center.

For Blush Sauce, in small saucepan, heat wine and cornstarch until thickened, stirring constantly. Spoon over tart to glaze. Refrigerate until chilled. Remove tart from pan.

Makes 8 servings

Tip: To keep fruit colors bright and prevent browning, dip cut fruit in a mixture of 1 tablespoon lemon juice and 1 cup water.

Picnic Pointers: Tart can be prepared up to 8 hours ahead of time. Keep chilled until serving by placing pie pan on top of a plastic bag filled with ice cubes.

Sugar-Plum Champagne Cocktail

   2 plums, sliced *or*
      2 California peaches, sliced
   1/4 cup sugar
   1 bottle (750 ml) pink Champagne

Roll fruit slices in sugar and place 2 or 3 slices in each of 4 glasses. Fill with Champagne.

Makes 4 servings

Tip: Turn this into a fruit starter for Sunday brunch by filling a Champagne glass with fruit slices. Top with Champagne.

For Great Picnic Fun

• *Choose the proper containers to arrive at your destination with hot foods still hot and cold foods still cold.*

• *Place dressings and sauces in leak-proof containers with vacuum-closing lids. For additional protection, place the containers in securely tied plastic bags.*

• *When packing fresh California peaches, nectarines and Bartlett pears, make sure the fruit is wrapped with a cloth to prevent bruising.*

• *Don't forget to pack a trash bag so that you can leave the great outdoors even greater than you found it.*

Sugar-Plum Champagne Cocktail and Elegant Country Fruit-Cheese Tart

Sunflower-Peach Cookies

1¼ cups all-purpose flour
1½ teaspoons baking powder
½ teaspoon ground allspice
½ cup margarine or butter,
    softened
1 cup packed brown sugar
2 eggs
1½ cups uncooked rolled oats
¼ cup hulled, toasted sunflower
    seeds
2 fresh California peaches, finely
    chopped (1 cup)
Hulled sunflower seeds
    (optional garnish)

Preheat oven to 350°F. Combine
flour, baking powder and allspice;
set aside. In large bowl, beat
margarine and sugar until smooth.
Beat in eggs. Beat in flour mixture
then oats. Stir in toasted sunflower
seeds and peaches. Drop by rounded
tablespoonfuls about 2 inches apart
onto lightly greased baking sheets.
Sprinkle with sunflower seeds for
garnish, if desired. Bake 12 to 15
minutes or until edges are browned
and center springs back when
touched lightly. Remove to wire
racks to cool.
                Makes about 2 dozen cookies

*Tip: To toast sunflower seeds, place
in single layer in cake pan. Bake at
350°F 8 to 10 minutes or until lightly
browned.*

*Picnic Pointers: Pack in unbreakable
container, separating layers with
waxed paper.*

*From top to bottom: Fruitful Slush,
Spicy Pear Cookies (see page 20),
Fruit-Filled Cookie Bars and
Sunflower-Peach Cookies*

Fruitful Slush

Refreshing and not too sweet.

3 plums, coarsely chopped
    (about 2 cups)
2 fresh California peaches or
    nectarines, chopped
1 can (6 ounces) frozen cranberry
    juice concentrate
20 ice cubes

In blender or food processor,
combine fruit and juice concentrate
and blend until smooth. Gradually
add ice and blend until slushy. Serve
immediately.   *Makes 8 servings*

*Picnic Pointers: Store in thermos
bottle.*

Fruit-Filled Cookie Bars

1 fresh California peach or
    nectarine, chopped (⅔ cup)
4 plums, chopped (1⅓ cups)
½ cup packed brown sugar,
    divided
1½ cups uncooked rolled oats
1 cup all-purpose flour
¾ cup margarine or butter, melted
1 teaspoon ground cinnamon
¼ teaspoon baking powder

In small bowl, combine fruit and
2 tablespoons brown sugar; set aside.
In medium bowl, combine
remaining ingredients. Press ½ of
oat mixture into 8-inch square
microwave-safe baking dish.
Microwave on HIGH 2 minutes.
Spread fruit mixture on top.
Crumble remaining oat mixture on
top of fruit; pat down slightly.
Microwave on HIGH 2 to 4 minutes
or until set; check after 2 minutes.
Let stand 20 minutes before cutting.
                    Makes 12 bars

*Picnic Pointers: Cut bars ahead of
time and leave them in the baking
dish.*

Spicy Pear Cookies

Take a big handful of these along whenever you pack up your knapsack.

COOKIES
½ cup margarine or butter, softened
1½ cups packed brown sugar
1 egg
1 teaspoon vanilla extract
2 cups all-purpose flour
1½ teaspoons baking powder
1 teaspoon ground cinnamon
1 teaspoon ground ginger
1 fresh California Bartlett pear, cored and finely chopped (1 cup)
½ cup chopped walnuts
½ cup golden raisins

POWDERED SUGAR ICING
1½ cups powdered sugar
2½ tablespoons lemon juice

Walnut halves (optional garnish)

For Cookies, preheat oven to 350°F. In large bowl, beat margarine and brown sugar until smooth. Beat in egg and vanilla. Combine flour, baking powder, cinnamon and ginger; mix into batter. Stir in chopped pears, chopped nuts and raisins. Drop about 2 inches apart by rounded tablespoonfuls onto greased baking sheets. Bake about 15 minutes or until edges are browned and center springs back when touched lightly. Remove to wire racks to cool.

For Powdered Sugar Icing, combine powdered sugar and lemon juice and mix until smooth. Spoon icing over cookies and top with walnut halves, if desired.

Makes about 2½ dozen cookies

Tip: For giant cookies, follow directions above. Drop by ¼ cupfuls about 3 inches apart onto greased baking sheets. Bake 20 minutes. Makes about 15 giant cookies.

Picnic Pointers: Pack in unbreakable container, separating layers with waxed paper.

Ginger Cake with Summer Fruit Sauce

An adaptation of gingerbread but with an exciting flavor difference.

2 packages (14 ounces *each*) gingerbread mix
1½ cups water
6 fresh California peaches, chopped (4 cups)
1 package (3 ounces) light cream cheese (Neufchatel), softened
Summer Fruit Sauce (recipe follows)

Preheat oven to 350°F. Grease two 9-inch round or square pans. In medium bowl, combine gingerbread mixes with water. Stir in peaches. Pour into pans. Bake 35 to 40 minutes or until toothpick inserted in center comes out clean. Cool 15 minutes. Remove from pans; cool on wire racks. Spread one cake layer with cheese. Place second cake layer on top. Spoon warm Summer Fruit Sauce over each serving.

Makes 10 servings

Summer Fruit Sauce

A delightfully refreshing sauce that's also wonderful on ice cream or shortcake.

    1 tablespoon cornstarch
    1 cup orange juice
    ¼ cup honey
    2 tablespoons margarine or butter
    1 teaspoon finely grated
        orange peel
    3 fresh California peaches,
        chopped (about 1⅔ cups)
    2 fresh California nectarines,
        chopped (about 1⅓ cups)
    1 plum, chopped (about ⅓ cup)

In medium saucepan, combine cornstarch and orange juice. Add honey. Bring to a boil and cook over medium heat 5 minutes or until thickened, stirring constantly; remove from heat. Stir in margarine and orange peel; mix well. Stir in fruit. *Makes about 3 cups*

Tips:
- *Summer Fruit Sauce may be prepared using only one kind of fruit.*
- *Sauce may be made in advance and refrigerated. Warm in microwave just before serving.*
- *This recipe travels well for picnics or for potluck dinners where your assignment is to bring dessert. For picnic occasions, the sauce can be served cold.*

Ginger Cake with Summer Fruit Sauce

Pear Bistro Picnic Salad

6 tablespoons olive or vegetable
oil, divided
3 chicken breast halves, skinned,
boned, cut into 1½-inch strips
½ cup walnut halves or pieces
Salt and pepper, to taste
2 tablespoons minced shallots or
green onions
2 tablespoons cider vinegar
2 fresh California Bartlett pears,
cored and sliced
8 cups assorted torn greens
(lettuce, fresh spinach, red
leaf lettuce or radicchio)
¼ cup crumbled blue cheese or
other cheese

In large skillet, heat 2 tablespoons
oil. Add chicken and nuts and sauté
until chicken is cooked through,
about 5 minutes. Remove to large
bowl; season to taste with salt and
pepper. Add shallots to skillet and
cook until translucent, about 2
minutes. Add vinegar and bring to a
boil, scraping up brown bits from
bottom of skillet. Remove from heat;
whisk in remaining 4 tablespoons
oil. Add pears and stir gently to
coat. Toss with chicken mixture.
Serve on bed of greens and garnish
with cheese. Serve cool or warm.
Makes 4 servings

*Picnic Pointers: Thoroughly chill
pear-chicken mixture after cooking
and store in unbreakable container
with tight-fitting lid; keep chilled.
Store blue cheese and greens in
separate containers.*

Marinated Picnic Salad

*This all-time favorite recipe is an
unusual combination of fruit and
vegetables.*

SALAD
2 fresh California nectarines,
thickly sliced and cut in half
½ pound fresh mushrooms,
quartered
1 cup cherry tomatoes, halved
½ cup pitted ripe olives, halved
⅓ cup diagonally sliced green
onions
1 jar (6 ounces) marinated
artichoke hearts, halved
6 cups torn mixed salad greens
(optional)

EASY HERB VINAIGRETTE
1 tablespoon olive or
vegetable oil
¼ cup lemon juice or white wine
vinegar
¼ teaspoon ground black pepper
1 teaspoon sugar
1½ teaspoons dried herb blend,
such as Italian seasoning or
herbes de Provence

In large bowl, combine nectarines,
mushrooms, tomatoes, olives and
onions. Drain and reserve marinade
from artichokes. Cut artichokes in
half and add to salad. In small jar,
combine marinade with vinaigrette
ingredients; shake well. Pour over
salad and refrigerate until ready to
serve. Serve on bed of salad greens,
if desired.   *Makes 6 servings*

*Tip: Recipe can be doubled or
tripled.*

*Picnic Pointers: Salad can be
prepared up to 8 hours ahead of
time. Store in container with tight
fitting lid. Before serving, invert
container to mix. Store torn lettuce
in plastic bag, if desired.*

Pear Bistro Picnic Salad

Easy Backyard Dining

Family Reunion (clockwise from top right): Mom's Summer Fruit Lattice Pie (see page 26), Mary's Fruit Platter with Dips (see page 26), Aunt Diane's Divine Cheesecake Bars (see page 30), Pop's Crusty Chicken (see page 27), Cousin's Berry Punch (see page 27) and Tangy Peach Salsa (see page 27)

Mary's Fruit Platter with Dips

Set this platter out early and let everyone feast on a good-for-you snack.

CREAMY CHEESE DIP
1 cup light sour cream
1 cup low-fat cottage cheese
1 teaspoon Dijon-style mustard
1 teaspoon minced garlic
½ teaspoon dried thyme
½ cup chopped walnuts or
    almonds, toasted
2 ounces blue cheese, crumbled
    (about ¼ cup) *or* 2 ounces
    light cream cheese
    (Neufchatel), diced
¼ cup chopped parsley
    Sliced green onions
    (optional garnish)

LIGHT 'N' LEMON DIP
2 cups low-fat lemon or lime
    yogurt
    Thinly sliced lemon peel
    (optional garnish)

FRUIT
4 fresh California nectarines,
    sliced
4 fresh California peaches, sliced
3 fresh California Bartlett pears,
    cored and sliced
1 plum, sliced
1 tablespoon lemon juice
    combined with 1 cup water

For Creamy Cheese Dip, in medium bowl, combine sour cream, cottage cheese, mustard, garlic and thyme. Stir in nuts, blue cheese and parsley. Spoon into serving bowl. Garnish with green onions, if desired. Refrigerate until ready to serve.

For Light 'n' Lemon Dip, spoon yogurt into serving container. Garnish with lemon peel, if desired.

For Fruit, dip sliced fruit into lemon water to keep fruit colors bright and prevent browning. Arrange on platter with both dips.
Makes 20 servings

Tips:
• *Yogurt can be easily thickened. Line a sieve with cheesecloth and place it over a bowl. Spoon yogurt onto cheesecloth. Cover and refrigerate; let drain several hours.*
• *Prepare Creamy Cheese Dip early in the day. For best results, slice pears just before serving. Peaches and nectarines can be sliced an hour or two in advance; dip in lemon-water mixture.*

Mom's Summer Fruit Lattice Pie

1 unbaked double 9-inch pie crust
10 fresh California nectarines or
    peaches, sliced
½ cup sugar
⅓ cup all-purpose flour
1 teaspoon finely grated
    lemon peel
    Milk and sugar (optional)

Preheat oven to 425°F. Line 9-inch pie pan with one crust. Cut remaining crust into ½-inch strips. In large bowl, gently toss nectarines with sugar, flour and lemon peel. Spoon into crust. Weave dough strips over top to form lattice crust. Seal and crimp edges. Brush lattice top with milk and sprinkle with sugar, if desired. Place on baking sheet. Bake 10 minutes. Reduce heat to 350°F and bake 45 to 50 minutes or until lattice top is golden brown and fruit is tender. Cool.   *Makes 8 servings*

Tip: *The crust will seem too full of fruit, but will cook down as it bakes.*

Pop's Crusty Chicken

ORANGE-GINGER MARINADE
1/4 cup orange marmalade
1/4 cup orange juice
2 tablespoons low-sodium soy
    sauce
1 teaspoon grated fresh ginger
    root *or* 1/4 teaspoon ground
    ginger
1 1/2 teaspoons Dijon-style mustard
1 clove garlic, minced *or*
    1/4 teaspoon garlic powder

CHICKEN
3 1/2 pounds chicken thighs and
    drumsticks, skinned
1 cup lightly crushed cornflakes
    Tangy Peach Salsa (recipe
    follows)

In small bowl, combine all marinade ingredients. Place chicken in zip-top plastic bag. Pour marinade over chicken; close bag securely, turning to coat well. Refrigerate 2 hours. Remove chicken from marinade and roll in cornflakes. Pat extra cornflakes on if necessary to make a solid coating. Place chicken in lightly oiled disposable aluminum foil pan; cover loosely with foil. Cook on covered grill over medium, direct heat 30 to 40 minutes or until cooked through. Uncover last 10 minutes. Serve hot or cold with Tangy Peach Salsa for dipping.   *Makes 6 servings*

Tips:
• *Chicken can be baked in a conventional oven. Prepare as above and bake in 350°F oven 30 to 40 minutes.*
• *Chicken can also be cooked in a microwave oven. Prepare as above. Cook in microwave-safe baking dish with thicker parts to outside edge of dish on HIGH 25 minutes or until cooked through. Turn pieces after 7 minutes and rotate dish after 20 minutes.*

Tangy Peach Salsa

4 fresh California peaches,
    chopped (about 2 1/4 cups)
1/2 cup orange marmalade
1/2 cup thinly sliced green onions
2 tablespoons cider vinegar
1 teaspoon grated fresh ginger
    root *or* 1/4 teaspoon ground
    ginger

In medium bowl, combine all ingredients. Refrigerate until ready to serve.   *Makes about 2 1/2 cups*

Tip: Serve as a savory sauce with lamb, pork or fish.

Cousin's Berry Punch

A crowd pleasing, refreshing drink.

8 raspberry herbal tea bags
2 cups boiling water
2 tablespoons sugar
2 cups cold water
4 plums, puréed (about 1 1/4 cups)
1 can (6 ounces) frozen lemonade
    concentrate
1 bottle (1 liter) lemon-lime
    soda, chilled

Place tea bags in large, heat proof pitcher. Pour boiling water over tea bags and let steep 5 minutes; remove tea bags. Add sugar and stir until dissolved. Add cold water, fruit purée and lemonade concentrate. Refrigerate until chilled. Just before serving, add soda.

Makes 2 1/4 quarts

Tip: Recipe can be doubled or tripled.

Serving Suggestion: *If desired, garnish each glass with a fruit slice and a few fresh raspberries.*

Warm Chinese Chicken Salad

ALMOND GINGER MARINADE

1 cup prepared Italian salad dressing
2 teaspoons low-sodium soy sauce
1 teaspoon minced fresh ginger root *or* ¼ teaspoon ground ginger

CHICKEN SALAD

2 whole chicken breasts, split, boned and skinned
8 cups torn mixed salad greens
¼ cup chopped fresh cilantro (optional)
¼ cup diagonally sliced green onions
5 fresh California peaches, divided
¼ cup toasted sliced almonds
2 tablespoons toasted sesame seeds (optional)

For Marinade, in zip-top plastic bag, combine salad dressing, soy sauce and ginger. Add chicken; close bag securely, turning to coat well. Refrigerate 30 minutes.

For Salad, arrange greens on serving plates. Sprinkle with cilantro. Top with green onions. Slice 3 peaches and arrange on lettuce. Remove chicken from marinade reserving marinade. Grill or broil chicken until browned and cooked through, basting occasionally with marinade. Halve remaining 2 peaches; baste with marinade and grill about 5 minutes. Slice chicken breasts and arrange chicken and grilled peaches on lettuce.

In small saucepan, bring remaining marinade to a boil (this can be done on the grill, if desired.) Add almonds and sesame seeds. Pour over salads and serve immediately.

Makes 4 servings

For Great Grilling

- *Light coals using lighter fluid, electric starter or chimney starter. Coals are ready when they are ash gray during daylight or glow at night. Spread coals in a single layer using long-handled tongs. For a lower temperature, spread coals apart. To make fire hotter, move coals close together and tap off ash.*

- *For **direct** cooking, arrange coals in a single layer directly under food. Use this method for quick-cooking foods, such as hamburgers, steaks or fish.*

- *For **indirect** cooking, divide and arrange coals to each side of grill. Place an aluminum foil drip pan under the food. Use this method for slow-cooking foods, such as roasts and chicken.*

- *Covering the grill lowers the heat and helps to keep grilled food moist and juicy.*

- *To make a disposable foil saucepan, mold 3 layers of heavy duty aluminum foil around medium saucepan or bowl. Remove saucepan and fold/roll edges down to form tight rim. Use to warm sauces.*

Warm Chinese Chicken Salad

Aunt Diane's Divine Cheesecake Bars

CRUST
1¾ cups chocolate wafer cookie
crumbs
¼ cup sugar
6 tablespoons margarine or butter,
melted

FILLING
3 packages (8 ounces *each*) light
cream cheese (Neufchatel),
softened
1 cup light sour cream
¾ cup sugar
2 teaspoons vanilla extract
2 tablespoons lemon juice
½ teaspoon finely grated
lemon peel
2 envelopes unflavored gelatin
½ cup water
5 plums *or* 3 fresh California
peaches, sliced and divided

For Crust, in medium bowl, combine crumbs and ¼ cup sugar. Stir in margarine. Pat into 13×9×2-inch baking pan; chill.

For Filling, in large bowl, beat cheese, sour cream, ¾ cup sugar, vanilla, lemon juice and lemon peel until smooth. In small saucepan, sprinkle gelatin over water; let stand 5 minutes. Heat over low heat, stirring to dissolve gelatin, about 2 minutes. Blend into cheese mixture. Spread 3 cups cheese mixture over crust. In blender or food processor, purée 3 plums or 1½ peaches to make 1 cup. Fold purée into remaining cheese mixture. Spoon over cheese layer; spread smooth. Refrigerate several hours or until set. Garnish with remaining fruit slices. Cut into bars to serve.

Makes 20 servings

Savory Grilled Peaches

You'll be hooked on this summer favorite side dish.

4 fresh California peaches,
halved

Cook peaches on covered grill over medium, indirect heat 4 minutes. Turn and cook an additional 4 minutes or until heated through.

Makes 4 servings

Tip: *Fruit that is still quite firm can be used successfully in most baked or grilled recipes. For added flavor, brush peaches during grilling with a marinade or sauce.*

Peach 'n' Cream Colada

Delicious on a warm afternoon.

4 fresh California peaches,
quartered
1 cup pineapple juice, chilled
½ cup cream of coconut, chilled
2 teaspoons rum extract
15 ice cubes
4 slices fresh California peaches

In blender or food processor, blend quartered peaches until smooth. Add remaining ingredients except peach slices and blend until slushy. Pour into glasses and decorate rim with peach slice. Serve immediately.

Makes 4 servings

Cocktail: *Substitute 2 ounces light rum for rum extract.*

Tip: *Cream of coconut can be found in most liquor stores or in some grocery gourmet sections.*

Nectarine Alexander

A creamy conclusion to any evening.

> 4 fresh California nectarines, quartered
> 2 teaspoons vanilla extract *or* 1 teaspoon almond extract
> 2 scoops (⅔ cup) vanilla ice cream
> 4 mint sprigs (optional garnish)
> 4 slices fresh California nectarine (optional garnish)

In blender or food processor, blend nectarines and vanilla until smooth. Add ice cream and blend just until smooth. Pour into glasses; garnish with mint sprigs and nectarine slices, if desired.   *Makes 4 servings*

Cocktail: Substitute 2 ounces brandy and 2 ounces white creme de cacao for vanilla extract.

Peach Perfect

Peaches make a deliciously special drink.

> 4 peaches, quartered
> 1½ cups low-fat milk
>   Dash of aromatic bitters
> 15 ice cubes
> 4 slices fresh California peach

In blender or food processor, blend quartered peaches until smooth. Add milk, bitters and ice and blend until slushy. Pour into 4 glasses. Garnish with peach slices.
Makes 4 servings

Cocktail: Add 4 ounces cream Sherry wine.

Iced Delights

That first icy spoonful of sweet, fruity crystals is so soothing on a steamy summer day. And, what could be a more natural companion for the cool desserts that follow than ripe, juicy California Summer Fruits®.

For best results, use very soft, sweet fruit in ice creams, sherbets and sorbets.

Sherbets *are sweetened fruit juices with milk used as part of the liquid. Other ingredients often include cream, egg whites or gelatin.*

The word ***Sorbet*** *is derived from the same origin as sherbet. Sorbet was originally an iced Turkish drink. Sorbets are soft ices, flavored with fruit or liqueur. They are traditionally too soft to mold.*

Ices *are sweetened fruit juices that have been frozen. Ices need to be "ripened." After the frozen dessert has been stored in the freezer for a few days, the texture becomes very hard. Ripening simply means softening the dessert to a smooth consistency to get the best flavor and texture. Ices with the most sugar or alcohol will tend to ripen the fastest.*

Granita *is a term used for what most people refer to as Italian ice. The name literally means granite which appropriately describes the pleasingly icy, granular texture of this frozen novelty.*

Basic Ice Cream Recipe

2 egg yolks
¾ cup milk
½ cup sugar
    Fruit Mixture (recipe follows)
½ cup sweetened condensed milk
1½ cups heavy cream

In large saucepan, beat egg yolks and milk; blend in sugar. Cook over medium heat, stirring constantly, until mixture lightly coats metal spoon. Do not boil. Cool. In large bowl, combine ingredients of Fruit Mixture of your choice. Stir in egg mixture, condensed milk and cream. Freeze in ice cream maker according to manufacturer's directions.

Makes about 1 quart

Fruit Mixtures

PEAR CHOCOLATE
5 fresh California Bartlett pears, cored and puréed
¾ cup semi-sweet chocolate chips, chopped

PEACHY PISTACHIO
5 fresh California peaches, puréed
1 cup pistachios, coarsely chopped
¼ teaspoon almond extract

NECTARINE BRANDY
5 fresh California nectarines, puréed
¼ cup apricot brandy
1 teaspoon finely grated lemon peel

Basic Sorbet Recipe

¾ cup apple juice or white grape juice or water
½ cup sugar
    Fruit Mixture (recipe follows)

In large saucepan, heat juice and sugar until sugar dissolves. Cool. In large bowl, combine ingredients of Fruit Mixture of your choice. Stir fruit mixture into sugar mixture. Freeze in ice cream maker according to manufacturer's directions. Thirty minutes before serving, process in blender or food processor and refreeze until serving.

Makes about 1 quart

Fruit Mixtures

PEACHY ORANGE
5 fresh California peaches, puréed
3 tablespoons orange juice
2 teaspoons finely grated orange peel

SHERRY NECTARINE
6 fresh California nectarines, puréed
¼ cup cream Sherry wine

NECTARINE LIME
5 fresh California nectarines, puréed
¼ cup frozen limeade or lemonade concentrate

BRANDY PEAR
5 fresh California Bartlett pears, cored and puréed
½ cup apple juice or white grape juice
3 tablespoons brandy

Tip: Omit freezing in ice cream maker and freeze in loaf pan. Thirty minutes before serving, process in blender or food processor and refreeze until serving.

Clockwise from top: Pear Zinfandel Ice (see page 34), Brandy Pear Sorbet, Peachy Orange Sorbet and Sherry Nectarine Sorbet

Basic Yogi-Pop Recipe

Fruit Mixture (recipe follows)
1 cup low-fat plain yogurt
½ cup white grape juice or apple
   juice

Purée Fruit Mixture of your choice.
In large bowl, combine yogurt, juice
and fruit mixture purée. Freeze until
mushy. Beat well and pour into
popsicle molds or small paper cups.
Insert wooden sticks or plastic
spoons. Freeze until firm.
Makes 10 to 12 pops

Fruit Mixtures

NECTARINE ORANGE
   5 fresh California nectarines,
      quartered
   1 orange, peeled and chopped
   1 tablespoon finely grated
      orange peel

PEACH BANANA
   5 fresh California peaches,
      quartered
   1 banana, cut into chunks

PEAR BERRY
   5 fresh California Bartlett pears,
      cored and quartered
   1 cup raspberries*

STRAWBERRY NECTAR
   6 fresh California nectarines,
      quartered
   1 cup strawberries, rinsed and
      hulled
   ½ cup white grape juice or apple
      juice

*Purée raspberries separately and
strain to remove seeds.

Guiltless Peach "Ice Cream"

7 fresh California peaches or
   nectarines, divided
1 envelope unflavored gelatin
2 cups low-fat milk
1 cup low-fat plain yogurt
½ cup sugar
1 tablespoon vanilla extract

Chop enough peaches to measure
1 cup. In blender or food processor,
purée remaining peaches to measure
2½ cups. In medium saucepan,
sprinkle gelatin over milk; let stand
about 5 minutes. Heat over low heat,
stirring until gelatin dissolves, about
2 minutes. Add all ingredients to pan
and mix well. Freeze in ice cream
maker according to manufacturer's
directions. Serve at once or pack into
freezer containers.
Makes 7 cups

Pear Zinfandel Ice

4 fresh California Bartlett pears,
   cored and chopped
½ cup Zinfandel or other red wine
½ cup sugar
¼ cup water
   Fresh basil (optional garnish)

In blender or food processor, purée
pears, Zinfandel, sugar and water.
Freeze in ice cream maker according
to manufacturer's directions. Garnish
with fresh basil, if desired.
Makes 4 servings

*Tip: Omit freezing in ice cream
maker and freeze in loaf pan. Thirty
minutes before serving, process in
blender or food processor and
refreeze until serving.*

Frozen Nectarine Yogurt

5 fresh California nectarines,
    chopped (3 cups)
1¼ cups water
¼ cup honey
1 tablespoon lemon juice
1 cup low-fat vanilla or plain
    yogurt
1 teaspoon almond extract

In medium saucepan, bring
nectarines, water, honey and lemon
juice to a boil. Reduce heat and
simmer until fruit is soft, about 10
minutes. In blender or food
processor, blend until smooth. Strain
liquid through cheesecloth or sieve.
Press remaining pulp to release
juices; discard solids. Refrigerate
juices until chilled. Whisk in yogurt
and almond extract. Pour into 8-inch
square pan and freeze until ice
crystals form around edges, about 45
minutes. Stir crystals into middle of
pan and return to freezer. When
lightly frozen, whip mixture with
electric mixer until light in color and
fluffy. Repeat freezing and whipping
process again. Spoon into storage
container and freeze until firm. Let
soften at room temperature 10
minutes before serving. Scoop into
chilled glasses.   *Makes 6 servings*

Peach-Mint Salsa

*Also great spooned over grilled
meat or fish.*

1 fresh California peach,
    chopped (about ⅔ cup)
⅓ cup chopped green onions
1 tomato, chopped
1½ tablespoons chopped fresh mint
¼ teaspoon chili powder

In small bowl, combine all
ingredients. Refrigerate leftovers.
            Makes about 1½ cups

Barbecued Chicken on a Bun

A satisfying meal in a bun.

1 teaspoon seasoned salt
⅛ teaspoon coarsely ground black
    pepper
2 whole chicken breasts, split and
    boned
4 buns, split and toasted
4 slices (1 ounce *each*) Swiss
    cheese
4 slices (1 ounce *each*) baked
    ham, warmed
Peach-Mint Salsa (preceding
    recipe)
Lettuce leaves
Savory Grilled Peaches (see
    page 30)

Combine seasoned salt and pepper.
Loosen one edge of chicken skin
and rub seasoning mixture
underneath skin. Cook chicken skin-
side down on covered grill over
medium, indirect heat about 30 to 35
minutes or until chicken is cooked
through. Remove and discard skin.
Serve chicken on buns topped with
cheese, ham and salsa. Garnish with
lettuce. Serve with Savory Grilled
Peaches.
        Makes 4 hearty sandwiches

Conventional Oven Method: *Prepare
as above. Roast skin-side up in
350°F oven for about 30 minutes or
until cooked through.*

Tip: *Sandwiches are delicious
served either hot or cold.*

Lime-Basted Lamb Kabobs

Lime makes the refreshing difference in this marinade.

LIME-HERB MARINADE
3/4 cup lime juice (about 6 limes)
1/4 cup olive or vegetable oil
1/3 cup sugar
1 teaspoon dried cilantro leaves
1 teaspoon fresh or dried rosemary
1 clove garlic, minced
1/2 teaspoon black pepper

LAMB KABOBS
1 1/2 to 2 pounds trimmed lamb, cut into 1 1/4-inch cubes
1 package (10 ounces) pearl onions, blanched and peeled
4 fresh California peaches, halved
1/2 cup non-fat plain yogurt (optional)

In large zip-top plastic bag, combine marinade ingredients. Reserve 3 tablespoons marinade. Add lamb and pearl onions; close bag securely. Refrigerate 30 minutes, turning bag every 10 minutes. Remove lamb and onions, reserving marinade for basting. Thread lamb and onions alternately onto 4 to 6 skewers.

Cook kabobs on uncovered grill over medium, direct heat, turning frequently and brushing with marinade, about 16 minutes for medium rare, 20 minutes for medium and 24 minutes for well done. Brush peaches with marinade and place directly on grill during last 8 minutes, turning after 4 minutes.

Combine reserved 3 tablespoons marinade with yogurt, if desired. Serve as a sauce with lamb and peaches.   *Makes 4 to 6 servings*

Tips:
• *To blanch onions, place whole onions in boiling water. Return to a boil and simmer about 6 minutes; drain and let stand until cool enough to handle. Trim stem end and skin will slip off easily.*
• *If using wooden skewers, soak in water 20 minutes before grilling.*

Summer Nectarine Chutney

Keep your cool and microwave this versatile chutney. Serve on sandwiches or as a relish with poultry, pork or lamb.

3 fresh California nectarines, cut into 1/2-inch chunks
1 onion, coarsely chopped
1/2 cup packed brown sugar
1/2 cup golden raisins
1/4 cup cider vinegar
1/2 teaspoon chili powder
1/2 teaspoon ground allspice
1/2 cup coarsely chopped almonds, toasted

In 2-quart glass measure, combine all ingredients except almonds. Microwave on HIGH 25 to 30 minutes, stirring every 5 minutes, until mixture is very thick and fruit and onion are tender. Refrigerate until chilled. Stir in almonds before serving. Refrigerate leftovers.
Makes 1 1/2 cups

Tip: Fruit that is still quite firm will work well.

Clockwise from top left: Anywhere Pear Frittata (see page 38), Lime-Basted Lamb Kabobs, Stuffed Fish Turbans (see page 39), Summer Nectarine Chutney and Herb-Grilled Turkey Sandwiches (see page 38)

Anywhere Pear Frittata

Enjoy this dish anywhere, anytime of day—at a backyard brunch or a campfire dinner.

2 fresh California Bartlett pears, cored and divided
1 tablespoon lemon juice combined with 1 cup water
2 tablespoons extra light olive or vegetable oil
¼ cup chopped onion
2 zucchini, thinly sliced (2 cups)
¼ teaspoon dried thyme
½ teaspoon lemon pepper seasoning
6 eggs, beaten
¼ cup shredded Monterey Jack cheese

Slice ½ of 1 pear into 6 slices. Dip in lemon juice mixture; set aside. Coarsely chop remaining pears. In cast-iron skillet on uncovered grill, heat oil over medium, direct heat. Add onion and sauté about 2 minutes. Add zucchini and sauté until vegetables are crisp-tender, about 2 minutes. Add chopped pears, seasonings and eggs, stirring occasionally until eggs are almost set. Smooth out mixture in skillet. Fan the 6 pear slices on top. Sprinkle with cheese. Continue cooking until eggs are set and bottom of mixture is slightly browned. Remove from heat and let rest 5 minutes before cutting. To serve, cut into pie shaped wedges with a pear slice in the center of each.   *Makes 6 servings*

Conventional Method: *Prepare as above and cook on top of range over medium heat.*

Tip: *Slices are most easily served by sliding a spatula in from the center (pointed end) of each slice.*

Herb-Grilled Turkey Sandwiches

A hearty do-it-yourself sandwich.

1 teaspoon seasoned salt
½ teaspoon mustard seed
½ teaspoon fennel seed
⅛ teaspoon coarsely ground black pepper
½ fresh or thawed, frozen, deboned turkey breast (about 2½ pounds)
Vegetable oil
8 whole wheat buns, sliced and toasted
Lettuce leaves
Summer Nectarine Chutney (see page 36)
½ cup light mayonnaise

Combine seasoned salt, mustard seed, fennel seed and pepper. Cut pocket in thickest part of breast and rub 1 teaspoon seasoning mixture inside. Loosen edge of skin and rub remaining seasoning mixture underneath skin. Brush turkey lightly with vegetable oil and place skin-side down on grill. Cook on covered grill over medium, indirect heat about 1½ hours or until meat thermometer inserted in thickest part reaches 170°F. Turn once after skin is well browned. Remove from heat and let rest 15 minutes before slicing.

To serve, slice turkey in direction of the seasoning-filled pocket. Serve on buns with lettuce, Summer Nectarine Chutney and mayonnaise.
Makes 8 hearty sandwiches

Conventional Oven Method: *Prepare as above and roast turkey breast skin-side up in 325°F oven about 1½ hours.*

Tip: *May be served either hot or cold. It is an easy do-ahead dish for either plain or fancy events.*

Stuffed Fish Turbans

6 plums, halved *or* 3 fresh
    California nectarines,
    quartered and divided
½ cup finely chopped onion
½ cup shredded Cheddar cheese
2 tablespoons finely chopped
    green bell pepper
2 tablespoons finely chopped
    fresh basil
¼ teaspoon finely grated
    lemon peel
¼ teaspoon lemon pepper
    seasoning
¼ teaspoon Italian herb seasoning
    or herb blend
4 long, thin fish fillets (see Tip)
1 teaspoon lemon juice
    Salt and pepper, to taste
4 sprigs fresh basil (optional
    garnish)

Slice 8 plum halves in half; reserve
for garnish. Chop remaining fruit
and combine with onion, cheese,
green pepper, chopped basil, lemon
peel and seasonings. Sprinkle fish
with lemon juice and season with salt
and pepper to taste. Divide fruit
stuffing among the fish fillets. Roll
up starting at the small end. Secure
with small wooden skewers. Place
upright on double thickness of foil.
Place reserved plum quarters
between fish turbans to allow for
more even cooking. Seal foil tightly
and place on grill.

Cook on covered grill over medium,
direct heat 25 to 30 minutes or until
fish flakes easily with fork. Serve
each turban with 4 plum quarters
and garnish with a sprig of basil, if
desired.   *Makes 4 servings*

*Conventional Oven Method: Place
turbans in baking dish; cover and
bake in 375°F oven 20 to 25 minutes.*

*Tip: If using shorter fillets such as
sole, place 2 fillets end to end,
overlapping slightly, to make an
attractive turban.*

Summer Angel Cake

1 prepared round angel food cake
2 egg whites
½ cup packed brown sugar or
    granulated sugar
2 fresh California peaches, sliced
2 fresh California nectarines,
    sliced
1 fresh California Bartlett pear,
    cored and sliced

With large serrated knife, cut cake
horizontally into thirds. In large
bowl, at high speed of electric mixer,
beat egg whites; gradually add
brown sugar until thick and fluffy,
about 5 minutes. Reserve several
pieces of fruit for garnish. Spread ½
of meringue on bottom layer of cake.
Arrange ½ of fruit on meringue. Top
with middle layer of cake and repeat
meringue and fruit layers. Add top
layer of cake. Garnish as desired.
Serve immediately.

Makes 8 servings

*Tip: To keep fruit colors bright and
prevent browning, dip sliced fruit in
a mixture of 1 tablespoon lemon
juice and 1 cup water.*

The Light Touch

Bountiful Brunch (clockwise from top right): Fresh Peach Muffins (see page 42), Four-Grain Pear Muffins (see page 42), Gingered Muffins (see page 43), Honey Peach Topping (see page 43), Creamy Brown Rice (see page 44) with No-Sugar Pear Berry Jam (see page 43), Summer Fruit (see page 43) and Peach Frosted (see page 42)

Peach Frosted

6 fresh California peaches, chilled and sliced
2 cups low-fat milk
1 pint low-fat vanilla yogurt
⅓ cup frozen orange juice concentrate, undiluted
6 mint sprigs or edible flowers (optional garnish)

Set aside 6 peach slices for garnish, if desired. In blender or food processor, place ½ of peaches, the milk, yogurt and juice concentrate; purée. Add remaining peaches and blend until smooth. Pour into glasses. Garnish with peach slices and mint sprigs, if desired. *Makes 6 servings*

Four-Grain Pear Muffins

Vegetable cooking spray
2 fresh California Bartlett pears, cored and chopped (2⅓ cups)
½ cup packed brown sugar
½ cup low-fat milk
½ cup vegetable oil
1 egg
¾ cup all-purpose flour
¾ cup yellow cornmeal
½ cup buckwheat flour or whole wheat flour
½ cup oat bran
¼ cup raisins
1 tablespoon baking powder

Preheat oven to 375°F. Coat muffin pan cups with vegetable cooking spray. In large bowl, beat pears, sugar, milk, oil and egg until sugar is dissolved. Combine remaining ingredients and stir into pear mixture until just combined. Spoon into muffin cups.

Bake 25 minutes or until wooden pick inserted in center comes out clean. Remove from oven and let cool 5 minutes. Turn out onto wire rack to cool completely.
Makes 12 muffins

Tip: Recipe can be doubled. Make one batch for now and freeze the other batch for later.

Fresh Peach Muffins

To eliminate the saturated fat often used in muffins, we've used extra-light olive oil—high in the "good" monounsaturated fat.

Vegetable cooking spray
3 fresh California peaches, chopped (about 1⅔ cups)
⅔ cup sugar
¼ cup extra-light olive or vegetable oil
¼ cup low-fat milk
1 egg
2⅓ cups all-purpose flour
⅓ cup flaked coconut
⅓ cup chopped walnuts
1 teaspoon baking soda
1 teaspoon finely grated lemon peel
½ teaspoon salt

Preheat oven to 375°F. Coat muffin pan cups with vegetable cooking spray. In large bowl, beat peaches, sugar, oil, milk and egg until sugar is dissolved. Combine remaining ingredients and stir into peach mixture until just combined. Spoon into muffin cups.

Bake 25 minutes or until wooden pick inserted in center comes out clean. Remove from oven and let cool 5 minutes. Turn out onto wire rack to cool completely.
Makes 12 muffins

Honey Peach Topping

4 fresh California peaches,
   coarsely chopped (about
   1½ cups)
1 cup sugar
⅓ cup honey
¼ teaspoon ground allspice
1 envelope (2 ounces) powdered
   fruit pectin

In 2-quart glass measure, combine
peaches, sugar, honey and allspice.
Microwave on HIGH, uncovered,
12 to 15 minutes, stirring every
5 minutes, until fruit is cooked. Stir
in pectin and microwave on HIGH
2 minutes longer. Pour into clean jars
or freezer storage bags; store in
refrigerator up to 2 weeks or freeze
up to 1 year.

Makes three ½-pint jars

No-Sugar Pear Berry Jam

10 fresh California Bartlett pears,
   chopped (about 9 cups)
1 package (10 ounces) frozen
   raspberries, thawed
2 envelopes (2 ounces *each*)
   powdered fruit pectin
2 tablespoons lemon juice
¼ cup powdered non-sugar
   sweetener (about 40 packets)

In heavy 4-quart saucepan, place
pears, raspberries, pectin and lemon
juice. Bring to a boil, reduce heat
and simmer, stirring constantly, 10 to
15 minutes until fruit is desired
thickness. Remove from heat and stir
in sweetener. Spoon into clean jars *or*
freezer storage bags. Cool
completely; store in refrigerator up to
3 weeks or freeze up to 1 year.

Makes 7 cups

Gingered Muffins

Vegetable cooking spray
2 fresh California nectarines,
   chopped (about 1⅓ cups)
1 cup sugar
½ cup vegetable oil or margarine
1 egg
1½ cups all-purpose flour
½ cup oat bran
2 teaspoons baking soda
¼ to ½ teaspoon ground ginger

Preheat oven to 375°F. Coat muffin
pan cups with vegetable cooking
spray. In large bowl, beat nectarines,
sugar, oil and egg until sugar is
dissolved. Combine remaining
ingredients and stir into nectarine
mixture until just combined. Spoon
into muffin cups. Bake 20 to 25
minutes or until wooden pick
inserted in center comes out clean.
Remove from oven and let cool 5
minutes. Turn out onto wire rack to
cool completely.

Makes 12 muffins

Summer Fruit

1 cup frozen orange juice
   concentrate, undiluted
½ cup water
2 tablespoons chopped candied
   ginger
1 tablespoon sugar
2 fresh California peaches, sliced
1 fresh California nectarine, sliced
1 fresh California Bartlett pear,
   cored and sliced
1 plum, sliced

In medium bowl, combine juice
concentrate, water, ginger and sugar.
Add fruit and toss gently to mix.
Refrigerate until chilled.

Makes 4 servings

Creamy Brown Rice

Try this satisfying rice dish for brunch or breakfast. It makes a great change from cold cereal.

1½ cups water
½ cup low-fat milk
1 tablespoon margarine or butter
¼ teaspoon salt
1 cup brown rice
   No-Sugar Pear Berry Jam or Honey Peach Topping (see page 43)

In medium saucepan, bring water, milk, margarine and salt to a boil. Stir in rice and bring to a boil again. Cook, covered, 45 to 50 minutes or until liquid is absorbed and rice is tender. Spoon into bowls and top with a generous spoonful of No-Sugar Pear Berry Jam.

Makes 4 servings

Fresh Peach Salsa

A mild and versatile salsa.

2 fresh California peaches, diced (about 1⅓ cups)
2 plums, diced (about ⅔ cup)
⅓ cup raisins
¼ cup diced red onion
1 to 2 tablespoons lemon juice
1 tablespoon chopped fresh mint
8 fresh flour tortillas, quarters or strips, warmed

In medium bowl, combine all ingredients except tortillas. Cover and refrigerate. Spoon onto tortilla quarters.   *Makes about 3 cups*

Tip: *Best if prepared a day ahead.*

Serving Suggestions: *Makes a delicious low-calorie topping for grilled chicken, pork, lamb or fish. Also great on quesadillas.*

Pear-Pepper Salsa

2 fresh California Bartlett pears, pared, cored and diced (about 2½ cups)
⅓ cup diced red bell pepper
⅓ cup golden raisins
2 green onions, thinly sliced
1 fresh jalapeño pepper, minced *or* 1 tablespoon canned diced jalapeño
1 tablespoon white wine vinegar
2 teaspoons minced ginger root *or* ½ teaspoon ground ginger
8 fresh flour tortillas, quarters or strips, warmed

In medium bowl, combine all ingredients except tortillas. Cover and refrigerate. Spoon onto tortilla quarters.   *Makes about 3 cups*

Serving Suggestions: *Makes a delicious low-calorie topping for grilled chicken, pork or fish. Also great on quesadillas.*

Mint-Nectarine Salsa

2 fresh California nectarines, chopped
1½ tablespoons chopped fresh mint
1 tablespoon lemon juice
8 fresh flour tortillas, quarters or strips, warmed

In small bowl, combine all ingredients except tortillas. Cover and refrigerate. Spoon onto tortilla quarters.   *Makes about 1½ cups*

Serving Suggestions: *Makes a delicious low-calorie topping for grilled chicken, beef, pork or fish. Also great on quesadillas.*

From top to bottom: Fresh Peach Salsa, Pear-Pepper Salsa and Mint-Nectarine Salsa

Dessert Fruit Pizza

    1 sheet (12-inch square) frozen
        puff pastry, thawed
    1 ounce shredded mozzarella
        cheese (about ¼ cup)
    ½ cup ricotta cheese
    ¼ cup golden raisins
    2 tablespoons chopped walnuts
    ½ teaspoon ground cinnamon
    ½ teaspoon ground nutmeg
    2 fresh California nectarines,
        sliced
    1 fresh California Bartlett pear,
        cored and sliced
    3 tablespoons orange marmalade,
        warmed

Preheat oven to 400°F. On large baking pan, place pastry; fold edges under to form ridge. Sprinkle with mozzarella. Top with small dollops of ricotta. Sprinkle with raisins, nuts and spices. Arrange fruit on top. Drizzle with marmalade. Bake 20 to 25 minutes or until pastry is puffed and brown.   *Makes 6 servings*

Smoked Chicken Pizza

    3 tablespoons yellow cornmeal,
        divided
    1 loaf (1 pound) frozen bread
        dough, thawed
    1 tablespoon olive or vegetable oil
    6 ounces Monterey Jack cheese,
        shredded (about 1½ cups),
        divided
    4 plums *or* 2 fresh California
        nectarines, sliced
    6 ounces shredded smoked or
        roasted chicken
    2 jalapeño peppers, seeds
        removed, thinly sliced
    2 teaspoons chopped fresh
        cilantro

Preheat oven to 425°F. In 10-inch oiled cast-iron skillet, sprinkle 2 tablespoons cornmeal. Stretch dough to fit bottom of skillet. Sprinkle with oil. Sprinkle with remaining 1 tablespoon cornmeal. Top with ½ of cheese, the fruit, chicken, peppers and cilantro. Top with remaining cheese. Bake 15 to 20 minutes or until cheese is melted.
      Makes 6 servings

Chinese Chicken Salad with Peaches

ORIENTAL DRESSING
    ¼ cup prepared Italian salad
        dressing
    2 tablespoons sugar
    1 tablespoon low-sodium soy
        sauce
    ¼ teaspoon ground ginger

SALAD
    1 quart prepared deli Chinese
        chicken or turkey salad
    2 fresh California peaches, sliced
    ½ head lettuce, thinly sliced
    1 can (3 ounces) chow mein
        noodles *or* 2 ounces rice
        sticks, fried
    ¼ cup peanuts or sliced almonds
        (optional garnish)

In large bowl, combine dressing ingredients. Add Chinese chicken salad and peaches. Toss lightly. Arrange lettuce on individual plates or serving platter. Sprinkle noodles on lettuce. Top with chicken salad mixture. Garnish with nuts, if desired.   *Makes 6 servings*

Top: Smoked Chicken Pizza;
bottom: Dessert Fruit Pizza

Tortellini and Artichokes in Garlic Cream Sauce

Extra quick in the microwave.

GARLIC CREAM SAUCE
    3 tablespoons margarine or butter
    3 tablespoons all-purpose flour
1½ cups low-fat milk
    ¾ teaspoon garlic powder

SALAD
    1 quart prepared deli tortellini
        salad
    2 fresh California nectarines or
        Bartlett pears, sliced
    1 jar (6 ounces) marinated
        artichoke hearts, drained and
        halved
    ⅓ cup freshly grated Parmesan
        cheese (optional)
        Parsley (optional garnish)

For Sauce, in 4-cup microwave-safe measure, microwave margarine on HIGH 45 seconds or until melted. Blend in flour. Slowly whisk in milk. Add garlic powder. Microwave on HIGH 3 to 4 minutes or until thickened, stirring every minute.

For Salad, in microwave-safe casserole, place tortellini salad. Cover with plastic wrap, venting one corner. Microwave on HIGH 4 to 5 minutes, stirring after 2 minutes, until heated through. Add nectarines and microwave on HIGH 2 minutes longer or until heated through. Stir in Garlic Cream Sauce. Garnish with artichoke hearts. Sprinkle with Parmesan cheese and parsley, if desired.   *Makes 6 servings*

Tips:
• *Deli tortellini salads will have a white or red based dressing; either are delicious in this recipe.*
• *To save time, use a prepared deli Alfredo sauce in place of the Garlic Cream Sauce and omit the Parmesan cheese.*

Pear Nut Bread with Citrus Cream Cheese

One or two toasted slices are great for breakfast.

PEAR NUT BREAD
    1 package (14 ounces) nut
        bread mix
    ⅛ teaspoon ground nutmeg
    1 fresh California Bartlett pear,
        cored and finely chopped
        (about 1¼ cups)

CITRUS CREAM CHEESE
    1 package (8 ounces) light cream
        cheese (Neufchatel), softened
    1 tablespoon finely grated orange
        peel

Grease and flour 8×4×3-inch loaf pan. Prepare bread mix according to package directions, adding nutmeg and *substituting pear for ½ the liquid required.* Bake according to package directions. In small bowl, combine cheese and orange peel. Serve Pear Nut Bread with Citrus Cream Cheese.   *Makes 1 loaf*

Sparkling Peach Pick-Me-Up

How easy can it get?

    1 fresh California peach,
        quartered
    1 bottle (10 ounces) club soda or
        sparkling mineral water
        Fruit Cubes (see page 12)

In blender or food processor, blend peach until smooth. Pour peach purée into tall glass. Add soda water and 1 or 2 Fruit Cubes.
          Makes 1 serving

*Sparkling Peach Pick-Me-Up and
Pear Nut Bread with Citrus Cream Cheese*

Quick and Creamy Cocoa Dip for Fruit

Whether you're a kid with a coloring book or an adult with a checkbook, this snack makes the task go faster.

> 1 carton (8 ounces) low-fat vanilla or honey yogurt
> 1 tablespoon unsweetened cocoa powder
> 4 fresh California peaches, plums, nectarines or Bartlett pears (or any combination), sliced

Combine yogurt and cocoa in serving bowl. Serve with sliced fruit.

Makes 4 servings

Tip: *To keep fruit colors bright and prevent browning, dip sliced fruit in mixture of 1 tablespoon lemon juice and 1 cup water.*

Summer Fruit Slices with Sparkling Mineral Water

Keep a supply of frozen fruit slices handy in the freezer. They lend a festive air to mineral water or any chilled beverage.

> 1 fresh California peach, nectarine or Bartlett pear, sliced
> 1 bottle (28 ounces) sparkling mineral water or soda water

Place fruit slices in single layer on foil or small baking sheet; freeze until firm. Place any fruit slice, or a mixture, into glass. Add mineral water.　　*Makes 4 servings*

Picnic Pointers: *Store fruit slices in unbreakable container.*

Sesame Ginger Pasta Salad

Transform a plain pasta salad into something quite special.

SESAME GINGER DRESSING
> 1/4 cup prepared red wine vinegar and oil salad dressing
> 1 to 2 tablespoons chopped fresh cilantro (optional)
> 1 tablespoon low-sodium soy sauce
> 2 tablespoons sesame seeds
> 1 to 1½ teaspoons ground ginger
> 1/4 teaspoon garlic powder

SALAD
> 1 quart prepared deli rotelli, fusilli or macaroni pasta salad
> 1/2 red onion, thinly sliced
> 2 fresh California nectarines, cubed
> 1/2 head lettuce, thinly sliced
> 1 can (4½ ounces) small shrimp, drained (optional garnish)

In large bowl, whisk all dressing ingredients to combine. Add pasta salad, onion and nectarines. Toss lightly. Arrange lettuce on individual plates or serving platter. Top with pasta salad mixture and garnish with shrimp, if desired.

Makes 6 servings

Tip: *Sesame seeds may be toasted for added flavor, if desired.*

Quick and Creamy Cocoa Dip for Fruit

Lemon Poached Pears with Chocolate Cherry Sauce

Lemon Poached Pears with Chocolate Cherry Sauce

LEMON POACHED PEARS
    4 fresh California Bartlett pears, pared
    2 cups water
    2 tablespoons lemon juice
    1 (4-inch) cinnamon stick
    2 whole cloves

CHOCOLATE CHERRY SAUCE
    1 cup semi-sweet chocolate chips
    ¼ cup brandy
    ½ cup fresh or frozen pitted cherries

For Pears, in large microwave-safe casserole, place pears, water, lemon juice, cinnamon and cloves. Cover with plastic wrap, venting one corner. Microwave on HIGH 5 to 7 minutes or until pears are just barely tender, giving casserole a ¼ turn after 3 minutes. Drain pears, discarding liquid.

For Chocolate Cherry Sauce, in small microwave-safe bowl, combine chocolate and brandy. Microwave on HIGH 1 to 2 minutes or until chocolate is melted. Whisk until smooth. Stir in cherries and microwave on HIGH another 1 to 2 minutes to heat through.

To serve, place pears on individual serving plates. Spoon Chocolate Cherry Sauce over pears.

Makes 4 servings

Tip: *Use a potato peeler to easily pare pears.*

Peachy Pasta Salad

SALAD
    1 package (8 ounces) bow tie or wagon wheel pasta
    2 tablespoons vegetable oil
    3 fresh California peaches, sliced
    1 red bell pepper, slivered
    ½ cup pecan or walnut halves
    ¼ cup non-fat plain yogurt

BASIL DRESSING
    ¾ cup vegetable oil
    ⅓ cup white wine vinegar
    ¼ cup chopped fresh basil
    2 teaspoons minced garlic
    ½ teaspoon salt

In large saucepan, cook pasta in boiling salted water with 2 tablespoons oil until tender, about 8 minutes. Drain and rinse under cool water. In large bowl, combine pasta, peaches, bell pepper, nuts and yogurt. In jar, combine dressing ingredients; shake. Pour dressing over pasta and toss gently. Refrigerate until chilled, if desired. *Makes 6 servings*

Tip: *If fresh basil is not available, substitute 2 tablespoons chopped fresh parsley and 1 tablespoon dried basil.*

Grilled Halibut with Zinfandel Sauce

Fish is always a barbecue favorite.

ZINFANDEL SAUCE
   3 tablespoons margarine or butter
   1/3 pound fresh mushrooms, thinly
      sliced
   1 cup Zinfandel wine
   2 fresh California nectarines,
      sliced
   3 tablespoons finely sliced green
      onions
   2 teaspoons cornstarch
   2 tablespoons water

FISH
   1½ pounds halibut steaks (4 equal
      pieces)
   Chives (optional garnish)

For Sauce, in medium saucepan or disposable foil saucepan, over medium heat, melt margarine. Add mushrooms and cook, stirring frequently, until liquid evaporates, about 8 minutes. Add wine, nectarines and onions and cook until nectarines are slightly soft. Combine cornstarch and water; whisk into sauce, stirring constantly, until slightly thickened. Set on side of barbecue to keep warm, if desired.

For Fish, cook halibut in oiled barbecue basket on uncovered grill over medium, direct heat 5 minutes on each side or until fish flakes easily with fork. Place on plates and spoon sauce over halibut; garnish with chives, if desired.

Makes 4 servings

Serving Suggestion: *Serve with brown or wild rice blend and steamed snow peas.*

Barbecue Basics: *See page 28 for making disposable foil saucepans.*

Peach Spritzer

Cool and breezy.

   2 fresh California peaches,
      puréed (1 cup)
   Crushed ice
   1 bottle (750 ml) white wine,
      chilled
   1 can (12 ounces) lemon
      lime soda

Divide peach purée among tall glasses. Fill 4 glasses with crushed ice. Add white wine and soda.

Makes 4 servings

Pear-Lime Freeze

   2 fresh California Bartlett pears,
      cored and quartered
   2 cups white grape juice or water,
      chilled
   1 can (6 ounces) frozen limeade
      concentrate
   5 ice cubes

In blender or food processor, blend pears until smooth. Add remaining ingredients and blend until slushy. Serve immediately.

Makes 6 servings

Cocktail: *Substitute 2 cups dry white wine for grape juice.*

Elegant
Entertaining

Delicious Dessert Buffet (from left to right): Brownie Pie with Quick Fruit Ice Cream (see page 57), Heavenly Peach Cake with Citrus Peach Sauce (see page 56) and Blitz Torte with Fruit (see page 57)

Heavenly Peach Cake with Citrus Peach Sauce

The delightful flavor combination of peaches and oranges makes this cake a sure-to-please winner.

CAKE
  1 package (18.25 ounces) yellow cake mix
1¹/3 cups orange juice, approximate
  1 teaspoon finely grated orange peel

FROSTING
  3 packages (8 ounces *each*) light cream cheese (Neufchatel), softened
3¹/2 cups (1-pound package) powdered sugar
  1 tablespoon finely grated orange peel

  3 fresh California peaches, thinly sliced
  Fresh mint sprigs (optional garnish)

CITRUS PEACH SAUCE
  2 fresh California peaches, divided
  2 cups orange juice
  2 tablespoons cornstarch

For Cake, preheat oven to 350°F. Grease and flour two 9-inch cake pans. In large bowl, prepare cake mix according to package directions substituting orange juice and orange peel for water. Beat until smooth. Pour batter into cake pans. Bake 25 to 30 minutes or until toothpick inserted in center comes out clean. Cool on wire rack 10 minutes. Remove from pans and cool completely. Cut each cake in half horizontally (see Tip).

For Frosting, in medium bowl, combine cheese, powdered sugar and orange peel. Beat until smooth. If necessary, add small amount of milk or orange juice to thin to spreading consistency.

To assemble, place 1 cake layer on serving plate and spread with about ¹/2 cup frosting. Top with second cake layer and another ¹/2 cup frosting. Reserve 6 peach slices for garnish. Cover frosting with remaining peach slices. Repeat layers of cake and frosting. Frost top and sides with remaining frosting. Garnish with reserved peach slices and mint sprigs, if desired.

For Sauce, purée 1 peach. In small saucepan, combine peach purée, orange juice and cornstarch. Bring to a boil, stirring constantly. Simmer 1 minute or until thickened. Refrigerate. Slice remaining peach and add to sauce.

To serve, place about ¹/3 cup sauce on individual dessert plates. Place cake slices on top of sauce.

Makes 10 servings

Tip: To cut cake layers in half evenly, mark center point at intervals with toothpicks. Use long, serrated knife or dental floss to cut cake using toothpicks as a guide.

Buffet Pointers: Prepare cake, frosting and sauce ahead of time and freeze. Thaw completely. Slice fresh fruit and assemble cake up to 4 hours before serving.

Blitz Torte with Fruit

MERINGUE TOPPING
  4 egg whites
  ¾ cup sugar

TORTE
  1 package (18.25 ounces) butter
    recipe golden cake mix
  ½ cup sliced almonds
  1 tablespoon sugar
  ½ teaspoon ground cinnamon
  1 fresh California peach, sliced
  2 fresh California nectarines,
    sliced
  1 fresh California Bartlett pear,
    cored and sliced
  1 plum, sliced

For Meringue, in large bowl, beat egg whites until soft peaks form. Gradually beat in ¾ cup sugar until stiff glossy peaks form. Set aside.

For Torte, preheat oven to 375°F. Grease and flour two 8-inch cake pans. Make foil collars for each pan (see Tip). Prepare cake according to package directions and spread in pans. Spread meringue over batter. Sprinkle with almonds, 1 tablespoon sugar and cinnamon. Secure foil collars around pans with string. Bake on lowest rack position in oven 35 to 40 minutes until meringue is well-browned and toothpick inserted in center comes out clean. Remove from pans and cool on wire rack, meringue-side up. Place one cake layer, meringue-side up, on serving plate. Arrange ½ of fruit on top. Place remaining cake layer, meringue-side up, on top of fruit. Serve each portion with a few slices of remaining fruit.

Makes 10 servings

Tip: *To make foil collars, tear off two 28-inch pieces of foil. Fold lengthwise into thirds.*

Brownie Pie with Quick Fruit Ice Cream

Delicious and oh, so easy.

BROWNIE
  1 package (23.5 ounces) brownie
    mix

QUICK FRUIT ICE CREAM
  2 fresh California peaches *or*
    4 plums, puréed
  1 pint vanilla ice cream, softened

Preheat oven to 350°F. Prepare brownie mix according to package directions and spread in greased 9-inch pie pan. Bake 45 minutes. Cool on wire rack. In medium bowl, stir puréed fruit into ice cream. Freeze until firm, 2 to 3 hours. Remove from freezer about 30 minutes before serving. To serve, cut brownie into pie-shaped wedges and top with a scoop of ice cream.

Makes 8 servings

Tip: *For easy serving, scoop ice cream ahead of time. Scoop each ball and place on waxed-paper-lined baking sheet or plate. Refreeze until ready to serve.*

California Chicken Salad

LEMON-MUSTARD DRESSING
  2/3 cup olive or vegetable oil
  1/3 cup lemon juice
  1 1/2 teaspoons dry mustard
     Salt and pepper, to taste

SALAD
  1 package (6 ounces) long-grain
     and wild rice blend
  2 3/4 cups chicken broth, divided
  2 whole chicken breasts, split,
     boned and skinned
  2 stalks celery, thinly sliced
  1 green bell pepper, chopped
  1/2 cup chopped red onion
  16 lettuce leaves
  3 fresh California peaches, sliced

In small bowl, combine all dressing ingredients; set aside. In medium, covered saucepan, cook rice and seasoning packet in 1 3/4 cups broth 30 minutes. Cool. Meanwhile, in large, covered skillet, poach chicken breasts in remaining 1 cup broth 15 to 20 minutes or until cooked through. Cool; shred chicken. Combine rice with celery, bell pepper and onion. Line serving platter or individual salad plates with lettuce leaves. Arrange 2/3 cup rice, chicken and peach slices on lettuce. Serve Lemon-Mustard Dressing separately.

Makes 4 servings

Tip: *If desired, toss shredded chicken with 1/3 cup dressing and toss rice mixture with remaining 2/3 cup dressing.*

Chicken with Peach-Champagne Sauce

CHICKEN
  1 whole chicken breast, split,
     boned and skinned
  2 teaspoons lemon juice
     Pepper, to taste
  2 fresh California peaches, sliced

PEACH-CHAMPAGNE SAUCE
  1 tablespoon margarine or butter
  1 tablespoon minced red onion
  1 tablespoon all-purpose flour
  1/4 cup Champagne or white wine

     Spinach noodles, cooked
        (optional)

For Chicken, in small microwave-safe baking dish, arrange chicken with thicker parts to the outside. Sprinkle with lemon juice and pepper. Cover with waxed paper and microwave on HIGH 5 minutes or until no longer pink and cooked through; reserve cooking liquid. Add peach slices to chicken and cook on HIGH 1 to 2 minutes longer.

For Sauce, in 4-cup glass measure, combine margarine and onion. Cook on HIGH 1 minute. Stir in flour and 3 tablespoons cooking liquid. Stir in Champagne. Cook on HIGH 3 minutes or until thickened, stirring after 1 1/2 minutes. Serve chicken and peaches on noodles. Spoon sauce over chicken. *Makes 2 servings*

Chicken with Peach-Champagne Sauce

Hearty Roast Beef, Pear and Pea Pod Salad

SALAD
  1 head lettuce
  10 ounces sliced rare roast beef, cut into strips
  2 carrots, peeled, cut into matchstick pieces
  3 fresh California Bartlett pears, cored and sliced
  1 small red onion, halved and thinly sliced
  10 ounces fresh Chinese pea pods (about 1¼ cups), trimmed
  ¼ cup pitted ripe or cured black olives (optional garnish)

MUSTARD VINAIGRETTE
  1 bottle (8 ounces) Italian salad dressing
  2 teaspoons Dijon-style mustard

On serving platter or individual plates, arrange lettuce leaves. Place remaining salad ingredients on top. In small bowl, combine vinaigrette ingredients and drizzle over salad.

Makes 4 servings

Tip: *To keep fruit colors bright, dip pear slices in Mustard Vinaigrette as you cut them, or cut pears just before serving.*

Poolside Fruit Salad Platter with Honey-Lemon Yogurt Dip

This works equally well as an appetizer, a salad or even as a refreshing dessert.

FRUIT
  2 kiwifruit, peeled and sliced
  2 plums, sliced
  1 fresh California nectarine, sliced
  1 fresh California peach, sliced
  1 fresh California Bartlett pear, cored and sliced
  ⅓ cup fresh blueberries (optional)

HONEY-LEMON YOGURT DIP
  1 cup non-fat lemon yogurt
  1 tablespoon honey
  1 strip lemon peel (optional garnish)

Line serving platter with kiwifruit. Top with remaining fruit. In small bowl, combine yogurt and honey. Spoon over fruit. Garnish with lemon peel, if desired.

Makes 6 servings

For Perfect Salads

To crisp lettuce: Pull greens apart and rinse in cool water; shake off excess water and store in plastic bag several hours or overnight. Because iceberg lettuce tends to "rust," place the entire head into a plastic bag with a damp paper towel and refrigerate several hours or overnight.

To crisp vegetables: Most vegetables will be crisp if rinsed in cool water and stored in plastic bags.

Top: Poolside Fruit Salad Platter with Honey-Lemon Yogurt Dip; bottom: Hearty Roast Beef, Pear and Pea Pod Salad

Four Fruit Antipasto Salad

HERB VINAIGRETTE
  2/3 cup vegetable or olive oil
  1/3 cup red wine vinegar
  1 tablespoon sugar
  1 teaspoon minced garlic
  1 teaspoon dry mustard
  1 teaspoon dried basil
  1/2 teaspoon dried thyme
  1/2 teaspoon salt

SALAD
  1 fresh California peach, sliced
  1 fresh California nectarine, sliced
  1 fresh California Bartlett pear, cored and sliced into wedges
  1 plum, sliced into wedges
  1 red bell pepper, cut into slivers (1 cup)
  1 package (5 1/2 ounces) plain or herbed goat cheese, sliced *or* 1 package (8 ounces) light cream cheese (Neufchatel), sliced
  1 cup pimiento-stuffed green olives
  4 cups torn spinach leaves

In blender or food processor, place all vinaigrette ingredients and blend until combined; set aside. Arrange all salad ingredients on bed of spinach leaves. Serve with Herb Vinaigrette.

Makes 4 main-dish servings or 8 first-course servings

Nectarine and Almond No-Bake Cheese Pie

  1 package (8 ounces) light cream cheese (Neufchatel), softened
  2 tablespoons sugar
  1/2 teaspoon ground cinnamon
  1 (6-ounce) prepared graham cracker crust
  1/3 cup slivered almonds, toasted (see Tip)
  3 fresh California nectarines, coarsely chopped (1 3/4 cups)
  2/3 cup apple juice, divided
  1/3 cup sugar
  1 envelope unflavored gelatin
  1/2 cup whipping cream, whipped

In small bowl, combine cheese, 2 tablespoons sugar and cinnamon; beat until smooth. Spread over crust. Reserve 1 tablespoon nuts for garnish, if desired. Top cheese mixture with remaining nuts; press into cheese slightly. Refrigerate until chilled. In medium saucepan, combine nectarines, 1/3 cup apple juice and 1/3 cup sugar. Cook over medium heat about 5 minutes, stirring frequently. In small saucepan, sprinkle gelatin over remaining 1/3 cup apple juice; heat over low heat, stirring until gelatin dissolves, about 2 minutes. Add gelatin mixture to nectarine mixture. Refrigerate to cool. Pour over filled pie crust; refrigerate several hours or until firm. To serve, top with whipped cream and remaining 1 tablespoon nuts, if desired.

Makes 8 servings

Tips:
• *To toast almonds, spread on baking sheet and toast in 350°F oven 7 to 10 minutes or until golden brown.*
• *To chill nectarine mixture quickly, place saucepan in a bowl filled with ice cubes and water.*

Four Fruit Antipasto Salad

Fast and Fancy Floating Meringue Islands

Now you can do these in less than 2 minutes in the microwave.

VANILLA SAUCE
   1 package (3¼ ounces) vanilla
      pudding mix, divided
  ½ cup low-fat milk
   1 to 2 teaspoons cream
      Sherry wine
   1 fresh California nectarine,
      puréed (about ½ cup)

MERINGUES
   2 egg whites
  ¼ cup sugar
  ⅛ teaspoon cream of tartar
      Pinch ground nutmeg
   3 plums *or* 2 fresh California
      nectarines, sliced

For Sauce, in small saucepan, combine ¼ package (2 tablespoons) pudding mix with milk. (Use remainder of package for another use, see Hint). Bring to a boil, reduce heat and simmer until thickened, stirring constantly. Remove from heat, stir in Sherry and nectarine; let cool.

For Meringues, in medium bowl, beat egg whites until frothy. Gradually add sugar, cream of tartar and nutmeg and continue beating until stiff and glossy peaks form. Spoon ½ of meringue into a tall, peaked mound onto double thickness of waxed paper or microwave-safe plate. Microwave on MEDIUM (50% power) 45 seconds, give ½ turn and continue cooking about 15 seconds longer or until meringue is softly set. If additional cooking is needed, cook in 15 second intervals. If using probe, cook until internal temperature reaches 140°F. Repeat process with remaining meringue.

To serve, place ½ cup sauce on each dessert plate. Place meringue on top of sauce. Make a circle of fruit slices around meringue. *Makes 2 servings*

Tip: Meringue will rise slowly as it cooks during first 45 seconds. During the next 15 seconds it should not be allowed to rise again. If overcooked it will collapse slightly and toughen. Serve meringue warm or let stand up to 1 hour.

Hint: For remaining pudding mix, combine mix with 1½ cups milk. Cook according to package directions. Makes 3 servings

Cheesecake with Brandied Peaches

 1½ cups water
 1½ cups sugar
   1 (4-inch) cinnamon stick
   4 fresh California peaches, halved
  ½ cup brandy
   1 frozen prepared cheesecake,
      thawed and sliced

In 2-quart glass measure, combine water, sugar and cinnamon stick. Microwave on HIGH 5 to 6 minutes or until syrup boils vigorously. Carefully add peaches and microwave on HIGH 4 to 6 minutes or until peaches are tender, stirring every 2 minutes. With slotted spoon, remove peaches to heatproof bowl. Microwave syrup on HIGH 10 to 12 minutes or until thickened. Pour brandy over peaches. Add enough syrup to cover peaches. Refrigerate until ready to serve.

Place cheesecake slices on dessert plates. Top with 2 peach halves and a little brandy sauce.

Makes 8 servings

Toffee-Topped Peach Pie

The crunchy praline topping makes this no-bake pie a special treat.

ALMOND CRUNCH TOPPING
- 1/3 cup granulated sugar
- 2 tablespoons water
- 1/2 cup slivered almonds, toasted (see Tip)

PIE
- 1 package (8 ounces) light cream cheese (Neufchatel), softened
- 1/3 cup powdered sugar
- 1/3 cup light sour cream
- 1/2 teaspoon vanilla extract
- 3 fresh California peaches, very thinly sliced, divided
- 1 (6-ounce) prepared graham cracker crust

For Topping, in small saucepan, combine granulated sugar and water. Cook until syrup turns a light golden brown, about 4 minutes. Add toasted nuts; pour at once onto buttered baking sheet. Cool. When cooled, break up and coarsely crush in food processor or blender (see Hint).

For Pie, in large bowl, beat cheese, powdered sugar and sour cream until smooth. Stir in vanilla and 1/4 cup Almond Crunch Topping. Place 2/3 of peach slices in pie crust. Spread cheese mixture over fruit. Sprinkle with remaining topping. Arrange remaining peaches on top.

Makes 8 servings

Tips:
- *After cooking the syrup, immediately rinse pan with hot water. The sugar syrup will dissolve easily.*
- *To toast almonds, spread on baking sheet and toast in 350°F oven 7 to 10 minutes or until golden brown.*

Serving Suggestions: Almond Crunch Topping is excellent to use over sliced peaches, ice cream or pudding.

Hint: For convenience, crushed English toffee candies may be substituted for the Almond Crunch Topping.

Elegant Summertime Salad

This salad boasts an unusual combination of nectarines with vegetables and cheese. An ultra-light dressing accompanies.

- Juice of 1 lime
- 2 tablespoons vegetable oil
- Freshly ground pepper (optional)
- 2 fresh California nectarines, sliced
- 1 tomato, cut into wedges
- 1 pink or white grapefruit, peeled and chopped
- 1 avocado, peeled, pitted and cubed
- 1/2 cup cubed sharp Cheddar cheese
- 2 cups torn lettuce

In small bowl, combine lime juice, oil and pepper. In salad bowl, combine remaining ingredients. Pour dressing over salad and toss gently.

Makes 4 servings

Tips:
- *Turn this into a heartier entrée salad by adding a can of drained water-packed tuna or salmon.*
- *Any favorite nut may be added to this salad. Dry-roasted varieties work especially well.*

Toffee-Topped Peach Pie

Peanut Butter 'n' Jam Building Block Cake

These whimsical cakes will be appreciated by kids of all ages.

> 3 packages (18.25 ounces *each*)
>   yellow cake mix
> **Chunky Nectarine Filling**
>   (recipe follows)
> **Peanut Butter Frosting** (recipe
>   follows)
> 1 can (16 ounces) creamy vanilla
>   frosting
> **Food coloring**
> **Fruit-shaped marzipan and
>   colored sugars
>   (optional garnish)**
> **Quick Fruit Ice Cream
>   (see page 57)**

Prepare each cake mix and bake in 12 × 8 × 2-inch baking pans according to package directions. Cool. Using long, serrated knife, cut each cake in half horizontally. Spread bottom layers with 1 to 1⅓ cups Chunky Nectarine Filling; replace top layer. Trim off outer edges and cut each cake into six 3-inch squares. Brush off loose crumbs.

Frost each cake square with about ⅓ cup Peanut Butter Frosting. With long spatula that has been dipped in hot water, smooth frosting around edges and corners.

Color portions of vanilla frosting as desired. Fill pastry bag fitted with small rose tip with frosting. Decorate each block as desired. Using a writing tip, add contrasting letters and numbers as desired. Place marzipan fruit on blocks, if desired. Serve with Quick Fruit Ice Cream.   *Makes 18 servings*

Tip: *Can be prepared 24 hours ahead of time. Refrigerate until ready to serve.*

Chunky Nectarine Filling

> 5 fresh California nectarines,
>   chopped (about 3 cups)
> 1½ cups sugar
>   ½ teaspoon ground cinnamon
>   ¼ teaspoon ground allspice
>   3 tablespoons water
>   3 tablespoons cornstarch

In 2-quart glass measure, combine nectarines, sugar and spices. Microwave on HIGH, uncovered, 15 minutes, stirring every 5 minutes. Combine water and cornstarch. Stir into nectarine mixture and microwave on HIGH 2 minutes longer or until thickened, stirring after 1 minute. Cool to room temperature.   *Makes 4 cups*

Peanut Butter Frosting

> 9 cups powdered sugar
> 1½ cups creamy peanut butter
> 1½ cups margarine or butter,
>   softened
>   1 cup low-fat milk
>   1 tablespoon vanilla extract

In medium bowl, beat all ingredients until smooth.   *Makes 6 cups*

Top: Peanut Butter 'n' Jam Building Block Cake; bottom: Quick Fruit Ice Cream (see page 57)

Nectarine-Strawberry Shortcake Torte

CAKE
2 cups buttermilk baking mix
2 eggs, lightly beaten
½ cup low-fat milk
¼ cup granulated sugar
  Finely grated peel of one
    lemon
1 tablespoon lemon juice

FILLING
1 package (8 ounces) light cream
    cheese (Neufchatel), softened
½ cup powdered sugar
4 fresh California nectarines,
    divided
1 pint strawberries, rinsed and
    hulled
1 envelope unflavored gelatin
¼ cup water
3 mint sprigs (optional garnish)

For Cake, preheat oven to 375°F. In large bowl, beat cake ingredients until just combined, about 30 seconds. Pour into greased 9-inch tart or cake pan. Bake 20 to 25 minutes or until toothpick inserted in center comes out clean. Cool on wire rack 10 minutes; turn out onto rack to cool completely.

For Filling, in medium bowl, beat cheese and powdered sugar until smooth. Purée 3 nectarines and all but 5 strawberries. Beat fruit purée into cheese mixture. In 1-cup glass measure, sprinkle gelatin over water. Microwave on HIGH 25 to 30 seconds; stir to dissolve. Stir into fruit-cheese mixture. Refrigerate until slightly thickened. Spread over top of cake layer. Slice remaining nectarine and arrange on top. Garnish with remaining 5 strawberries and mint sprigs, if desired. Refrigerate until ready to serve.

Makes 8 servings

Summertime Cooler

4 fresh California nectarines,
    divided
1 package (10 ounces) frozen
    strawberries, thawed
1 cup water
1 bottle (750 ml) Champagne *or*
    1 bottle (28 ounces) ginger
    ale, chilled
8 mint sprigs (optional garnish)

In blender or food processor, purée 3 nectarines, strawberries and water. Strain through cheesecloth or fine sieve. Discard pulp. Pour fruit juice into punch bowl or individual glasses. Add Champagne. Slice remaining nectarine. Float slices in punch bowl or individual glasses. Garnish with mint sprigs, if desired.

Makes 8 servings

Gourmet Cheese and Fruit Appetizer

A delightful do-it-yourself appetizer.

**Variety of specialty cheeses
    (allow 2 to 3 ounces per
    person)
Fresh California peaches,
    nectarines and Bartlett pears
    (allow 1 piece per person)
Variety of crackers (allow about
    6 per person)
Variety of whole nuts in shells**

Serve with several appetizer knives or cheese slicer as needed for the cheese. Place a small cutting board and paring knife out for cutting fruit.

*Top: Summertime Cooler;
bottom: Nectarine-Strawberry
Shortcake Torte*

Kids' Favorites

Jungle Dinner (clockwise from top): Campfire Cobettes (see page 75), Chicken Drum Beaters (see page 75), Tropical Swamp Cooler (see page 75), Fruit Ketchup (see page 74), Tiger Cookie Pie (see page 75), Frog in a Jungle Salad (see page 74) and Spicy Slithering Snakes (see page 75)

Frog in a Jungle Salad

Who's this guy peaking out of the pond? He looks good enough to eat!

   6 cups boiling water
   2 packages (6 ounces *each*) lime
      gelatin mix
   1 package (6 ounces) lemon
      gelatin mix
4½ cups cold water
   1 cup shredded lettuce
   4 fresh California Bartlett pears,
      cored and halved
   1 package (8 ounces) light cream
      cheese (Neufchatel), softened
 ½ cup calorie-reduced mayonnaise
   2 plums, divided
   1 marshmallow, cut in quarters
      horizontally
   1 fresh California peach
   2 brown coated candies
   6 to 7 yellow coated candies

1. Refrigerate a 13 × 9 × 2-inch baking dish until chilled.

2. In large bowl, pour boiling water over lime and lemon gelatin mixes. Stir about 2 minutes to dissolve. Add cold water and refrigerate until syrupy. In chilled baking dish, add 2 cups of prepared gelatin and lettuce. Arrange 6 pear halves in "pond." Cut the remaining pear into pieces and fill in gaps or "holes."

3. In medium bowl, beat cheese and mayonnaise until smooth. Cover the pears with cheese mixture. Slowly pour remaining gelatin around "frog" being careful not to splash gelatin on the cheese covering. Leave some of the frog's face above the gelatin "water." Refrigerate several hours or until gelatin is firm.

4. With a toothpick make a light outline indicating where the eyes and mouth will be. Cut 1 plum in half; flatten the rounded side slightly by cutting off a small piece. Place a plum half for each eye. Top each plum half with 1 marshmallow slice (eat the other two). Thinly slice peach and remaining plum and form the mouth as shown in the photograph (see page 72). Refrigerate until ready to serve.

5. Just before serving, put the brown candies on the marshmallows for the eyes. Use yellow candies to make frog freckles.

Makes 12 servings

Fruit Ketchup

You'll love this new kind of dipping sauce.

   6 plums, puréed (about 1¾ cups)
      or 3 fresh California peaches
      or nectarines, puréed
      (about 1½ cups)
   1 cup sugar
 ½ cup cider vinegar
1½ teaspoons ground cinnamon
 ½ teaspoon ground mace or
      nutmeg
 ¼ teaspoon ground ginger
 ⅛ teaspoon ground cloves
 ⅛ teaspoon salt

In 2-quart glass measure, combine all ingredients. Cover with plastic wrap, venting one corner. Microwave on HIGH 10 to 12 minutes or until slightly thickened, stirring every 4 minutes. Refrigerate until chilled. Store up to 2 weeks in refrigerator.

Makes about 2 cups

Campfire Cobettes

3 tablespoons margarine, softened
4 ears fresh corn, cleaned and
   halved
Salt and pepper, to taste

Spread about 1 teaspoon margarine on each cobette. Sprinkle with salt and pepper to taste. Wrap cobette in foil. Place around edge of grill. Cook in covered grill about 20 minutes or until tender, turning often. Garnish as desired. *Makes 4 servings*

Chicken Drum Beaters

8 chicken drumsticks
Salt and pepper, to taste
Fruit Ketchup (recipe at left)

Season chicken with salt and pepper. Cook on covered grill over medium, indirect heat (see page 28) 30 to 35 minutes or until cooked through, turning once. Serve with Fruit Ketchup for dipping.
Makes 4 servings

Spicy Slithering Snakes

1 package (8 ounces) refrigerator
   crescent rolls
1 fresh California peach, cut into
   8 slices
16 raisins
Ground cinnamon

Separate rolls and stretch slightly. Place peach slice on wide end and roll up to resemble a snake. Pull dough to make snake longer, if desired. Place on baking sheet. Press two raisin "eyes" into dough and sprinkle lightly with cinnamon. Bake according to package directions until dark golden brown.
Makes 8 snakes

Tropical Swamp Cooler

This refreshing drink is good any time of the day.

3 fresh California nectarines,
   puréed (about 1½ cups)
1½ cups orange juice
1 bottle (10 ounces) club soda,
   chilled
Ice cubes
Colored straws (optional
   garnish)

In pitcher, combine purée and orange juice. Just before serving add soda water. Place ice in glasses. Fill with Tropical Swamp Cooler. Serve with straws, if desired.
Makes 4 servings

Tiger Cookie Pie

Easy to make! Easy to bake!

1 package (20 ounces)
   refrigerated oatmeal or
   chocolate chip cookie dough
1 quart vanilla ice cream
4 fresh California nectarines,
   sliced
½ teaspoon ground cinnamon

Preheat oven to 350°F. In bottom of 10-inch pie plate, spread cookie dough. Bake 18 to 20 minutes or until brown. Cool; freeze. Remove ice cream from freezer and let soften 30 minutes. Spread ice cream over cookie layer flattening top. Return to freezer. In medium bowl, toss nectarines with cinnamon. Place nectarines on top of ice cream. Cut and serve immediately.
Makes 8 servings

Pop-Up Muffins

A favorite with kids. The fruit actually pops up as they bake.

1 package bran muffin mix
3 fresh California nectarines or
plums, cut into wedges

Prepare bran muffins according to package directions. Fill greased muffin cups ⅔ full. Place a fruit wedge on batter in each muffin cup. Bake according to package directions.

Makes about 12 muffins

Creamy Peach-Pineapple Smoothie

A tangy, morning eye-opener!

1 fresh California peach
1 can (6 ounces) pineapple juice
½ cup non-fat vanilla yogurt

In blender or food processor, purée all ingredients. Blend until smooth. Serve immediately.

Makes 2 servings

O.J. with Fruit Cubes

Keep a supply of Fruit Cubes handy in the freezer. They add great flavor to any breakfast juice.

8 Fruit Cubes (see page 12)
3 cups orange juice

Place 2 of any flavor Fruit Cubes, or a mixture, into glass. Add orange juice. *Makes 4 servings*

Silly Peach Smiles

This will bring a smile to everyone at the table.

1 fresh California peach
Creamy peanut butter
Mozzarella or Monterey Jack
cheese, cut to make "teeth"

Quarter peach into wedges. From the skin-side, cut each wedge almost through to make lips (don't worry if you slip and cut all the way through). Open peach "lips" and spread with peanut butter. Press cheese "teeth" into peanut butter to form smiles. *Makes 4 smiles*

Sleepy Head Pears

6 slices processed American
cheese food
3 slices toasted bread
1 fresh California Bartlett pear,
cored and sliced

Place 1 cheese slice on toast. Lay pear slices evenly across cheese. Place remaining cheese slice on top of pears like a top sheet. Microwave on MEDIUM (50% power) about 15 seconds or until one edge of cheese "sheet" can be turned back.

Makes 3 servings

Clockwise from top left:
O.J. with Fruit Cubes, Pop-Up Muffins,
Silly Peach Smiles and Sleepy Head Pears

Fruit Smoothies

A great, healthy snack.

**2 fresh California peaches,
nectarines or Bartlett pears *or*
4 plums
1 cup non-fat plain yogurt
1 cup low-fat milk**

In blender or food processor, purée all ingredients until smooth. Serve immediately.   *Makes 2 servings*

Peach Chocolate Soda

**2 fresh California peaches,
divided
2 tablespoons sugar (optional)
4 scoops chocolate ice cream
2 bottles (10 ounces *each*) peach-
flavored or club soda, chilled**

Slice 1 peach. Set aside for garnish, if desired. In blender or food processor, purée remaining peach and sugar until smooth. Place 2 tablespoons purée and 1 scoop ice cream into each glass. Fill with soda. Garnish with peach slices.

Makes 4 servings

Quick Fruit Leathers

**3 fresh California peaches,
nectarines or Bartlett Pears *or*
6 plums
4¹/₂ teaspoons sugar
Plastic wrap, for microwave**

In blender or food processor, blend fruit and sugar until smooth. Pour fruit purée into microwave-safe bowl and cook on HIGH 8 to 10 minutes or until purée is reduced by about half. Lay a piece of microwave-safe plastic wrap on a 10-inch microwave-safe plate. Evenly spread ¹/₄ cup fruit mixture to a 6¹/₂-inch diameter circle. Make sure edges are not too thin or they will scorch. Elevate plate on top of inverted (upside-down) microwave-safe saucer. Microwave at MEDIUM (50% power) about 5 minutes or until leather is no longer sticky in center. If more cooking time is needed, cook at MEDIUM in 25 second increments, watching closely so that leather does not burn. Carefully place plastic wrap with fruit leather on wire rack to cool. Let stand at room temperature overnight to dry. Repeat with remaining fruit purée. Roll up leathers in plastic wrap. Store at room temperature for up to 1 week.

Makes 6 or 7 fruit leathers

Sunshine Method: *Follow directions above through cooking fruit purée in microwave. Let cool. On plastic wrapped trays or cookie sheets, spread fruit into a 6¹/₂-inch circle or rectangle ¹/₄-inch thick. Cover pans with cheesecloth. Place pans in direct sunlight for 12 to 24 hours until dry. Fruit leather is done when edges pull back from plastic and center is not sticky.*

*Assorted Quick Fruit Leathers and
Fruit Smoothies*

Quick & Easy

Instant Desserts (from left to right): Peach Slices with Speedy Fruit Sauce (see page 82) and Pound Cake with Nectarine and Honey Vanilla Yogurt (see page 82)

Peach Slices with Speedy Fruit Sauce

1 fresh California peach, sliced
2 tablespoons frozen whipped topping, thawed
  Speedy Fruit Sauce (recipe follows)

Arrange peach slices on 2 dessert plates. Top with 1 tablespoon whipped topping. Drizzle with ¼ cup Speedy Fruit Sauce.

Makes 2 servings

Speedy Fruit Sauce

2 plums, finely chopped
1 tablespoons packed brown sugar or honey
1 tablespoon orange-flavored liqueur or brandy (optional)

In 1-quart glass measure, combine all ingredients. Microwave on HIGH about 6 minutes, stirring every 2 minutes until thickened.

Makes ½ cup

Pound Cake with Nectarine and Honey Vanilla Yogurt

1 package (10¾ ounces) frozen pound cake
3 cartons (8 ounces *each*) low-fat vanilla yogurt
3 tablespoons honey
6 fresh California nectarines, sliced

Let cake thaw 15 minutes. Slice cake into 8 slices. In small bowl, combine yogurt and honey and spoon over each slice. Top with nectarines.

Makes 8 servings

Tip: This serves 1 as easily as it serves 8. Just use 1 slice of pound cake; freeze remainder for later. Combine ⅓ carton yogurt and 1 teaspoon honey. Slice 1 nectarine.

Nectarine Ambrosia

An old-fashioned favorite.

3 fresh California nectarines, sliced
1 orange, peeled and sliced into rounds
1 plum, sliced
2 tablespoons brandy or peach liqueur (optional)
1 tablespoon sugar
½ cup shredded coconut, toasted (see Tip)

In large bowl, gently combine fruit, brandy and sugar. Sprinkle with coconut.

Makes 4 servings

Tip: To toast coconut in microwave oven, arrange coconut in thin layer on double thickness of paper toweling. Microwave on MEDIUM (50% power) 4 to 5 minutes or until golden brown, stirring every 2 minutes. Watch carefully to prevent scorching.

Quick and Easy Ideas

Cool Summer Supper - Avoid cooking on a sultry summer evening by serving cold shredded cooked chicken topped with sliced fresh California peaches, chopped nuts and dollops of chutney and sour cream.

East Indian Luncheon - Spread a mixture of cream cheese, chopped parsley and chutney or salsa on pumpernickel bread. Top with wedges of fresh California peaches. Serve open-face for a tasty patio luncheon.

Luscious Finale - Soften vanilla ice cream and mix in almond-flavored liqueur, licorice-flavored liqueur or rum, to taste. Freeze. Scoop into fresh California nectarine halves and garnish with fresh mint sprigs.

Low-Calorie Elegance - Cheer up dieters with this colorful pear salad idea! Halve a fresh grapefruit, scoop out the fruit and combine the citrus sections with fresh California Bartlett pear cubes. Serve in hollowed-out grapefruit shells, drizzle with kirsch and top with cottage cheese or yogurt.

Peaches and Cream - A universal favorite! Fold fresh California peach slices into sweetened whipped cream. Serve in long-stemmed dessert glasses. Calorie counters can use half whipped cream and half yogurt.

Fresh Peach Mousse Cake

Fresh Peach Mousse Cake

  ¾ **cup whipping cream**
  ¼ **cup sugar, divided**
  ½ **teaspoon vanilla extract**
  ¼ **teaspoon almond extract**
  3 **egg whites**
  1 **package (10¾ ounces) frozen pound cake, thawed**
  3 **fresh California peaches, sliced**
    Mint sprigs (optional garnish)

In large chilled bowl, whip cream until stiff, gradually beating in 2 tablespoons sugar and the extracts; set aside. In medium bowl, beat egg whites with remaining 2 tablespoons sugar until stiff. Carefully fold egg whites into whipped cream so as not to reduce volume; refrigerate until chilled. Cut cake horizontally into 3 layers.

Reserve 5 peach slices for garnish. Place one cake layer on serving plate. Spread with ⅓ of mousse and ½ of remaining peach slices. Repeat layering, ending with mousse. Refrigerate until chilled. Garnish with reserved peach slices and mint sprigs, if desired.   *Makes 8 servings*

Homemade Peach Syrup

1⅓ cups sugar
1 cup water
6 fresh California peaches or
    nectarines, sliced
1 tablespoon cornstarch (optional)
2 tablespoons water (optional)
1 teaspoon vanilla extract

In 2-quart glass measure, microwave sugar and water on HIGH 3 minutes. Add peaches and microwave on HIGH 10 minutes or until peaches are tender. Strain through cheesecloth or strainer. Squeeze fruit gently to release juices. Discard pulp. Return liquid to glass measure and microwave on HIGH 10 minutes to reduce liquid. If syrup is too thin, continue to microwave until desired consistency. Or, dissolve cornstarch in water. Whisk into syrup and microwave 1 minute or until thickened. Whisk again. Repeat if necessary. Stir in vanilla.

Makes about 1½ cups

Peaches with Brown Sugar

Delicious as is, or use as a versatile topping.

6 fresh California peaches, sliced
2 tablespoons packed brown
    sugar

In large bowl, gently toss peaches and sugar. Let stand 10 minutes to blend flavors.   *Makes 6 servings*

Serving Suggestions: *Serve over pound cake, ice cream or toaster waffles. If desired, top with non-fat plain yogurt, light sour cream or whipped topping.*

Vanilla Yogurt with Sliced Fruit

Use any flavor of yogurt; they're equally good.

1 carton (8 ounces) vanilla yogurt
1 fresh California nectarine,
    sliced

In short wide glass or bowl, layer yogurt and fruit.

Makes 1 serving

Tips:
• *Use one fruit or a combination of two or more.*
• *If fruit is tart, mix it with a teaspoon of honey or brown sugar.*

Toaster Pancakes and Sliced Fruit

This recipe works equally well with either pancakes or waffles.

3 frozen prepared pancakes
1 cup sliced fresh California
    peaches, nectarines, Bartlett
    pears and plums
¼ cup Homemade Peach Syrup
    (recipe at left), warmed

Toast or microwave pancakes according to package directions. Place on warmed plate. Top with fruit and Homemade Peach Syrup.

Makes 1 serving

Tip: *Use one fruit or a combination of two or more.*

Top: Vanilla Yogurt with Sliced Fruit;
bottom: Toaster Pancakes and Sliced Fruit

Chocolate-Nectarine No-Bake Cheese Pie

Elegant, easy and positively guaranteed to be a crowd pleaser.

1 package (8 ounces) light cream cheese (Neufchatel), softened
¼ cup sugar
½ teaspoon vanilla extract
1 (9-inch) prepared chocolate crumb crust
2 fresh California nectarines, sliced
¼ cup semi-sweet chocolate chips *or* 1 tablespoon grated unsweetened chocolate
⅔ cup orange marmalade or ginger preserves, warmed

In small bowl, beat cheese, sugar and vanilla until smooth. Spread over bottom of pie crust. Arrange nectarine slices on top of cheese mixture. Sprinkle with chocolate chips. Glaze with marmalade. Refrigerate until chilled.

Makes 8 servings

Angel Surprise Cake

1 prepared round angel food cake
1 carton (16 ounces) vanilla or honey yogurt *or* 1 cup whipping cream, whipped
2 fresh California nectarines, sliced
2 fresh California peaches, sliced
Raspberries (optional garnish)

Cut a channel 2 inches deep out of top of cake, leaving outer and inner rim intact. Tear half of removed cake into pieces; set aside remainder for another use. In medium bowl, combine cake pieces and yogurt and spoon into cut-out channel. Top with half of fruit. Garnish with raspberries, if desired. To serve, slice cake and spoon remaining fruit on top. *Makes 8 servings*

Peaches with Vanilla Sauce and Raspberry Sauce

Thanks to the microwave oven this recipe is super-fast!

POACHED PEACHES
2 tablespoons almond-flavored liqueur
1½ teaspoons lemon juice
½ teaspoon vanilla extract
2 fresh California peaches, halved

VANILLA SAUCE
1 cup low-fat milk
1 piece (1-inch) vanilla bean, split lengthwise
2 tablespoons sugar
3 egg yolks, beaten*

RASPBERRY SAUCE
1 cup raspberries, puréed
1 tablespoon sugar

For Poached Peaches, in 2-quart microwave-safe bowl, combine liqueur, lemon juice and vanilla. Add peaches, cut-side down. Cover with plastic wrap venting one corner. Microwave on HIGH 2 minutes. Turn peaches over and microwave on HIGH about 1 to 2 minutes or until peaches are tender. Transfer peaches to plate; refrigerate until chilled. For glaze, microwave poaching liquid on HIGH about 2 minutes or until reduced to about 2 tablespoons.

For Raspberry Sauce, in small microwave-safe bowl, place raspberries and sugar. Cover and microwave on HIGH about 2 minutes or until mixture boils. Strain through fine sieve to remove seeds. Cool.

Left: Peaches with Vanilla Sauce and Raspberry Sauce; right: Angel Surprise Cake

For Vanilla Sauce, in 1-quart glass measure, add milk. Scrape seeds from vanilla bean into milk, then add bean. Microwave on HIGH about 2 minutes or until milk boils. Discard bean. Stir in sugar until dissolved. Stir a small amount of hot liquid into egg yolks; whisk egg yolks into hot liquid. Microwave on HIGH 45 seconds then whisk for 30 seconds. Microwave on HIGH about 45 seconds or until mixture coats spoon. If necessary, strain through sieve or strainer to remove lumps. Place plastic wrap directly on surface of sauce to prevent skin from forming; refrigerate until chilled.

To serve, arrange 1 peach half on each plate. Brush with glaze. Spoon Vanilla Sauce around peach. Drizzle Raspberry Sauce onto Vanilla Sauce.
Makes 4 servings

Preserving

Preserves To Go (clockwise from top right): Pickled Nectarines (see page 90), Peach Ketchup (see page 90) and Summer Fruit BBQ Chutney (see page 90)

Summer Fruit BBQ Chutney

2 fresh California Bartlett pears, cored and chopped (about 2 cups)
4 plums, chopped (about 1⅓ cups)
⅓ cup packed brown sugar
⅓ cup cider vinegar
3 tablespoons raisins
2 teaspoons finely grated lemon peel
1 teaspoon ground ginger
2 drops hot pepper sauce
3 tablespoons chopped green bell pepper

In medium saucepan, combine all ingredients except green pepper. Bring to a boil; reduce heat and simmer, uncovered, 30 to 40 minutes, stirring occasionally, until mixture is thickened. Add green pepper; cook 5 minutes. Cool. Pour into clean glass jars. Store up to 3 weeks in refrigerator.

Makes about 2 cups

Serving Suggestion: *This is delicious served with beef, pork, lamb and fish.*

Pickled Nectarines

1 cup sugar
½ cup cider vinegar
½ cup water
⅛ teaspoon salt
1 (4-inch) cinnamon stick
1½ teaspoons whole cloves
½ teaspoon whole allspice
7 fresh California nectarines, halved (about 2⅓ pounds)

In large non-aluminum saucepan, combine all ingredients except nectarines. Heat to boiling. Add nectarines and return to a boil. Reduce heat and simmer until nectarines are just tender, about 5 minutes. Pour into clean glass jars. Refrigerate until chilled. Store up to 3 weeks in refrigerator.

Makes about 1 quart

Serving Suggestion: *Pickled fruit is a refreshing side dish or condiment and goes equally well with sandwiches or elegant entrées.*

Peach Ketchup

Who says that ketchup has to be made with tomatoes? Try this for a gourmet touch at any barbecue.

3 fresh California peaches or nectarines, puréed (about 1½ cups)
1 cup sugar
½ cup cider vinegar
1½ teaspoons ground cinnamon
½ teaspoon ground mace or nutmeg
¼ teaspoon ground ginger
⅛ teaspoon ground cloves
⅛ teaspoon salt

In medium non-aluminum saucepan, combine all ingredients. Bring to a boil, reduce heat and simmer 20 minutes, stirring occasionally, or until mixture is reduced to 2 cups. Pour into clean glass jar. Store up to 3 weeks in refrigerator.

Makes about 2 cups

Tip: *See Fruit Ketchup (page 74) for microwave directions.*

Brandied Pears

1½ cups water
1½ cups sugar
½ of (4-inch) cinnamon stick
3 cardamom seeds or whole
    cloves
4 fresh California Bartlett pears,
    cored and halved
½ cup brandy

In 2-quart glass measure, combine water, sugar, cinnamon and cardamom. Microwave on HIGH 5 to 6 minutes until liquid boils vigorously. Carefully add pears and microwave on HIGH 4 to 5 minutes, stirring gently after 3 minutes, until pears are tender. With slotted spoon, remove pears to heatproof bowl. Discard spices. Microwave syrup on HIGH 10 to 12 minutes or until thickened; cool. Pour brandy over pears. Add enough syrup to cover pears. Store up to 3 weeks in refrigerator.   *Makes 4 servings*

Tips:
Syrup may be flavored with lemon or orange peel, whole cloves, vanilla bean or candied ginger.

Four peaches or nectarines may be substituted for pears.

Serving Suggestion: Serve as a side dish with meat and fish. Or, top with a dollop of whipped cream and serve for dessert.

Lemon-Nectarine Vinegar

Deliciously subtle on salads.

3 fresh California nectarines,
    chopped (about 1½ cups)
2½ cups white wine vinegar
½ cup sugar
    Pinch paprika (optional)
1 strip lemon peel

Clockwise from top right: Lemon-Nectarine Vinegar, Ported Peaches (see page 92), Peach Freezer Jam (see page 92) and Brandied Pears

In 2-quart glass measure, cover fruit with vinegar. Let stand 8 hours or overnight. Strain through cheesecloth pressing fruit to release juices; discard pulp. Add sugar and paprika. Return vinegar mixture to glass measure. Microwave on HIGH 5 minutes. Strain through cheesecloth. Pour into clean glass jars; add lemon peel. Store up to 3 months in refrigerator.
        Makes about 3 cups

Peach Champagne Preserves

In large bowl, combine peaches, sugar and nutmeg. Let stand 10 minutes until juices run, stirring occasionally. In small bowl, combine pectin and lemon juice; add to peach mixture and stir 3 minutes. Ladle into clean half-pint glass jars *or* freezer storage bags. Label. Let stand at room temperature 24 hours. After about 5 hours, stir each jar gently to evenly distribute fruit. Store up to 3 weeks in refrigerator or up to 1 year in freezer.

Makes 5 half-pints

Peach Champagne Preserves

Serve as a topping on ice cream or pancakes.

    4 fresh California peaches, sliced
    4 fresh California nectarines, sliced
    1 cup sugar
    3/4 cup Champagne
    1 envelope (2 ounces) powdered fruit pectin
    1 tablespoon lemon juice

In large saucepan, combine all ingredients. Bring to a boil and cook 1 minute. Pour into clean pint glass jars, *or* into freezer storage bags. Store up to 1 week in refrigerator or up to 3 months in freezer.

Makes 2 pints

Ported Peaches

    1 1/2 cups Port wine
    3/4 cup Zinfandel wine
    1/2 cup packed brown sugar
    1 piece (1-inch) cinnamon stick
    4 whole cloves
    8 fresh California peaches or nectarines, halved

In 2-quart microwave-safe bowl, combine all ingredients except peaches. Microwave on HIGH 6 minutes or until boiling. Carefully add peaches. Microwave on HIGH 7 minutes or until peaches are tender. Using slotted spoon, pack peaches into clean glass jars. Discard spices. Microwave syrup on HIGH 5 minutes, or until syrup thickens slightly. Pour over peaches. Store up to 3 weeks in refrigerator. *Makes about 3 pints*

Peach Freezer Jam

This recipe makes a soft homemade-style jam with unpeeled fruit.

    4 fresh California peaches, finely chopped (about 2 1/4 cups)
    3 1/4 cups sugar
    1/4 teaspoon ground nutmeg
    1 (3-ounce) pouch liquid fruit pectin
    5 tablespoons lemon juice

About Preserving

Contemporary preserving takes advantage of modern appliances: Microwave, freezer and refrigerator. Today's smaller families and reduced kitchen storage means we just need a few jars of any one recipe to keep us content until next year's bounty.

Peak Availability
Peaches are available April through October. Supplies peak twice; first in late May and early June, and then again mid-July through August. More than 120 varieties are grown.

Nectarines are available late April through September. Supplies peak late June through August. More than 150 varieties are grown. Later in the season nectarine varieties tend to be clingstone.

Bartlett Pears are available July through December. Supplies peak August through mid-October.

Pitting
To pit freestone fruit (flesh does not adhere to pit), cut along the seam or suture, twist neatly in half, remove pit with spoon. To pit clingstone fruit (flesh adheres to pit), slice into the pit and cut the fruit away in wedges.

Peeling
In general, there is no need to peel the fruit before preserving. Should you wish to peel follow these directions. Fill a 2-quart glass measure with 1 quart water. Microwave on HIGH 8 to 11 minutes or until water boils. Immerse fruit, a few at a time, in boiling water; let stand 30 seconds. Immediately immerse fruit in cold water. Gently slip off skin.

Freezing
Wash fruit. Peel, if desired. Halve and remove pits; cut in half and into 4 slices. Dip in a mixture of 1 tablespoon lemon juice and 1 cup cold water. Pack in single layers in 1-quart freezer bags; seal, removing as much air as possible. Arrange in single layer on shelf in freezer. Freeze firm, then stack for storage.

Use Clean Containers
Whatever size jars you use to keep preserves, be sure they are clean and free of nicks and scratches. Wash glass jars and lids thoroughly in hot soapy water.

To Store Longer Than 3 Weeks
Ladle fruit mixture into clean glass canning jars, leaving 1/2-inch headspace. Place lids and rings on jars. Process jars in 170°F water bath for 10 minutes, making certain that water level is 2 inches above jars. Remove jars from water. Let cool undisturbed. Lids are sealed when center is firm to touch.

Index